Literature and the Experience
of Globalization

Also available from Bloomsbury:

Literature After Globalization, Philip Leonard
Mapping World Literature, Mads Rosendahl Thomsen

Literature and the Experience of Globalization

Texts Without Borders

Svend Erik Larsen

Translated by John Irons

Bloomsbury Academic
An imprint of Bloomsbury Publishing Plc

B L O O M S B U R Y
LONDON · OXFORD · NEW YORK · NEW DELHI · SYDNEY

Bloomsbury Academic

An imprint of Bloomsbury Publishing Plc

50 Bedford Square	1385 Broadway
London	New York
WC1B 3DP	NY 10018
UK	USA

www.bloomsbury.com

BLOOMSBURY and the Diana logo are trademarks of Bloomsbury Publishing Plc

First published 2017

British Library Cataloguing-in-Publication Data
A catalogue record for this book is available from the British Library.

ISBN:	HB:	978-1-3500-0756-7
	ePDF:	978-1-3500-0830-4
	eBook:	978-1-3500-0757-4

Library of Congress Cataloging-in-Publication Data
Names: Larsen, Svend Erik, 1946- author. | Irons, John, 1942- translator.
Title: Literature and the experience of globalization : texts without borders / Svend Erik Larsen ; translated by John Irons.
Description: London ; New York : Bloomsbury Academic, 2017. | Includes bibliographical references and index.
Identifiers: LCCN 2017010880| ISBN 9781350007567 (hb) | ISBN 9781350007574 (epub)
Subjects: LCSH: Literature and globalization. | Globalization in literature.
Classification: LCC PN56.G55 L37 2017 | DDC 809/.933552--dc23 LC record available at https://lccn.loc.gov/2017010880

Cover design: Liron Gilenberg/ironicitalics.com
Cover image © blackred/iStock

The book has been supported by Aarhus University Research Foundation

Typeset by Integra Software Services Pvt. Ltd.

To find out more about our authors and books visit www.bloomsbury.com. Here you will find extracts, author interviews, details of forthcoming events and the option to sign up for our newsletters.

Oh the world's so big, so big,
John, my little Johnnie,
far more than you'll ever twig,
John, my little Johnnie.

(from a Danish children's song)

Contents

Introduction:
A Cultural Duck-Billed Platypus

How and why do we read literature in a globalized culture with a new and expanding media landscape? Globalization is a catchword with many meanings. Sometimes the word is used more to express our own enthusiastic or dismissive attitude towards a world in motion than to describe global realities, and at times, it simply floats off on the surface of an everyday fast-talking stream of speech. At the same time, however, 'globalization' is a clearly defined technical term within economics, politics and other domains. Globalization impinges on so many aspects of our life that the word cannot be restricted to particular specialist areas. Conceptually it is still open-ended, waiting to be made concrete and relevant to our everyday lives. It is this unfinished process in which literature actively participates, and to which this book is a contribution.

I hope that the book will convey the impression that literature is more profoundly involved in the globalized cultural processes than a mere supplier of literary images and counter-images of a globalized world's airports, docu-fiction from developing countries and the social drama of protest movements. Of course, present-day literature bandies topical global themes around: rootless and marginalized people, journeys from place to place, financial dramas, terror activities, power of the media and religious conflicts. And, of course, many texts are openly critical of the power play of globalization, the breakdown of values, wars and poverty, and changes to human communities.

Yet, first of all, literature deals with the human experiences of globalization, more than with the obvious manifestations of the globalization. These experiences are felt everywhere, although in different ways. Otherwise, globalization would not be global, but only local or regional. Such experiences concern the transformation of the basic building blocks of human culture and existence like our sense of place, body and movement in time and space, and the pressure to be able to translate languages and other cultural systems in a multifold network of cultural encounters as well the revision of the meaning of personal and collective memories. By confronting such issues with the immediate effects of globalization that are easily turned into thematic clusters, literature fills the themes with human life and strong emotions that we cannot do without if we want to become involved in them.

Moreover, literature contains more than just topical themes with an emotional appeal evoked by their existential impact. It also places the experience of globalization in a wider historical and cultural context than the functional contexts of contemporary economics and politics. Literature has always roamed across borders between cultures and languages in translations, linguistic influences, media, motifs, genres and symbols. It disrespectfully assumes that globalization has always existed. It behaves like a cultural duck-billed platypus, a border-crosser that does not occupy a neat place within the normal boundaries of our cultural and mental map. Such creatures have a rosy future ahead of them. The little platypus has outlived dinosaurs, sabre-toothed tigers and aurochs in the long history of our planet.[1]

The cross-border movements accelerated after Gutenberg started to print books in fifteenth-century Europe. Books could go everywhere, smuggled or openly disseminated, longer than the spoken words. For that reason, literature has always been on the scene wherever new cultural understandings and meanings are emerging, and where traditions are being opened up, also in today's manifold cultural transformations. It provides the cross-border global movements with certain meanings that the obvious themes alone do not supply, concentrating as they do on our immediate present age. Literature brings with it the long cultural tradition for cross-border activity into modern globalization, which thereby gains new meanings and a deeper historical perspective.

It would be naïve, though, to pretend that power and money are not involved in the relation between literature and globalization. With or without the inclination of the authors, literature is packaged in both; it is not merely the battleground of ideas and of new experiences. The institutions that lubricate the connection between works, society and the public are undergoing marked changes: education systems, campaigns by ministers of culture, book fairs, private and public distribution networks, author support schemes, authors' rights, international awards and so on. We are talking about cultural power, considerable power. Nor should one forget that economic market conditions help determine what is written and read: the concentration of publishing firms, the relation of books to large media conglomerates, film rights, copyrights, TV programming and so on. We are talking about big money, really big money.

This book, however, does not intend to concern itself with such relations but to concentrate on the reading of literature. Centre stage is the physical pleasure at being surprised by the detail and the feeling of being spellbound when discovering the vista that opens up beyond known horizons. This is how literature expands the abstract circuit of globalization by giving it a historical dimension and turning it into a concrete, individual experience. In both the narrow, specialist conceptions of globalization and in the fashionable stream of speech, these two dimensions are normally lacking. But without them, we cannot relate to globalization as a concrete cultural process of which we ourselves are a part, and which we ourselves help to shape. Literature, with all its compelling effects, attempts to get us to understand the world in that perspective, cutting across its existing borders. Literature is independent, global thinking.

Thinking shapes a sense of totality, and so do texts. For that reason, I have sought to introduce only a few texts, some large, some small. At times, I also refer to fragments and extracts, but I hope I will succeed in making the reader want to read the works in their totality. Literature on globalization's terms cannot be boiled down to a few texts. But even if I had included ten times as many, it would have been only a glass of water in the Kalahari Desert. Rather one good work than ten quotations, twenty names and thirty titles.

The nine chapters of the book have been conceived as a cohesive sequence. Fortunately, though, readers are ungovernable and can choose to do whatever they like. For that reason, the individual chapters concentrate on one delimited subject, so that even those who like to jump around have something to land on. All foreign titles are quoted the first time they appear in the text; then I use the translated title and quote, if possible, from the English editions, which can be found in the bibliography. All non-English quotations have been translated and all quotations from European languages have been checked with the original.

The reader who does not wish to use the references can simply read without being interrupted by heavy footnotes or references. Hence, those interested in proceeding further on their own will find in the notes to each chapter a brief reader's guide to references I have used and some supplementary information. If some readers wish to look over my shoulder, the bibliography also indicates the fictional and non-fictional works I have leaned my head on. If others feel this list is too long, bear in mind that it could have been lengthened from Tórshavn to Tasmania.

Teaching, lectures, chapters and articles have been the springboard for parts of the book. Before I hand the book on to its readers, I would like to thank all those who have listened, read and aired their views. More specifically, I would like to thank colleagues I have worked with within the Department of Comparative Literature at Aarhus University from 1998 to 2014. It has been a privilege beyond what I deserved. Also, I would like to thank my colleagues at the Centre for Comparative Literature and Cultural Studies, Monash University, Melbourne, who have contributed with a roof over my head, a place to work in peace, a library and discussions during the writing of the Danish version of the book in spring 2007. My thanks also extend to my colleagues at the School of Literature and Journalism at Sichuan University during my service as Yangtze River Visiting Professor in 2016 when I revised it for this edition. This revision was made possible by the kind support of Aarhus University Research Foundation. And first of all, thanks to my translator, John Irons, whose rare gift for also translating poetry can be witnessed in Chapter 8, and to my friend Susan Bassnett for her comments.

The book is dedicated to my grandchildren, Frederik, Maja, Sara, Freja and Emilie. You have managed to get me to look, once more, at my world as if for the first time. You will grow up with globalization as a part of your everyday life, a time when maybe e-mails will be back in the past, the TV will belong to the Stone Age and the mobile phone will be something people tried to kid you into believing in. But books have been and will be there, always.

Copenhagen and Chengdu, November 2016

Part One

Globalization in a Literary Perspective

1

The Breathing of Culture

Texts without borders

In 1849, the nineteen-year-old Frederick Sinnett, of Anglo-German extraction, travelled from England to Australia to work as an engineer. During the seventeenth century and slightly beyond, the area was a battleground for French and British colonization – with the Dutch on the sidelines. It was rugged and unknown, best suited to the convicts the British deported there once they had thrown their Dutch and French competitors to the sharks. It was also impenetrable for the Europeans because of its climate and terrain, but less because of its indigenous people. They were simply not reckoned with, and certainly not as those to whom the country belonged. The savages did not understand such things. So the country did not belong to anyone and could simply as a *terra nullius* be declared to belong to those who shouted loudest in English, French or German, or shot farthest (Lindqvist 2007). The indigenous people, though, did not find the place any more strange, impassable or hazardous than indigenous peoples do in all other continents that they call home. Like the Europeans when at home, they had the deep-rooted conceptions of their places and their relationship to them expressed in myths, tales, laws and rules. These were just different from those of the Europeans. At that time, the major European powers, and later the United States, were only just discovering the continents that were to become the arena of modern globalization in all its cultural breadth.

Like other places colonized by the Europeans, most of the Australian whites lived in a belt along the coasts. Some farmed slightly further inland, others set themselves up as merchants, and yet others were former convicts, missionaries, adventurers and gold-diggers. Not what a European would call civilization. The blacks were simply not taken into account. But, on the other hand, it was a place to be civilized, from a European point of view. From the outset, modern globalization has been both a geographical and a cultural process. The young Sinnett agreed with all this, but without the brutality that otherwise flourished. He stopped being an engineer in the geographical expansion of the European colony and became an enterprising journalist managing the issue of cultural expansion.

Sinnett was in no doubt that literature is a necessary and indispensable part of the process and not first to be introduced after elementary material protection of a rudimentary life has been established. It is already there as a part of this. Sinnett wrote in 1856 under the title 'The Fiction Fields of Australia':

> MAN can no more do without works of fiction than he can do without clothing, and, indeed, not so well; for, where climate is propitious, and manners simple, people often manage to loiter down the road of life without any of the 'lendings' Lear cast away from him; yet, nevertheless, with nothing between the blue heaven and their polished skin, they will gather in a circle round some dusky orator or vocalist, as his imagination bodies forth the forms of things unknown, to the entertainment and elevation of his hearers. To amend our first proposition, then, works of fiction being more necessary, and universally disseminated, than clothing, they still resemble clothing in this, that they take different shapes and fashions in different ages. (Sinnett 1966: 21)

Sinnett would have understood the nine-year-old Digger, who almost 150 years later lives somewhere in the Australian outback that also belonged to Sinnett's surroundings. They are still found there, such places that make the back of the moon seem like home. Precisely there, the fundamental need of the narrative appears without any shadow. Digger features in one of the novels by the Lebanese-Australian David Malouf, *The Great World* (1990). He narrates quite literally for dear life, even though his mother gets rather annoyed when he sets his younger sister Jenny's imagination alight:

> The moment he saw [his mother] he knew how angry she would be. But he couldn't help himself. Coming to the edge of some extraordinary possibility, he would let himself claim it, put it into words: if he didn't, the force of

it, huge and expanding in his head, might make him go flying off from the centre of himself. What he did now, shamefaced at being caught, was explode in giggles. (Malouf 1990: 30)

His mother is also finally placated in this way, and they all laugh together. Literature is not the wild fantasies and big words of a single individual. It is a concrete act when it is narrated and shared with an audience. It catches hold of us and can also catch hold of the situation and change it: Jenny's excitement, his mother's anger and Digger's urge to narrate end up as shared laughter. Literature is a cultural spinal cord that links places and cultures, an integral part of all cultures, where it shapes people and histories. Sinnett knows this, Digger does this. This book follows in their footsteps.

And there is a power behind the borderless words of literature. It is the strength of words that causes the works of writers to continue their way out into the world despite all national borders, and in doing so to shift the borders between the known and the unknown on the readers' inner map. The works decide the cultural agendas, even if the writers are imprisoned, go into voluntary or forced exile or are censured and killed. The holocaust victim Anne Frank was unable to get outside a door. But her diary could, and it continues to move around in the outside world. It occupies its acknowledged place in literature despite the narrow walls of her hiding place. The German Thomas Mann left Nazi Germany for the United States, but his works surpassed other writers on their German home pitch by several lengths and subsequently added a Nobel Prize to his early lead. The same applies to the Russian Alexander Solzhenitsyn, who wrote books that became both Russian and global major works.

An increasing number of such writers are appearing on the scene. They come from one place, live voluntarily or involuntarily in other places in the world and perhaps move on again, writers such as the Afghan Atiq Rahimi in Paris, the Iranian Azar Nafisi in Baltimore, the Chinese Xiaolu Guo in London or the Nigerian Chimamanda Adichie in New York. Their books get translated, become bestsellers and are perhaps turned into films, even though they do not gain a foothold in their native countries – as yet, and even though quite a few are less known to us – as yet. But it will not stay that way. Writers from the near and far East, from the former European colonies in

Africa and elsewhere and from such multicultural regions as the Caribbean are those who, in a globalized world, are already in the process of shifting the borders inside our heads and native countries in a global perspective, just as the European writers did when Europe was the world.

It was this European-dominated colonial world that Sinnett lived in prior to modern globalization. First and foremost, he wanted to show Europeans that the rough settlers balancing on the outer edge of the known world had literature that could be judged by the same yardstick as back home in Europe. Even though it was not possible to point to an Australian Shakespeare, the area belonged to what was then regarded as the European world culture. Sinnett's text, however, also shows his unconscious historical limitation. In his essay, he declined to take the mindset of the indigenous people into consideration, although he nevertheless had to refer to them in order to support his assertion of the global importance of literature. Even the naked Aboriginals cannot help but listen to a black narrator, he concludes in the above quotation.

Today, literature does not only pass the border between mother country and colonies. In modern globalization, all the geographical and cultural borders are involved that come into contact with each other in the criss-cross movement of literature, but without any fixed cultural centre of gravity. The Russian-American Vladimir Nabokov wrote a global bestseller with *Lolita* in 1955. In an interview in *Playboy* in January 1964, he talks about how he himself has been in constant motion:

> I am an American writer, born in Russia and educated in England where I studied French literature, before spending fifteen years in Germany. I came to America in 1940 and decided to become an American citizen, and make America my home ... I propelled myself out of Russia so vigorously, with such indignant force, that I have been rolling on and on ever since. (Nabokov 1973: 26, 27)

To the question as to why he always lives in furnished hotel suites, he replies that he does not want to get stuck in his own things and places.

Here things have clearly happened, 100 years after Sinnett made his reflections on the periphery of the Europeanized world. Nabokov too has admittedly a European linguistic and cultural background and makes use of it. Nobody can do anything else than make use of a personal background, no matter where one comes from. Unlike Sinnett, however, he makes conscious choices. He chooses to become an American citizen, but also chooses a basic, unceasing movement out into the world. It is not rootlessness he is talking about, but about how at each place where he finds himself, he experiences the border between the local and the global as a border that is *his*. That is what he deals with, linguistically and culturally, in his works. The unskilled Sinnett and the sophisticated Nabokov lived with their separate backgrounds in different phases of the long cultural process of globalization. But it applies to both of them – and to this book – that literature is also involved in shaping the process, so that we can understand it as being *ours* wherever we happen to be.

Culture in the garb of language

Even though Nabokov does not plague us with his private agonies, crossover authors and publishers pay and paid a price for their deplacements. This also applied to Sinnett. He left Europe with the initial signs of tuberculosis, worked under severe conditions in his attempt as a journalist to create a cultural self-awareness in a country that was mainly a European convict colony, and died as early as 1860 before reaching forty. Writers do not, however, pay a greater price than all others who go beyond known borders. Others who try out their strength in a foreign country by going beyond cultural, linguistic and social borders in their education, work and entire life are not given anything for free either. As individuals, writers are no more interesting than other mould-breakers. They are all everyday globalists in a common cultural process. Writers are just better able to tell their story and use language that makes the stars fall out of the sky.

Nor does Nabokov tell us about his private life, but about the conditions that shaped him as a writer. When he says, 'I am living in Switzerland for purely private reasons', it is not a piece of information but a discreet 'What business is it of yours?' (Nabokov 1973: 28). So there is good reason to keep focused on writers' texts rather than their personal fate. They can write so that other people's and their own experiences become larger than their individual lives and the individual horizons of their readers. This is not because literature is a special language. On the contrary, it is due to the fact that literature uses the language we also use to order a beer, have a row, encourage our children, lie about money we owe or find words for our emotions and our world view. Language also actively interacts with all the other media we use for such purposes. And literature naturally does so as well. Novels are turned into films, and literature learns from films how it can refine its use of points of view and modes of narration.

Yet, media and activities such as images, gestures, sounds, games and sport cannot manage without language. Sport can be controlled by whistles and arm movements, but the rules for how the game is to be played must be written down in language. Even my silent body language requires language for me and others to make us aware that this is something *my* body is doing. Film, TV and digital images are full of language in what we see, but even more in what lies behind their coming into existence in shooting scripts, manuscripts, story boards and contracts.

The strongest linguistic medium, the book, will not be eradicated by other media. But its role alters in relation to the other media that are used in our culture. To include our open and uncertain experiences with globalization in our use of language means that we can articulate them in the medium that most subtly shapes our everyday life, its trivial doings, its highlights and our thoughts about how life is progressing. Culture uses the lungs of language to breathe.

Cultures, however, do not share a common language. No matter how universal the experiences and opinions are that languages get hold of, they are thereby also anchored in the place where this language functions. Images, sounds and gesture go beyond cultural borders without always paying attention to them. But when literature crosses over, we cannot avoid noticing in language the tension between local understanding and global perspective. We talk about the whole world, but use a local language to do so, and this world permeates our language, both its meanings and its vocabulary, in the form of technical words, other loan words and perfectly common expressions and idioms. France has an overt policy of whitewashing smuggled goods from other languages – but it cannot prevent the cross-border practice of language. Languages that are used are never pure, nor is the literature that makes use of them. A love affair between language and literature as something purely national is an unconsummated love relationship that has nothing to do with the real life that language and literature lead. This life is profoundly promiscuous.

That is why translations are an important part of literary activity, particularly in a globalized context. Via translation, we not only transfer utterances and forms of utterances more or less correctly from one language to another. It challenges and develops our very ability to express ourselves in all the languages that are involved in the translation, our own language included, and thereby expands their cultural register on their home ground. Bible translations in Europe in the sixteenth and seventeenth centuries meant more for a crossover expansion of the capacity of the European languages as written and cultural languages than the internal developments of the individual languages. The Greek and Latin biblical texts that the translators made use of are themselves translations. Languages develop because they are used to speak of a world that is larger than those who use them, and languages cannot avoid intermeshing when they meet in situations that cut across the limitations of the language users. The border between the local and the global passes straight through the middle of language, and we express this border every time we speak.

That is why languages also have open borders and are constantly shifting them. Mixed languages result that later may acquire the status of national languages, and these languages will in turn gradually be sucked up by others. That is how Pidgin, Creole and Yiddish work together with today's language of many migrant groups around the world. They are shaped as sub-languages as a mixture of several languages that have not been completely mastered, but the mixtures work in practice. Since the languages help create necessary relations between shifting populations in a particular location, they eventually rub off on each other and on the main language of that location to the effect that both the jargon and the main language mutate. A common language emerges that can be spoken at many levels. That is how Afrikaans came into being in South Africa and Swahili spread in a belt across Central Africa. In the Mediterranean area, in the Middle Ages, a cocktail was used of early Italian that was close to Latin, mixed with Greek, Turkish and Arabic, which became a practical common language for trading and communication at a supra-regional level and also by those countries that took part in the crusades. This hotchpotch was referred to as a *lingua franca*, a term that is still in use today.

So those who believe that English is the main language of globalization are wrong. Firstly, English is already many different types of English today. Just look at the spelling check programme on the computer: British, American, Australian and a number of other variants. Secondly, these stable variants are in a minority. The global English that can successfully be used to improvise at meeting places of globalization are varieties of broken English, a *lingua franca* that is just as much a hotchpotch as that of the Middle Ages. That is the language all of us master, if this is the correct verb, but it can very easily seem confusing when ten or so various forms of broken English are being spoken at one and the same time. But then, we improvise, and as a rule do so successfully without any central reference to standard English grammar. The former director of IBM, Jean-Paul Nerrière, has dubbed this practical language of communication *globish*. He drily notes that it functions everywhere, but that peoples with one of the main types of English as their native language are at a handicap (Nerrière 2005).

It is this broad linguistic and cultural palette that literature operates with when using language. The inner strength of language has always been that understanding is more important than formal correctness, even though linguistic purists often claim the opposite. This strength is the linguistic springboard of literature. Literature is not global because it takes place in airports or some far-distant country, nor because it deals with international terror networks or voyages in the Pacific. Such literature only comprises what we could call *global literature*, a recent literary subgenre just like Victorian literature, high modernism, magical realism from South America or Southern literature from the United States. It is a particular group of texts with a certain thematic and perhaps a formal affiliation that is located in a demarcated historical period close to our own age. Global literature is both exciting and relevant and will appear in this book. But it is not the concern of this book. This book does not deal with how we read a particular type of literature, but with how we can use literature from various times and places to relate actively to the global and rift-filled cultural processes we find ourselves in. The focus is not on a textual theme but on reader involvement and a wider historical perspective.

In the age of globalization, all locations are close areas for some people and at the same time distant areas for others. All locations display their own special traces of the same globalization process, and all locations can be the starting point for understanding this process. When literature uses language, it is not some external medium that is polished with rhyme, rhythm and exciting actions and characters. Instead, it makes us aware that the meeting between the local and that which lies further away from the tips of our noses takes place most subtly in language and with language. Literature operates as a jack-of-all-trades in the global cultural workshop of language.

So literature is only apparently distinct from normal language. It uses imagery and invents strange characters and irrational occurrences; it alters set patterns for time and space – indeed, it almost goes beyond everything we can confirm in the physical world. It 'bodies forth the form of things unknown', as Sinnett has just said. However, literature does not make use of other linguistic characteristics than those which language already has in store, when we fantasize about unattainable holidays and lottery wins. But it has a greater self-awareness about what it does with language than we have in our everyday lives. And it shows this directly in its material delight in language. In literature, linguistic self-awareness steps into the foreground so that language can acquire a central cultural function: to transcend the boundaries of what we expect, but in such a way that we notice that this is taking place with the same language that we use when organizing the world we know.

This self-conscious use of language is the aesthetic side of literature. People often associate aesthetics with glossy wrapping paper that has nothing to do with the contents inside. But all practical work must concentrate on its material to have an effect. A mechanic has to master his tools and know the durability and suitability of his materials. A bicycle repairer must know how a saddle is imprinted by the rear end that is placed on it. Concentration on and also delight in the material do not take us away from the matter in hand but straight to it, also in literature.

If this sounds abstract, just consider how rhyme and wordplay immediately catch a child's attention and cause it next time to fetch a particular book among all its toys just to enjoy again and again the magic of the sound and sight of words. Aesthetics is what makes a text something concrete that we can sense and feel: the sound, the feel of a book, its layout, the rhythm of the book that is repeated in our body, something particular that we can tell others about and return to ourselves. Without aesthetic effects, a text would merely be one of the cardboard cut-outs that look like books on the furniture dealer's showcase shelves.

A rapper without aesthetic self-awareness – forget it! He improvises freestyle with a maelstrom of rhyme, rhythm and wordplay on a theme that otherwise would not interest us for the 60 seconds it takes. It is concrete and effective language work with a top-tuned aesthetic self-awareness during an MC Fight Night that would have got Shakespeare to incorporate it into his plays on the spot. The opening of *Romeo and Juliet* (1594) is actually already pure battle rap. Shakespeare was a match for rappers when it came to wordplay and rhyme about sex, the body, men and women of both sexes and ethnic coarseness.[1]

That aesthetics should be some kind of red herring that art in particular is good at is a recent conception of aesthetics. The original meaning is concrete and does not particularly apply to art. The Greek word *aisthesis* means, quite simply, sensory experience, as opposed to abstract thought, *noesis*. Greek words ending in *–is* normally refer to an activity. So the aesthetic deals with everything to do with the objects around us, natural objects or those that are man-made, of which we process our experience with our senses. Art came to play a special role among the objects we produce ourselves. The hidden forms and principles that govern nature were revealed to our senses in art. The Greek statues, which have been imitated down through the history of European culture, did therefore not depict particular bodies to the Greeks. They made the ideal forms of the body visible and perceptible to us, so that each of us could nevertheless gain a concrete experience of the hidden dimensions via our senses and experiential antennae. It was only later that art came to be regarded as the most important, and for some even the only aesthetic medium and was no longer considered to be merely a particular instance of concrete, individual sensory experience.

I intend to retain the original meaning of the word aesthetics. When literature operates consciously with its aesthetic effects, there is only one intention, which is not an escape from reality. On the contrary, the relations that are otherwise abstract or inaccessible are made concrete, accessible and relevant to the individual reader. Aesthetics is bridge-building between these two dimensions of our experience and is therefore a central cultural function of literature. Aesthetic self-awareness is what gets the text to look the individual reader straight in the eye: 'Hey you, sitting there reading right now – you're the one I'm talking to'. The Polish-English writer of the seven seas, Joseph Conrad, expresses this in his manifesto-like preface to *The Nigger of the 'Narcissus'* (1897):

> All art ... appeals primarily to the senses, and the artistic aim when expressing itself in written words must also make its appeal through the senses, if its high desire is to reach the secret spring of responsive emotions. (Conrad 1950: ix)

It is these springs Digger is scooping up from when his mother becomes angry, Jenny excited, he himself exalted and all of them end up giggling.

Later, Digger also describes reading in that light. As an adult he becomes a slave labourer as a Japanese POW in Malaysia during the Asia-Pacific War until 1945. His comrade Mac is also interested in reading, and when he is beaten to death, Digger gets his letters from Iris back home. He knows them by heart:

> The letters were just a few hundred words. But the words themselves were only part of it. / Reading took time. That was the important thing. Constant folding and refolding had split the pages, and in the continuous damp up here the ink had run and was hard to read. Each time he took them out, especially if his hands were shaking and wet, he ran the risk of damaging them. But he liked the look of the unfolded pages, their weight – very light they were – on his palm. Even the stains were important. So was the colour of the ink, which differed from letter to letter, even from page to page of the same letter, so that you could see, or guess, where Iris had put the pen down in mid-sentence to go off and do something. So what you were reading was not just words. (Malouf 1990: 145)

It is the concrete experience with all his senses that grips him when reading, both when Iris imagines a larger world to herself somewhere else, and when he feels the writing paper. It is Iris' sensory experience, here and now every time Digger reads the letters, which opens up a larger world beyond the words. That is also how it is when we hear the words, feel the book, see the sentences in black on white. The reading is both a repetition and a unique experience. It does not need cola and popcorn with it as in the cinema or in front of the TV, where we do not have a direct sensory experience of a screen. Literature is therefore not a cultural phenomenon with more or less aesthetic glitter that we can ignore, so that we can enjoy the usual meaning of the words and their deeper significance. No, literature is a cultural phenomenon *because* it is an aesthetic phenomenon, for it is in that way that it sets in motion the individual reader's sensory experience of text and world.

The medium of literature in that process is language, a medium we all share. For that reason, literature is also part of a culture's shared resources, even though not everyone reads it and not everyone has an equally large vocabulary or command of language. The same applies to films. Although not everyone goes to the cinema or watches DVDs, films strongly influence our shared visual outside world in ads and commercials, fashion and the organization of the cityscape. Literature also profoundly influences the language everyone uses, readers of literature or not, when its effects continue to circulate outside literature. Expressions, images, sayings, ideas, realizations that are part of our everyday language, without our always thinking about it, have grown on the wide-ranging continents of literature. When literature broadens the world, it is not just some world or other or somebody's world that this applies to, but *our* world. If language is culture's lungs, literature is the deep breathing that maintains the supply of oxygen.

This book talks about why and how we can read literature with globalization as a perspective, also literature which belongs to the past but which is the precondition for how we understand this perspective. The basic view of the book is that literature is not first and foremost a collection of texts with global literature as one group, but is an active linguistic and cultural function with aesthetic effects. We can only understand its importance today by looking at it in relation to our globalized cultural conditions, and in relation to other forms and histories of expression and media that also cause our concrete experiences with these conditions to cut across the world we are familiar with.

'Seeing things for the first time'

If some people feel that they are going to read yet another introduction to how one reads literature, they are absolutely right, but with a new condition, and thus different from other introductions. The explosive opening up of the world's borders in recent years has created new crossover vistas and made regional life global, as, for example, triggered by migration, climate changes, nature conservation, energy supply and religious conceptions. But new barriers have also been put in place where regionalization has strengthened local self-awareness. In a broad sense, new cultural themes and challenges have been created, and thereby new frameworks for the way literature can influence things. That situation calls for new introductions, also others besides mine.

When the borders of culture shift, it not only leaves a mark on the new literature. Even though the texts already standing on the shelves are unchanged, their meaning to us changes, because we have different cultural horizons when we read them and because their aesthetic effect is new every time it hits us, also when new media emerge next to the book. Globalization is not without a history, even though it punctures the speech bubbles of known local history about life as celebrated in a variety of open air museum villages around the world. But it encourages us to look for other and older texts and prerequisites than those that normally lie at the top of the pile on the book seller's desk. Works we have previously failed to notice, and others that we have read with different eyes, have also helped to build the open cultural platform where we now hesitantly stand. Globalization was already under way before we saw it clearly enough to be able to give it a name (Osterhammel and Petersson 2009). Among the texts and the material that cultural history has already laid around today's cultural platform, globalization also invites us to reconsider our choice of texts and interpretations from the past so we can use them again to make banisters and railings helping us to keep our balance in the situation where we are now.

For that reason, we are to read not only the new literature but also existing literature anew. In the former European colonies, including the United States, it has in particular been the indigenous literary tradition that came to the fore, from both before and after colonization. This rediscovery has given their history greater cohesion for the present inhabitants with mixed colonial roots. Part and parcel of this process is an often painful awareness of the fact that the colonies belonged to those originally living there, before the colonial powers copiously helped themselves from the vast buffet of raw materials and cultural products that was laid out. Via difficult negotiations and court cases, some of the indigenous peoples are now getting some of their rights recognized and are having some of their lands reapportioned to them, occasionally accompanied by apologies. The past cannot be re-established, but in this way history can be rewritten and put into practice today on global conditions by keeping history alive on new conditions. This is not an unqualified success, but without the age-old narratives and other forms of artistic expression that have kept the blacked-out tradition alive, nothing at all would have happened. The traditional texts have also now come alive by crossing cultural borders and conceptual barriers, even though the literary history that has screened them mainly did so with the aim of enclosing them as exotica in national and other local arenas. An introduction that does not encourage people both to understand contemporary literature and to restructure traditional texts and concepts is not an introduction to literature on the conditions of globalization.[2]

On the occasion of Mozart's 250th birthday in 2006, Slavoj Žižek pointed out the necessary risk we run when we look at tradition with new eyes. We risk losing it. In this case, he refers to a new performance of *Così fan tutte*, which is a radical intervention in the performative tradition of the opera:

> Each … intervention is a risky act and must be judged by its own immanent standards. Only one thing is sure: the only way to be faithful to a classic work is to take such a risk – avoiding it, sticking to the traditional letter, is the safest way to betray the spirit of the classic. (Žižek 2007: s.p.)

This risk also applies to literature. In 1958 the Australian Nobel Prize winner Patrick White describes the process in his essay 'The Prodigal Son': 'Writing, which had meant the practice of an art by a polished mind in civilised surroundings, became a struggle to create completely fresh forms out of the rocks and sticks of words. I began to see things for the first time' (White 1989: 16). Literature can get us to look at things we know and traditions we are familiar with as if we were seeing them for the first time.[3] It is our chance to make it *ours* again in a new way, and to see the known as something else that for the first time can be formulated in *our* language. Globalization forces us to do so today and literature actually does it with us.

Tradition is the way a present time acquires a historical perspective, also the present time of globalization. However, this book does not contain a cohesive description of the history of culture, literature or ideas up to the present day. Globalization is neither the provisional final station of the long, straight road of history nor certain economic operations here and now without a history. It is a reason to reinterpret parts of history, so that it becomes a resource for us today. I therefore make use of texts that have been read before, and concepts that have been used before, but give them other perspectives. And therefore I present historical contexts in relation to concrete texts and issues, not as accounts of clear historical trajectories, but opening general perspectives of literary relevance from concrete events. But along the book, these contexts will gradually cover large sections of European cultural history, selected, re-used and also used for new interpretations.

The book does not deal with what metaphors, narrators or genres are. Nor are there any model readings from the top icing layer of the cream cake down through layer upon layer until we reach the deeper meanings at the bottom of the macaroon. All readings are selective and focused on the experience of globalization. Nor do I conduct a comprehensive discussion of earlier schools of literary criticism. I assume that work has already been done by many readers and can be accessed on book shelves.

There are also topically prevalent points of view regarding literature that one will search for in vain in this book. The relation to national histories of literature and national literary canons is mainly indirectly present, even though many people in recent years spend a lot of time and effort with canon formation. That works of art, particularly linguistic ones, are traditionally conceived on the initial basis of their national affiliation, possibly with a few words about international dissemination or influence, is contrary to the very nature of literature. Literature has always been a model for global thinking that makes the constitutive exchange between local experience and the world outside concrete. Under fluctuating historical conditions, this model has been given a different content, but it has always functioned in such a way that we can use this form of thinking on new conditions.

The national expression is only a knot that for a short while binds together all the cross-cultural threads that are the real life-lines of literature. The most important purpose of national literary history in a globalized world ought to be to show how the local literature opens up, and has always done so, towards a world outside, an opening that allows any local area to come into existence at all. It was not the world outside Verona that killed Romeo and Juliet but Verona's monumental inwardness. Literature nurtures our capacity to avoid paying what Amitav Ghosh in *The Glass Palace* (2000) refers to as 'the price of a monumental inwardness' (Ghosh 2000: 349).

Nor is there much to be found in my book for those who are interested in portraits of the world's great writers and their biographies. This field is studied by many people at present and gives rise to many exciting initiatives in the grey zone between fiction and reality and between the writer as a creator and as a social individual. This book prioritizes texts, and every writer is regarded as William Shakespeare. We fortunately know very little about him, while at the same time his texts go straight for the jugular. He writes texts that with their forms, motifs and ideas are involved in the broad cultural contexts outside the texts, and that take their readers with them on their journey.

World literature

Those who want to get an answer to the question of what the perfectly globalized work of fiction looks like, will be disappointed. In recent years, the world literature paradigm has framed a difficult discussion of value in a globalized framework.[4] Yet, world literature does not indicate quality but function. World literature comprises all forms of literature that actually exist and are used in a way that creates new connections between historical periods, between texts and genres and between local and cross-border phenomena. No literature *is* just world literature, but all literature in all local languages *can become* it by the way we use it and through the interpretations of the world it invites, when we as readers accept that invitation. This occurs when literature transcends cultural boundaries determined by place and time: literature is always locally anchored and yet crosses borders at the same time. Texts do not become world literature by being incorporated into a canon of world literature but by shifting the border markers of the languages in which they are written. All texts do this, but some texts do it better than others. Ibsen is not more theatre than a school play, but better theatre. The good works are not more world literature than the others either. They are simply better at being it. It is such texts that I have chosen in this book.

There are of course perfect works of art that break through the boundaries of space and time. We are unable to forget them. They strike us dumb with admiration, possibly almost fear. They are new each and every time we meet them when our knowledge, attitudes and total life-experience and cultural surroundings are undergoing change. Some of us would be hard put to live without them, but it is certain that we would be unable to live if we solely wanted to live next door to perfection.

Perfection does not automatically make them world literature. It does not say anything about the participation of literature and language in cultural processes. It is wonderful to stumble across such a work as an exception, but in literature – as in the rest of existence – it is unusable as a set norm for practice. Many authors who we could not do without would fail abjectly. There is excess fat in works by Honoré de Balzac, at times a need for a gang of clearers in Charles Dickens, spot cleaning needs to be done in Homer and Dante, and in Leo Tolstoy there are places rather like trousers that need to be taken up before their bottoms fray too much. All of them stand in the midst of a cultural process they have no overview of, and they take us with them into it. It is its confusing lack of clarity they write about, not its clarification and no perfection. Hence the awe that strikes us.

Globalization confronts literature and readers with new challenges that are determined neither by the literature nor by the readers themselves. These challenges arise in the encounter between the requirements and needs that a globalized cultural arena under development has and the resources offered by literature and language. In this encounter, new cultural conditions can draw on forgotten or unknown resources in literature and tradition, and with these resources literature can in turn enable *us* to better formulate the cultural processes of globalization, because without us, wherever we happen to be, they do not take place at all.

Some people would have us believe that the local and the global are totally interactive, so that now all of us are *glocal*. This linguistic neologism is smarter than it is wise, and it only makes one more appearance in this book. The term casts a veil over the fact that the relation between the local and the global is a process full of breaks, interruptions and unsolved conflicts evolving when borders are moving in yet unknown directions. It calls for circumspection and insight to make a cohesive interconnection out of this process. Literature is not a question of a seamless glocal interconnection, but of this open process. Literature is a form of expression at our disposal for investing human experience in the broader processes of globalization that determines our local lives.

In that situation, there are two basic attitudes to reading. Harold Bloom asks, as do I: How and why are we to read literature? But in his preface to the book *How to Read and Why?* (2000) he answers differently. The reader is a lone wolf whose concentration on himself or herself is increased through reading. Gradually, the reader is raised above time and space in order to strengthen a sense of selfhood under the aspect of eternity. Reading runs parallel to personal life. Maturity and the perfect reading only come ultimately. I was on the point of saying: when it is too late. There is here a silent assumption that various stages of life and experiences can be assessed in relation to the same yardstick for maturity and its coincidence with the old-age pension. But if I behave like an OAP at the age of twenty five, I am overmature. And if I play at being young with young people when I am seventy years old, I am immature. With or without literature there is no ideal maturity as a normative common denominator.

This book represents a different point of view: Bloom is of course right in saying that both literary works and readers are unique phenomena that can roam through space and time, literature in its meanings and we in our imagination. However, like the reader, literature is always anchored outside itself, is historical. To look oneself ever more deeply in the eye without gaining a greater glimpse of the world outside is a higher form of blindness. The subject of the next chapter is globalization, not as an abstract process but as a concretely experienced cultural process and thus a challenge to literature and its readers.

Globalization Becomes Everyday Life

Newcomer High School

When I went into the classroom in April 1989, I did not know that I was entering globalization,[1] and when I came out again, I did not know that I had been there. But I knew that I had experienced something new. The place was Newcomer High School in San Francisco, which from 1980 to 2010, received immigrant children – 'newcomers' – in a successful immersion programme.[2] Along with eleven other representatives from just as many European countries, I was then on a one-month trip around the United States as an 'international visitor', at the invitation of the United States' Fullbright programme. 'International' – I knew that word. That also included me. But what I witnessed in that classroom was something else. Today, I would call it 'globalization'. In 1989, the word was only just starting to enter the language, but not my language.

I was together with two other participants, Clas from the Netherlands and Stjepan from the then Yugoslavia. Clas described the situation as follows:

On the white computer screen, we saw the heads of Osiris, Horus and other Egyptian gods lined up without their bodies. Immediately underneath were a series of bodies that walked, stood or sat, some with sceptres or fans in their hands.

'By clicking on the mouse the pupils can place the heads on the bodies. In the same way, they can identify the names of the gods written in hieroglyphics. They can also learn to write their own names in hieroglyphics', the teacher explained.

'But this is only for the ablest pupils. We spend practically all our time with most of those in the class on Greek and Roman civilisation. They are the most important basis for the Spanish-speaking pupils from Latin America such as those in this class.'

'And is Spanish the native language of most of the pupils, Mr. Ostrovski?' I asked.

'Yes.'

'And what is the largest ethnic group at Newcomer High School?'

'Chinese.'

'How come?'

'Most Chinese pupils from Peru are Spanish speakers'. (Larsen 1990: 59, 60)

The children and the teacher were not international in the same way as I was. I just went out the door back home and danced into the international arena. It rested securely on national poles. A solid pole rammed down for each nation with an international dance floor above, where we could invite each other to dance and glide out onto the floor in mixed formations and local rhythms, in our case, one representative per nation. The international is something that takes place, as the word implies, between well-defined national entities in various combinations. This international world was simple. It was just big although well structured, but also exciting by being different and a little dangerous at certain points, as when I was living on the edge of Rio de Janeiro's slum or felt uncertainty creeping in under my skin on the streets of Johannesburg.

But I could leave the international scene again when the music stopped, and return home. There a Danish back garden was waiting for me, also part of the big world, but not mixed up with it. Here I could digest everything until the international music called me to the floor again. This was a rather simple operation. At home, on the other hand, the world was complex, but in its completely local way: children at school, off to sport or music, working hours and professional ambitions, a tolerable relationship with the bank and workmen's bills and involvement in community life on the school board and similar places.

When the two siblings Abdullah and Fatima came into my son's class after my trip to the United States, things changed. They were stateless Palestinians from Lebanon and were just two of several migrant children at the school. Abdullah had a shot hole in his shoulder, but didn't flaunt it. That was just the way it was. But the other children looked at it with shocked surprise. Their parents did not speak Danish, and their father was probably sick, in the head that is, my son understood, and Abdullah was not allowed to drink soft drinks after football during Ramadan. TV images, parents chatting over the newspaper, an echo of local politics, war films and pirate toys shifted from unreality to reality, became a part of the already-complicated mechanisms of the children's everyday lives, mostly as a slight spoke in the wheel, but now no longer just events outside in the international world.

All of this was everyday at Newcomer High School, and not just a single broken spoke in the wheel resulting from a few new arrivals. It was everyday for everyone, not a special everyday, just everyday. The ethnic, linguistic and national complexity was not only prevalent in the class. It also structured the life of each individual person as the ordinary basis for life at home and in the school. Naturally, it had its everyday problems, just like in the different everyday complexity that formed the ordinary basis in *my* children's school. But the Newcomer complexity was not a particular issue or subject of discussion. It was just there. It was *us*, the visitors, who saw problems and asked the questions in the class, but without getting an overall answer. Today, I would call the answer globalization.

Conceptions of globalization

But one cannot simply find a relevant answer to our questions in a dictionary. 'Globalization' is not a word or a term, but an open issue. It is not a clearly demarcated phenomenon with a definition we must get to learn and that only applies to certain regions in the world, certain forms of knowledge and certain specially selected experiences, such as those we had in San Francisco.

In Antiquity, Aristotle attempted in his book on metaphysics to define what nature is (1941: 1014b15–1015a19, cf. Cohen 1996). That was then the only conception of the global, that is, the framework for human existence that of necessity comprises everyone. But, without further ado, he abandoned the attempt to provide a stable definition that comprised nature in all the relevant contexts. There are a number of definitions, he says, because nature has many actual effects that cannot simply be lumped together into one whole – nature is the basic substance, nature is form, nature is force, nature is raw material, nature is basic elements, nature is cosmos – and more besides. The divisions do not then mean that nature *is* fragmentary, but that the various definitions serve different particular purposes. No single definition can exhaustively determine what nature or similar phenomena are, for we are unable to do so, Aristotle says. But each of the definitions is pragmatic; it is made to provide us with certain tools so that we can relate to the phenomenon in particular situations – acquire knowledge about it, use it in practice, distinguish it from other things and so on. In other words, the use of complementary knowledge is necessary to approach such phenomena, including today's globalization. I will come to this particular complementarity that involves literature a little further ahead.

It is also a pragmatic, or contextualized, conception of that kind of knowledge we have to use to embrace globalization. And there is definitely no single one that can cover all aspects of globalization at one and the same time. There are several conceptions in circulation that are not necessarily incorrect, but that do not fit our present requirements: we must get hold of one that can be used when dealing with literature. One standard conception of globalization views it primarily as an economic phenomenon. If we maintain an economic definition as the basic, or even the only correct or relevant one, we overlook the overall cultural effects of the globalization process. Instead, religious and ethnic clashes tend to be translated into economic problems in order to find a political solution. Globalization then mainly becomes something we can manage after a crash course in economics, and not a comprehensive dynamics that challenges our whole world of experience.

It made good sense to monopolize the definition in that way during an earlier phase of modern globalization, because economics has been an activating impetus, also for the regional inequalities and social misery that have followed in its wake. It was via economics that globalization became visible as a global connectivity across the borders we usually deal with in economics and politics. It also made good sense to say 150 years earlier that the industrial revolution resulted from capitalism, science and technology. But as soon as industrialization led to changes to the family structure, it no longer made any sense to say that technology was responsible for my neighbour getting divorced. Economic development is perhaps the main cause of globalization, but economics no longer establishes a sufficient explanation of globalization in its present form as a complex cultural process.

Another conception states that globalization first and foremost describes what is taking place in particular parts of the world, the highly developed societies like Europe, the United States, parts of Asia, the Shanghai area and the São Paulo area, and quite a few other places as well. From that point of view, globalization will probably be broader than the economic conception, but it will still be relevant only for those who live where globalization is supposed to be a reality. This conception suggests that globalization divides up the world, with some being left on the tailboard of globalization or being thrown off the vehicle completely. As a totality, globalization is this obstacle course with winners and losers. Even with this broader conception, which is not wrong in a certain sociological context, we still find ourselves within the narrow borders of economics, but with a still unsatisfied need to be able to understand its cultural consequences for all.

A third conception claims that globalization first and foremost has to do with a starker contrast between the local and the global. The local is static, tradition bound, locked in linguistically and culturally defined regions, while the global is dynamic, outward looking, functional and transcends borders independently of local history. The local is then often viewed as a resistance to globalization, and globalization as an assault on the local.

Globalization is, however, nothing at all if it does not manifest itself locally. Where else should it manifest itself? After all, everyone lives locally, even if they live in different local environments in all their life time. We are global where we happen to be, the local being the platform where we experience global processes and from which we participate in them. I am not just global, but I am so with Denmark and Europe as my platform. People can have houses and flats at various localities, but not everywhere. Local culture only means something, and has always only meant something, in a confrontation with what lies outside it. A local culture that has been unable to cope with this confrontation as a constitutive aspect of its particular way of being local has never survived as a local culture, only as a reservation, also before globalization became highly topical. The most exciting literature in any local language, translated or original, have always dealt with this constitutive relation between the local and the translocal, which now is extended to be global.

From that point of view, we do not get very far by asserting that globalization is first and foremost a process that via common conditions within such domains as economics, the media, communication, transport and lifestyle makes the world more uniform by levelling out cultural and local differences and distinctive characteristics. It is correct that globalization differs from other types of dynamic, international networks we know from history, back to the trade routes of Antiquity, wars, the building of empires and colonizations that all belong to the prerequisites of globalization. Today, global networks make up a far broader spectrum of our individual and common life than comparable processes in the past, and also involve far more people and institutions.

Yet, if one believes that common global conditions automatically create a uniform cultural life everywhere, the misunderstanding easily arises that counter-movements, such as the nationalist movements in the Western world or the so-called Islamic State, position themselves outside globalization. It is, however, obvious that without texting, Facebook, Twitter, other social media and general access to cyberspace they would not function. By being opposed they are also part of the globalized world and are defined by the new differences and contrasts that globalization also creates. Globalization does not create a homogenous global society, but establishes certain uniform conditions for different local developments. As a cultural process, globalization is first and foremost the formation of such differences, some of which at this point in time are turning against the effects of globalization and becoming conflicts determined by globalization.

Globalization as everyday experience

When trying to assess the significance of globalization for culture and literature, we should not start with the particular causes or structures of globalization. We should start by looking at the variety of experiences it creates for everybody. The changes produced by globalization call for innovative thinking 'not just about the scientific elite, the trendy creative class or entrepreneurial superheroes but [one] which recognises the contribution that everyone can make as consumers, citizens and creators', the British think tank Demos notes in *The Atlas of Ideas* (Leadbeater and Wilsdon 2007: 51). Globalization first meets us mainly as a new complexity in everything we come across in our everyday lives, also when we do not think about it that way: food, environment, the media, clothing, work, public subjects of debate, use of language, all of which are complex globalized phenomena. It is this everyday experience, with conflicts, hopes and fears generated on globalized conditions that form literature's feeding ground. Here it has a concrete springboard for the global perspectives as well as a concrete anchoring for the structures and conditions of the global world, which is the world of the anonymous globalists and of the children at Newcomer High School. And it is ours.

Sometimes most people fail to notice the complexity of their immediate everyday surroundings. They too become routine. At other times, some people react spontaneously, randomly and not always appropriately to an everyday uneasiness, without waiting to understand the causes of the events they are reacting towards. It all just becomes too much, and the reaction is fuelled from somewhere that has nothing to do with globalization: it is certainly not appropriate to react with religious fanaticism or a celebratory revival of a pre-industrial past to global economic fluctuations, nor is it well motivated. But it happens and even more so in the twenty-first century. Global relations interact with what is already present in people's heads and everyday lives, such as religion, despite the fact that this content is not connected in any other way with globalization apart from the fact that it clashes with its effects. This non-uniformity is, however, also a real part of the complexity of globalization.

Just like other cultural processes, global cultural processes therefore represent three interrelated cultural challenges. These are also dealt with by literature, but literature reshapes them using its own tools and potential. It is these tools and potential that this book mainly deals with. The three challenges address our patterns of experience, models of knowledge and forms of communication.

1) *The challenge to patterns of experience:* 'No one experiences globalisation in all its complexity, but globalisation is significant insofar as it reshapes the daily lives of billions of people. Increasingly, the larger world is present locally', the publishers of *The Globalisation Reader* (2004), Frank Lechner and John Boli, write in the section 'Experiencing Globalisation' (Lechner and Boli 2004:

106). Globalization does not mainly influence the concrete individual things and events we perceive with our senses. Nor does it have an unmediated impact on our knowledge. First and foremost, it affects our experience of the world around us. Experience is different from both perception and knowledge. *Perception*, or observation, refers to the fact that we register certain things with the senses with which we happen to be equipped. The sensory experience merely confirms that we are located in a physical world co-present with things and people. *Experience* on the other hand deals with actual occurrences of which we have sensory evidence, but which we do not only observe but also participate actively in by using practical skills that we can repeat. Experience is interactive. If someone asks me to tell him how to tie a tie, I have to reply that I am unable to. But give me a tie and I'll show you how to do it. I do not exactly know *what* I am able to do, but I certainly know *that* I am able, and I can prove it again and again. That is experience. Lastly, *knowledge* is all that we can abstract from the observations and experiences and express in language. It can be used so that we can choose between right and wrong within various fields of knowledge, assess our choice and express it in terms of a principle. Knowledge enables us to repeat not only what we are able to do, but also to move the boundaries of both what we can observe and what we can experience.

The point of departure for literature is always the experience in the concrete texts and with the texts, for both writer and reader, or, in other words, the interpretational practice. The experience provides the basis for knowledge and is a prerequisite for literature's particular way of being involved in culture's various forms of knowledge. Experience qualifies the elementary perception of more or less detailed textual observations, so that the encounter with the text is not only a neurological fact but becomes an experience of our participation in a physical world. Literature can only effectively grapple with globalization when it is grasped as an everyday experience, and only then can literature contribute to how we shape that experience. In Chapter 1, I therefore emphasized 'aesthetic experience' in the broad meaning of the term. This is the only meaning that is relevant for literature when faced with the experience of globalization.

Experiences form patterns that make the individual experiences cohere. To have experience of a car does not only mean that I have seen it or sat in it, but that I know I can do something with it. Experience of a car means that I can drive it, have tried to finance it, know the fluctuations in petrol prices and the rhythm of the check-ups; I may even be knowledgeable about handling tools. In this way, the experience of a car forms a pattern of experience. But when the change in petrol prices that I notice at the petrol station is linked to late effects of the series of wars in the Middle East or to the price of crude oil in Rotterdam, and when the car licence fee I actually see in my statement of account changes because of an environmental tax and international agreements about CO_2 emissions, then my pattern of experience with the car has altered, and the coherence of my experience has been broken, even though my old car is still the same, and I know that the door has to be given an extra push to shut properly.

Such rifts occur in all major cultural changes, also prior to globalization. This was the case when the Europeans came to present-day South America: everyone experienced something, no one experienced everything, both because it was an unknown area and because the forms of understanding they brought with them collapsed. The new, however, was indisputably real, on both sides of the Atlantic. Those who set out found themselves in the middle of an unknown world of which they had no previous conception, although this forced itself on them, with fauna, flora, peoples and societies they could not have imagined in their wildest imagination. And those who remained at home saw strange objects and things that came home with the ships, or heard incredible tales about what certain people had definitely experienced, or who at any rate knew reliable individuals who had seen mermaids and amazones with their very own eyes. The known border between the local and all that lay outside it disintegrated. The European homeground was also transformed, politically, economically and culturally. Some became even more fanatically local and force-fed the new world with the local norms of the colonial powers. Others opened up their eyes to new understandings of humanity, nature and society. And literature was an integral part of the process, struggling to mould the imagination of the unknown into known forms of presentation or in new ones.

The patterns of experience also changed when industrialization and urbanization got under way in the early nineteenth century, first in Europe and later elsewhere. Everyone could personally feel how society changed in relation to nature, family, beliefs, body, place, travel, economics, forms of government, power and education, but no one experienced everything or how everything was interconnected. Everything whirled around on the roundabout of early modernization. Literature joined in this roundabout with such writers as Charles Dickens, Honoré de Balzac, Walt Whitman, Charles Baudelaire, Edgar Allan Poe and many others who we still read. They wrote about the mysterious, explosive and inevitable things they experienced long before they knew what those things were or whether they were something positive or something negative. It was all so confoundedly real and confusingly dominating. That is also how Shakespeare approached his world in the Renaissance.

If the writers had felt they had a clear picture of the world, we would scarcely have been interested in reading them today, and they would perhaps not even have bothered to write about it, but simply lived their everyday lives. Via literature, they brought what was new within the experiential horizon of the individual readers. What was new could now also become *their* world, even though they did not quite know what to do with it. Literature particularly processes patterns of experience, not individual experiences. It is because earlier literature from near and far challenges such patterns that they can acquire renewed topicality.

It is inevitable that we use patterns of experience with which we are already familiar to interact with new experiences before we can turn them into some kind of knowledge, although we know they do not match completely. This is the way we use history to gain a piecemeal grasp of a changing reality. This type of interaction is not unique to literature, but also applies to all kinds of science. It happens by way of metaphors and images before the stage of more adequate conceptualizing is reached that can produce knowledge.[3] When electricity was referred to as current in the nineteenth century, it was a way a known pattern for liquids to pass through a pipe was exploited to imagine what happens when electricity is transported through a cable. It was wrong, as we now know, but in everyday language, we still call it a current, based on the old pattern of experience for natural flows. A more recent reference to a hole in the ozone layer does the same: it inscribes a newly detected phenomenon into known patterns of experience. We experience it as a hole, while it is actually a reduced concentration of a certain chemical substance.

Such cases are pre-scientific borderline cases in the practice of science, but in literature, they are part and parcel of its basic way of working. The text has to include an appeal to something of the experience, the ideas and the media knowledge we have in advance. If one is to understand the sentence "'Hamlet was mad", one must [...] have seen mad people or read about them', the American philosopher Charles Peirce once said, using the expression 'parallel observation' (1998: 494, 209). I would prefer to say instead *supplementary experience* – 'experience' because we do not only draw on something we have observed but also to something related to habitual practice, and 'supplementary' because the experience is not only a parallel to text and images but reflects our interaction with the texts in order to understand them.

The appeal to supplementary experiences already in place is the necessary prerequisite for our ability to understand the texts, even though we have never been or have had the possibility of being at Newcomer High School or inside any of the fictitious universes I intend to unravel in the following chapters. But it is also the necessary condition for our being able to be provoked. For the texts pull our experiences in new directions. We may not be provoked by what is written there, but are affected by what it does to the supplementary experience we invest in our reading. The texts get us to look at the supplementary experience we invested in the reading, as if seeing it for the first time.

Most often, literature will demand *maximum* supplementary experience of the reader, as in such poetry as haikus or Emily Dickinson's poems. Other types of presentation presuppose a *minimum* of supplementary experience. This applies to the guide to online payment using my credit card or to my new washing machine. Preferably, everything I need to know ought to be there. More than any other form of expression, literature systematically moves up and down the ladder between minimum and maximum supplementary experience – between surrealism and documentary fiction, say – forcing us all the time to be ready to change our conception of the nature and scope of the supplementary experience the text is appealing to. It is this register that is activated when we read literature from other cultures and historical periods. Those who know the texts and their cultural background supplement with less experience than readers from outside, who have to open up to experiences they perhaps did not know they had at all. And then literature really becomes exciting in today's transnational cultural landscape.

(2) *The challenge to models of knowledge:* No individual sciences or spheres, let alone theories and methods, have told us once and for all what globalization

is in all its complexity. If that had been the case, we could simply have formed society, our daily lives and the cultural arenas of globalization according to these directions. But important changes in our knowledge requirements take place today so rapidly and so radically that the traditions that ensure the necessary continuity of individual spheres of knowledge can only process them with difficulty. 'All the models we use to predict inflation have broken down – it is one great chaos', Professor of Economics Jacob Brøchner Madsen of the University of Copenhagen stated in the Danish daily *Politiken* already on 25 April 2005, a few years before the crisis of 2008, which confirmed it.

Globalization is thus not only a challenge to our patterns of experience but also to the models of knowledge on which we rely, and the way in which we combine them to provide a tenable interpretation of experience. The strength of science is that it divides and systematizes the areas we are to know something about, so that the resulting knowledge is as specific and unambiguous as possible. That which is irrelevant is consistently removed from the field of vision, and one looks at economics, language, atomic structures, religion and bacteria separately. But such globalized phenomena as the turmoil in the Middle East, waves of migration or climate changes demonstrate that the border between essential and non-essential knowledge shifts rapidly and cannot be contained within known models of knowledge. Apart from acquiring concrete new knowledge about particular areas of reality, the new task is also to discover how we combine what we actually know, cutting across areas, methods, theories and subject areas, and thereby gain important new knowledge that can broadly be understood and accepted.

To grasp this situation as the necessary framework for the use of knowledge on cultural conditions and not only the conditions set by the sciences that produced the knowledge in the first place, is a challenge intensified by globalization. Across research domains the need for scientific knowledge beyond disciplinary boundaries in the case of, for example, climate change and its social effect is solved in various cross-disciplinary scenarios involving different disciplinary models of knowledge that are all reshaped in order to be compatible on scientific grounds. In contrast, the cultural challenge is to bring together complementary models of knowledge inside and outside the scientific area that resist complete compatibility, but which, nevertheless, have to be taken into account as alternative and incompatible models, which co-exist as crucial for knowledge to play a role from politics to everyday action in today's society.

Literature's approach to knowledge matches this situation. Literature does not focus on the right knowledge, rather on the maybe contradictory models of knowledge that are actually accepted and used, rightly or wrongly, consciously or unconsciously. Even in science-based societies such as ours, it takes more than solid knowledge to convince people to stop smoking, change their diets and save water when brushing their teeth. And there are some people who would risk their lives for models of knowledge that others would not even count as knowledge, but as superstition. Honour killings or religious self-sacrifices are a reality that must be understood, even though we do not understand, let alone agree with the dogmas that underlie them.

Scientific knowledge cannot avoid working in such mixed cultural contexts of individual unpredictability, cognitive uncertainty and an understanding of reality far removed from science. Such conditions for the social function of knowledge are rarely decided by science. But it is this intricate universe of knowledge which all of us live in, and it has become larger and more complex in a globalized world. The concrete models of knowledge, their contradictions and actual effects are the focus of literature, not the correctness of the individual components.

With a term borrowed from the physicist Niels Bohr, I would call such models *complementary models of knowledge*. To a group of biologists when at a convention in 1938, Bohr was to argue what recent discussions in nuclear physics on the principle of complementarity could say to other disciplines about human knowledge (Bohr 1961). Biologists can examine living organisms as composed of atoms and particles as is every physical object, but the price paid is that they have to abandon explaining what it means that they are alive. Here, life is a prerequisite that cannot be made a subject for cognition. If, on the other hand, one wishes to understand the organisms, such as humans, as alive, one has to include factors beyond physics, such as urge, intentionality, memory, language, instinct, environment, habitat. Bohr's point is that one cannot simply put two types of knowledge together and get a single, more comprehensive knowledge, for one does not ask questions on the same conditions in the two cases. One has to accept that an understanding of a number of phenomena calls for several kinds of knowledge, each of which is correct in itself, but which cannot be synthesized on one common denominator. They are, Bohr says, using a term that has become world famous, 'complementary'. In literature, such complementary models can coexist. So, literary texts function by the use of supplementary experience and complementary knowledge.

3) *The challenge to forms of communication:* It is self-evident that the demands to communicate experience and knowledge increase under such conditions. More communication courses are on offer than there are subjects to communicate; the number of focus groups to investigate users and voters exceeds the population; and politicians replace their shadows by spin doctors. All this expresses the fact that there is no one good form for communicating knowledge, messages and practical experiences, but that everyone has to use and understand several different forms. Laymen or experts, all of us share certain common questions. How can we communicate a complex experience of reality in a simple way but without oversimplifying? How can we communicate an idea of security so that it does not mean more surveillance but more open space for movements and communication? How can we communicate doubt so that it does not result in despair but a strengthened orientation towards the future?

It is not hard to see that communication has to take account of a number of elements at the same time: What subject do we want to communicate, to whom, using which media and pedagogical techniques, in what situation, on the basis of which conditions of reception, from which perspective? And more elements besides. The coherent totality of all of these elements is what I call a *form of communication.* Such a totality can have a form that is fairly fixed. We know what elements to take into account in a TV communication today and how they form a whole. We knew the elements that defined class teaching in school up to about twenty years ago. As long as the single elements are fixed, we can consider them separately and assess their contribution to the whole. But if new sub-elements are involved, a new subject or a new medium for example that call for taking a fresh account of both the sender's and recipient's skills and preassumptions, we will also need to reconsider the form of communication as a whole, including all its components, old and new.

This was the case in, for instance, communicating information about AIDS, and it also occurs, for example, in the use of digital media in teaching. But we can also run into new composite forms of communication we have not seen before, and can begin to have doubts about which elements are actually brought together here. The use of blogs, search engines, block chains, texting and chatrooms and social media in general create new global forms of communication the structure, function and consequences of which we have not yet been able to grasp fully, let alone control, and which we therefore have difficulty in using purposefully as reliable forms of communication. Some have even regarded the whole lot of them as contradicting knowledge and promoting a post-factual society.

Globalization challenges both the individual elements and the forms of communication in their totality. First of all, this problem concerns the authoritative basis for the communication. Can we trust what we find via Google or Baidu? What the TV news broadcasts say? The minister's spin-doctors? The identity of senders of mails, sms, tweets and so on? The knowledge that derives from new didactical principles in education and from interdisciplinary disciplinary projects? As long as the elements and the overall form of communication are relatively constant at any historical moment, we do not inquire about the authority behind the communication. It follows automatically, as long as we do what we usually do when communicating in a qualified way, or, as an old Danish proverb says, 'No matter how large the church, there is always a priest at one end.'

However, this trust may be abused on a global scale by phishing mails from disguised senders who, if anyone is careless enough to respond, receive information that allows them to hack your computer and server. The confidence in the established forms of communications is even more profoundly challenged by the emergence of so-called 'fake news', maybe mixed with hacking. Old-fashioned rumours were mostly of a local nature, or at least with a limited circulation, and grounded in detectable human motivations. In contrast, fake news go global via a blend of social media, market economy and hacking with no motivation beyond sensation, demonstration of technological skills and easy money, but still they have a global effect which may even present an potential global threat. The identity of authors and their locality, background and context vanishes in cyber space and the circulation of fake news pays off via ads on phoney websites that appear as reliable look-alikes of news channel. If efficient lying presupposes a sufficient knowledge of the truth (Frankfurt 2005), fake news producers could not care less. When caught red-handed, this is just an occasion to produce new fake news. Later, the fake news may be repeated by traditional news media, which then, unintentionally, add their authority to the hoax and maybe trigger new scams, thus jeopardizing the entire reliability of public information. The 2016 presidential election in the United States generated a global awareness of this problem and added political manipulation to it; but beyond this particular event, the effect is that the general reliability of our forms of communication disseminating vital information with a global impact is caught in a vicious circle of global proportions.[4]

The challenge to forms of communication imposed by globalization is precisely directed against the basis of authority. In schools, the background of the pupils changes because of the influence of globalization on childhood and adolescence as well as family background, and this situation of course includes the effects of migration. The students' consumption of media and use of language differs from just a few years ago. Their patterns of experience are not the same; their models of knowledge evolve in new directions. Today more than ever before, forms of communication must therefore incessantly be selected and reselected, and together with assessment of outcome, also assessment of working processes and choice of communication strategies has therefore become an integral part of most forms of communication.

There is no point in searching for a wall-to-wall authority, which we can roll out each time we are to pass on experience or knowledge, be it a belief system supported by an institution, a political ideology supported by a party or a universal pedagogical formula comprising all schools. Nor can schools make do with teaching pupils to write one form of their native language, the right one. They have to learn that communication depends on subject matter, situation and audience and calls more for culturally determined choices than communication techniques.

Since no one on his or her own can experience or personally develop knowledge about the global world of which we are a part, everyone, experts included, is always dependent on experience and knowledge from a variety of sources and transmitted through many different media and caught by the cognitive uncertainty that is produced by this situation. Human reality has always been mediated, but the mediation in the globalized reality is more complex than ever. To refer mindlessly to 'science is of the opinion' does not provide an authoritative basis of communication that is beyond doubt; it only provides an indispensable partial contribution. In literature, however, doubt of communicative authority is no aberration; literature always seizes direct hold of the clash between an authoritative basis and competing media and messages in the manifold forms of communication that globalized culture makes us dependent on. Who has the authority to speak here? Throughout history, this question has been essential to literature as communication and it plays an important cultural role in a globalized culture.

The three challenges I have mentioned here are not just a somewhat random selection of the furnishings in the buildings of culture. They form their underlying foundation. They cannot be ignored without the house collapsing or standing unfinished, with abandoned tubs of cement and empty scaffolding. Culture builds on the experiences we make and the knowledge we use in order to make the experiences cohere in patterns of experience and models of knowledge. These we communicate to each other in forms that enable us to test their validity with others. Experience, knowledge and communication are the cornerstones of cultural structures.

The cultural process of globalization challenges the basic structure we are familiar with. When experiences are new, open-ended and uncertain, and yet impossible to ignore, then words, concepts and forms of expression in which we can contain them also become inquiries and experiments in relation to what we usually do. The communication must try out several paths at the same time, so that together we can start to relate to the new experiences. Literature helps to maintain and renew the basic structure, because it does not mainly have to do with the meanings that words *have* but with the meanings that experiences *acquire* through them. Of course, literature is not always the strongest or most important factor in every situation. Nor is it the only one. But it is always an indispensable factor. The 70 per cent water in our bodies and its microscopic four to five grams of iron are equally indispensable for our survival.

Spanish Chinese from Peru

Back at Newcomer High School, we may ask Li-Tsu Fernandez, Mario Fu or Cathy Yang how they dealt with these challenges to their experience, knowledge and communication. In all likelihood, they would look at me as if I was a man who had wandered by mistake into the ladies' toilet. They did not have globalization as a school subject or topic. It was simply their life, and, over a wide range, it permeated the concrete details of their everyday lives. Nevertheless, it was these three challenges that they inadvertently were relating to, even without thinking about it.

They sat there separately with their mixed *experiences* of family life and family history. Chinese, Spanish and South American highways merged when they had to work out, which experiences of a place of belonging, values and traditions towards which they had to choose to orient themselves. They did not do this in a general or abstract way, but in relation to actual experiences of how dwelling, family, parents' jobs, friends, school and spare time had changed by their arrival in the United States, without their being able to grasp the larger contexts of the experiences, let alone gain an overview of them. The patterns of experience were conveyed beyond the horizon of the individual pupil, and as far as some of the patterns were concerned they reached back to earlier generations beyond their own memory. There was not any necessary inner cohesion between the elements, except for the fact that most of these elements for more or less random, murky historical reasons were actually collected together in precisely *their* lives where they are now.

And their teacher, Mr. Ostrovski, was also moving along on the same highway. The name betrays an East European history that runs parallel to that of the children. His experiences of place, tradition and values have also been radically transformed by personal and shared choices and coincidences and are active at precisely the spot where he now experiences their impact. I took a sidelong glance at one of my fellow visitors, Clas Ruyssevelt. Some branch or other of his family had also emigrated and taken the name Roosevelt. And I thought of my other co-visitor, Stjepan, who phoned home every day to the then united Yugoslavia to check if it still existed. It did, but only for a short amount time after our encounter in 1989. That was before I knew that there was going to be a war and the Balkans would come to be split up. But he already knew that, for it was nothing new to him or his family.

He was born in the Balkans and grew up in the United States with his grandparents, but travelled home to get education and a job. Since the age of ten, he had lived permanently with his brother in the Croatian district of

New York, up in Queens. All of them, including the brother who remained in New York, were shadow Croatians, just as others were shadow Serbians. When he returned to study at the university, Stjepan spoke a mixture of children's and old people's Croatian, so he had to have language training in his native tongue. But he knew English all right. Half of his family lived in the United States, having come as refugees after the Second World War, although it was not always the same half. Some of them travelled back and forth for a while, living several years on either side of the Atlantic, also his parents. As for the schoolchildren, to say 'this is where I belong' was not something that was self-evident to him.

My name is just Larsen, as is the name of quite a few Danes. My family crept ashore on the west coast of Jutland at some point, although they had moved a bit further east after a couple of generations. I live where none of my family members ever lived, first in Odense then in Copenhagen. Both places have been as much 'home' to me as the then non-existing Croatia Stjepan returned to. We are just 'at home' in different ways. Perhaps I am the one who is slightly out of place. My home was perhaps a part of globalization without my realizing it. And what did that mean? That was something to take a close look at when I returned – well, home (Larsen 2016b).

The children at the school also dealt with the challenge to their *models of knowledge*. Was there anything at all in the way of cohesive common knowledge that was simply passed on to them, apart from a technical proficiency in English? The choice of historical subjects, Egyptian gods and ancient Greek and Roman culture did not seem an obvious one, despite Mr. Ostrovski's vague reference to the children's common European background since they happened to talk Spanish, although the history of European colonization actually played a more important role when the family histories of the children were formed. But the real reason for the choice of subject, Mr. Ostrovski remarks, was neither the content nor the children's assumed cultural background. It had solely been determined by the pedagogical level and what the teacher decided to be relevant.

On that basis, what he taught became understandable knowledge. Greek and Roman mythology was something all of them could manage, while Egyptian gods was for the proficient ones, we were told. Basic knowledge requirements then were never something given, but had to be chosen throughout, and the choice was not decided by tradition but by the situation. It was doubtful whether it ever became a model of knowledge. I thought of my children back home. Perhaps they were having a Danish or History lesson right now. Those subjects naturally also challenge our knowledge. But choices had been made in advance, without any further justification, because it lay within a well-known and common model of knowledge for Danes. Perhaps these choices also ought to be justified more closely?

The choice of the *form of communication* was a striking challenge. There was no common language that was self-evident. That is how things are in every globalized context. And if there is a common language, it is not certain that it is always the most appropriate one. Here it was Spanish, but it ought to be English, since hieroglyphics hardly encourage common verbal interaction. Images could be made use of, however. The children were carrying out a fundamental cultural activity that goes deeper than language: choose, combine, give it a name and do this with the media you have at your disposal in your culture. In this instance: choose head and body, combine them, look at the name in hieroglyphics, write your own name and do all this by touching a keyboard and clicking on a mouse. It is not the mediation of a common culture, but an exercise in building up culture as a game on the basis of common cultural conditions. Here, the game is a form of communication in a new cultural situation that as yet does not have a context.

And the kids certainly join in the game, giggling when they deliberately combine wrongly. The Internet is still waiting just round the corner, but they reproduce precisely the way in which the net builds up information, knowledge and cultural context. This way is basic for how experience, knowledge and communication are part of present-day globalization processes. Global knowledge and experience are inextricably linked to this media communication. Game or not, the media have to get under our skin if we are to take an active part in the exchange of information and knowledge, one where we constantly have to select, combine and validate. No one can ever experience everything that is necessary to know something about from a global point of view. One is dependent on the mediated transmission of other people's knowledge, opinions and experiences – not only when one occasionally asks for it, but all the time. Whether or not we can keep our daily job round the corner depends on the Asian markets, the price of oil in the Middle East, the New York stock exchange and the effect of the volatile oil prices. Communicated knowledge about such relations is now part of our immediate everyday life.

Although the children at Newcomer High School were to be helped to integrate in a new cultural context, they were already prepared for globalization before it had really got under way. In 1989, I had just got a computer for the first time back home and was a bit unsure about what the whole thing was about. At that point in time, it had definitely not changed anything in my way of communicating, or amassing knowledge let alone my experiences, apart from introducing a foreign element into my life that I had to become familiar with.

There is no cultural master template

The school class is a concentrated image of globalization. The image shows that these children are going to form their lives in a world that demands choices, on conditions that are more dynamic and changing than those that have characterized the lives of earlier generations, including language and place, even tradition and history. The latter sounds contradictory at first glance, but it is an unyielding condition for many people in a multicultural society that they will have to choose the tradition to which they wish to belong. Indeed, the choice situation is even more radical, for also the natural basis of our lives is partially made up choices, from global risks in the environment via genetic modification of plants to individual plastic surgery and straightening irregular teeth with braces. It is this fundamental cultural process of choice that the children set in motion, still as a game, by clicking the mouse while playing together in class.

Globalization is a process that probably creates uniformity, but the three challenges of experience, knowledge and communication also intensify known differences and create new ones that call for choices. Changes in patterns of experience and models of knowledge are the result of choices, ours and other people's. Forms of communication mainly mediate this condition, right down to the banal use of the mouse. Standard communication situations also lead to individual choices. This applies at the simple everyday level: pick up the phone, call a company, your community health centre or a public authority and listen to the various choices given to you by the digital voice so as to get you through to the relevant person to talk to; all the while you guess as best you can, sometimes making the wrong guess and having to return to the main menu. And if you have to wait, you are often presented with all sorts of other wonderful things the firm can offer you to choose between. Or given music that I at any rate would hardly have chosen to pain my eardrums, but others have.

The person who has to choose also comes under pressure. Choosing means subsuming responsibility: 'Click on the mouse and write your name in hieroglyphics!' 'Yes, but how?' 'Just try for yourself!' – If the choices, apart from involving combinations and confusion, also end up being personal and binding, this means that those clicking are aware of how basic even the simplest and most innocent choices are, and what demands it makes on the chooser. The mouse does not click itself. Someone does so and sets consequences in motion that far exceed a click that lasts a fraction of a second. A bomb released by a drone or a global virus attack on the Internet are started by the same sort of click. Perhaps that perspective is way above the children's heads, but not beyond their context and the reality of which they are a part. And not only the children here, my children and I at home are part of that reality. If we are not, we will become so. If we are unaware of this, all the worse for us. That too is a choice.

One can say that this situation indicates the contours of a new collective global culture for individual choices. Not for individualists in the traditional sense, where we made a choice and were held responsible for all the premises and the consequences, also those we knew nothing about. We could simply have thought twice about it, we would be told. From that point of view, we were personally responsible for both the course and the content of our journey through life. We often made the difficult choice of taking part in something or remaining outside and taking the consequences of both. We could simply have made a different choice. I chose to travel to the United States and also to return home again.

But the pupils do not choose in that way and are not individuals in that way. Not because they are children, but because their conditions are different. No matter how much they think twice about things, they cannot know the premises and consequences. What fixed models are there for Spanish-speaking Chinese from Peru in the United States? For they are not Danes in Denmark. Even so, the ball lies at the feet of every single child. To use the title of a

Danish interview book by Camilla Mehlsen and Filip Laus, *Globalisterne* [The Globalists] (2007), they are globalists:

> Globalisation is neither vapid, abstract nor frighteningly impossible to grasp. On the contrary, it is extremely concrete. Globalisation is carried out by Lars, Camilla, Morten, Søren and Mette – and all the others we meet in this book. … And globalisation also has to do with you, for it is the result of your choices, your purchases and your film and internet habits. … 'You should talk to my teenage son about what globalisation means for his everyday life in Dubai', Jacob Illeris says to us. 'He wouldn't call it globalisation, but that's what it is, it is the basis for much of what he does every single day.' (Mehlsen and Laus 2007: 182 and 183)

So each time we make a concrete choice, on a small or a large scale, in details, in jest or in all seriousness, we also make a choice in principle about our identity and our cultural basis, often without realizing it. When the children, chatting away, click back and forth between heads and bodies, they unconsciously demonstrate in practice that history and tradition are not only something one *has* but something one is obliged to *choose*. This doubleness between detail and basis, between conscious and unconscious choices is not a complication of everyday life. It is the simplicity of everyday life, a type of 'banal cosmopolitanism' (Beck 2006: 10). Literature makes this self-evident quotidian life something concrete and conscious in the texts so we can see it, and maybe qualify other choices.

What the Newcomer children are practising in their small computer exercises is something else than learning about the great figures of history who make fundamental and difficult choices and become models of identification. Instead, they are learning themselves to choose how they build up open-ended situations in which they place themselves in partially unpredictable situations full of dilemmas that they have to learn to judge in relation to surroundings, earlier situations, other individuals, other possibilities, other information, relevant and irrelevant effects. Globalization offers no master template or craft apprenticeship, only invites imagination, experiment and improvisation. This is what literature presents to us and practises itself. Hardly strange that the former president of Seoul University Un-Chan Chung predicts that 'The values of openness, disinterestedness, and cooperation will come to be seen as equally important as market principles and global standards' (Leadbeater and Wilsdon 2007: 16).

Perhaps some of the Newcomer pupils will be future advocates and practitioners of these values. When this book is published, they are old enough to be, and they are prepared early. They ought not to perform limited actions with a predetermined responsibility, modelled on other persons and their actions. They ought to choose improvised situations with frayed edges. But those they are also responsible for. We do not choose because we *have* a responsibility. But we *acquire* a responsibility because we choose and are obliged to do so. We are alone, but not isolated. What we are going to form is the individuality of globalization. Here, the children do not choose if they are to be included or not. They *are* included.

I sent a few thoughts off to Denmark. It lay there as usual. The very concept of the distinctive nature of the local is not revoked by globalization. The only thing that is revoked is the idea that the distinctiveness of the local is developed and strengthened by being isolated. For in the light of globalization the distinctive nature of the local is decided by the way in which we make our locality the vantage point of a larger world of other local cultures and their norms. The individual children at Newcomer High School live in various different places at one and the same time – China, Peru, the United States. The same applied to Stjepan and maybe Mr. Ostrovski. They had to choose to get that world to cohere with their personal and family experience and the local histories that underlay them. And this would be the case no matter where they chose to settle down in the future. Just like the cash dispenser I used somewhere: 'The world at your feet, your banking at your fingertips'. I cannot recall where the dispenser stood. But when I find it, I will know it is the same cash dispenser at the same street corner, no matter where in the world it stands.

I also realized that I was not simply going home at some point. Returning home was also a choice. I could choose not to or be forced to, just as the families of the children and Mr. Ostrovski had perhaps once been, and Stjepan perhaps would be. Returning home was to choose to confirm that it was there that I belonged. But it could have been a different choice and perhaps will be one day, without that necessarily being a larger break than staying at home. To choose another place could be an unexpected consequence I did not foresee when I pressed a button and said yes to a trip to the United States. Now though, I had to relate to this.

I came to think of my Swedish maternal grandparents who chose to leave for Denmark in the 1890s, and my uncle, who took the decision to emigrate to Canada in the 1920s. I had not exactly been thinking of them until now. I had always regarded them as exceptions. Perhaps that is wrong, perhaps they exemplify the new normal. Yet, they always remained migrants and local at the same with different references, hybrid Danish Swedes and Canadian Danes. Or maybe Swedish Danes and Danish Canadians? The majority of people the world over, possibly everyone, experience, despite material, cultural and religious dissimilarities, such differences that call for choices, no matter whether they are, high or low, rich or poor, Danish or migrant, the Western modernist or the suppressed toiler of the developing world, male or female, children or adult. Even those who have never heard of globalization, never chosen to live on its conditions and never moved from the spot. The naive conception of early colonization that countries did not belong to anyone when Europeans had not set foot there no longer applies, not even as an illusion. The entire planet, inhabited or not, is now subject to international conventions. They are the frameworks of our choices of place.

Not everyone, however, has the same opportunity to choose, only the same obligation. Experiencing demands is not the same as having power over them, even though both are harsh facts in the same reality. We are admittedly all in the same boat, but we are in separate lifeboats, if there are enough of them. This complex of conscious and unconscious choices, detail and basis, experience and power, equality and inequality, individuality and heterogeneous communities, identity and responsibility in a global perspective are the great thematic garner of literature. It is made use of in both new and old works that cut across their local borders, but all of them give the individual reader a concrete experience here and now of border-crossing trajectories.

The next chapter turns the attention directly to literature: How does literature, in terms of the conditions of globalization, take up the three challenges I have just discussed? The chapter attempts to *develop* a mutual connection between globalization and literature, not talk about a connection that already exists. It doesn't. So as to concretize this connection I give it the form of a dialogue between two recurring main characters neither of whom have any preconceived opinions about what such a connection looks like.

One of them is the late German social scientist Ulrich Beck. He rightly has a global reputation for having supplied comprehensive and inquiring, but definitely not simple, analyses of globalization as a broad social and cultural phenomenon. The three major subsections of the chapter follow the three cultural challenges of globalization: patterns of experiences, models of knowledge and forms of communication, which Beck analyses under three headings: the cosmopolitan, the risk society and reflexive modernization. But the concretization which literature and other aesthetic phenomena give of the complexity is not covered by his abstract social science. Complementary knowledge is acquired. This is provided by the second main character of the chapter, the storyteller Karen Blixen, better known under her pen name as Isak Dinesen. She has never heard anyone say globalization, but she knows something about experience, knowledge and communication in a wider transnational context, among other things by activating a supplementary experience from her European background to understand the foreign African continent she writes about in her memoirs *Out of Africa* (1937).

Literature as a Challenge to Globalization

Patterns of experience

The world citizen

In 1789, the French Revolution took the whole of Europe by storm. This was shortly after the United States had seceded from Britain. Both events involved attempts to put human rights and other expressions of liberty into practice. They were referred to as universal; today, one could be tempted to use the term 'global'. Although contested, these rights are still the only transnational guidelines for our acts across all forms of borders worldwide. And in general, we often refer with good reason to the Enlightenment period when trying to find tools with which we can actively relate to globalization, but there are disagreements as well.

On one of the first heady days in August 1789, before the revolution went completely off the rails and ended in a bloodbath on the guillotine, Joachim Heinrich Campe was in Paris. He was a liberal-minded writer, an educator and a publisher from Hamburg. He stood in the gardens of the Palais Royal, the epitome of a public space at the time. It was a social place of refuge with shops, cafés and gambling dens and girls who were either out walking or 'walking the streets', and where one could also glimpse Paris fashion and air political views; if macchiato, sushi and caipirinha had been known at the time, that is where you would have found them. Campe could hardly stand still from sheer enthusiasm.

This Garden ... is rightfully in more than one respect referred to as the 'Capital of Paris', and regarded as the centre of not only the city but of the entire kingdom ... Anyone who ever since birth had not been outside this wonderful and magical place, could pride himself on not being inferior in knowledge of humanity and the world, or of any kind of enjoyment and pleasure – apart from an enjoyment of nature – to anyone else, even if that person had travelled the length and breadth of the entire surface of the globe … A Parisian would cease, the moment he entered this place, to be a Parisian and a Frenchman; he would for that moment become a complete Republican, a World Citizen, who knew of no bourgeois or conventional limitations and fetters. (Campe 1790: 72–74)

Here, at one particular place, everything is present at one and the same time. Nature or non-nature, it makes no difference. Campe experiences himself as a universal individual, a world citizen, and feels almost able to touch the whole world. The basic experience of the world citizen almost erupts from places like this where the whole world is gathered together into one concrete experience.

In the early eighteenth century, the varied and explosive experiences of great discoveries from near and far started to be gathered into words, concepts and theories that then could be transmuted into common social principles and be widely disseminated. For Europeans, and quite a few others, the whole world started in Europe, with the rest of the world being an extension of the universal European perspective. In turn, impressions, products, peoples and raw material from this world subsequently arrived in Europe as in a cultural laboratory, where it was transformed into production, knowledge, views of humanity and societal structures, which then once more were disseminated to apply to the whole world. Europe was the centre of this globalizing roundtrip in the run-up to modern globalization. Things and thoughts of highly diverse origins were harmoniously united. The rest consisted of rings in the water around Europe.

Inspired by Diogenes from Greek Antiquity, the world citizen was also called a cosmopolitan, at the same time belonging nowhere and everywhere and detached from local societal concerns. *Kosmos* is the old Greek concept of the universe. It gathers together both all the concrete elements from sand between one's toes to stars before one's eyes, and at the same time all the basic principles that hold the universe together. Here, the big city becomes the iconic place for this experience. *Polis* is also Greek and means not only a city but also a city state. As early as the fourth century BCE, Aristotle described in his *Politics* such a social and geographical structure which had an actual city, especially

Athens, as its centre, and a surrounding area that was governed from there. *Polis* is thus both the physical city and an urbanized society. In miniature, *Polis* has the same form as *kosmos*. Cosmopolitans came into contact with the kosmos when they resided in the polis, and could experience themselves as being at the centre of the universe. That was what Campe experienced in Paris which opened for a new globalized pattern of experience.

Cosmopolitans were not necessarily great travellers. The *salons* were as genuinely cosmopolitan as any other place. There were seafarers, explorers and colonial governors who carried out the hard graft. But on the basis of their own and other people's knowledge, the cosmopolitans created a coherent whole out of the experiences. They operated at the interface between science and the cultural debate, between knowledge and communication. Yet, they did travel, but mainly between the major European cities, a few went to America and others to the colonies. Stable routes had been established across the Atlantic and navigable routes to other colonies. But they mainly travelled so as to get together with other cosmopolitans. They took the world order upon themselves with the major international cities as their point of departure, cities where one moved in high circles, in studies, coffee houses, clubs and at the public gatherings that were now gradually being allowed. Here one was a world citizen. In London, the Irish writer Oliver Goldsmith went to a pub in 1763 – certainly not for the first time – and listened in contempt to the bragging local regulars expressing their national prejudices about all European countries except Britain. Goldsmith had travelled, or rather toured around Europe and he would rather much prefer 'the title of a citizen of the world, to that of an Englishman, a Frenchman, a European or any other appellation whatever' (Goldsmith 1992: 97).

Regional and national peculiarities were boundaries and in particular prejudices that had to be overcome. The cosmopolitans thought in terms of social principles that were to apply to everyone, and they were developed under the prevailing conditions as the principles we still use when we try to regulate the globalized world: universal human rights, democratic principles, freedom of speech, gender equality, general principles of upbringing and education, reforms of society as an ongoing process and also the idea of a global social order to regulate conflicts.

But some places were better than others, for example, Paris or the landscapes that started to tempt citizens out into nature. In both environments, one experienced the world in its totality and saw it from above in its universal naturalness. On that basis, valid principles for everyone were formulated. In the world's first major interdisciplinary collective knowledge project, the French Encyclopedia of 1755–1780, common knowledge was collected together that could spread out in all directions. It was a gigantic collective knowledge and dissemination project, an eighteenth-century Wikipedia. For the first time, it was admitted that no one single person, the polyhistor, could collect all relevant knowledge. The knowledge-based network thinking of globalization was maybe not born but at least conceived here.

On such a basis, it ought also to be possible by common effort to construct certain locations and societies on virgin soil as confirmation of the fact that universal harmony could be achieved. In the United States, Paris and elsewhere, people set about realizing this project. But truly virgin soil normally meant the colonies, America, Africa, Australia and the Pacific Islands. Utopian ideas almost tripped over each other. No one imagined that the universal principles could be practised by everyone, though. Certain peoples and places were simply too wild and too close to animals and nature for them to be able to practise it themselves. The thousands of years of prehistory in colonial areas were not conducive to universal principles and could thus be ignored. But for those who had the prerequisites, that is, the Europeans, it was possible. And then they could, of course, bring in the others from the cold to a suitable location in relation to the European centre.

There were of course conflicts: first, between old and new structures in the individual societies. The French Revolution did not go off quietly. Then, there were the new, cosmopolitan-oriented countries that had to fight for the same planet with its raw materials, riches and markets in order to become cosmopolitan, and finally, between the cosmopolitan elite and the masses, who were beginning to flex their muscles as a united force before they became the classes of the industrial society. Not to mention all those who were to be Europeanized elsewhere with the aid of clothing, religion, beatings and glass beads.

But the actual way of thinking did not have built-in conflicts and clashes. Conflicts were passing faults that would disappear as developments continued.

One only had to weigh up things carefully and organize an increasing number of locations that could serve as examples of how the universal principles could gain concrete, local life. The inexhaustibility of nature was changed into society's inexhaustible potential for progress, a straight line of development like the never-ending highway Chaplin waddles along when the film ends and our dream continues.

Everyday cosmopolitans

Ulrich Beck has provided new definitions of basic concepts from the Enlightenment period in order to understand fundamental cultural and social characteristics of globalization. One of the concepts he examines, takes apart and reassembles in a new way, is precisely this cosmopolitan experience.[1] What does it feel like to be present in the globalization, to experience a global location? This is one of the key questions he asks in his book *Cosmopolitan Vision* (2004) [Der kosmopolitische Blick]. The first thing he does is to turn Campe's experience upside down. The world citizen proceded directly from his concrete experience to a universal idea that was to trim the experience until all frictions and differences disappeared or were assigned a subordinate place. But as we know from twentieth-century Europe and elsewhere, the tensions that exist between the harmony of the utopia and the conflicts of the experience cannot be 'cosmopolitized away' without the shedding of blood.

So Beck takes the opposite tack. The cosmopolitan outlook is a way of looking at the actual diversity of reality, not towards a utopian uniformity. By means of that outlook, one describes the actual social and cultural differences of regions and places on the basis of certain principles that enable us to understand this composite nature as an everyday reality. Contrasts do not mean a lack of order but a lack of one order and of one universal harmony. It is that form of complex order his cosmopolitan outlook tries to glimpse. To include the global dimension in this experience calls for an extra interpretative effort. It does not remove conflicts or differences, but places them in perspective. Globalization is not a utopian aim outside the reality all of us have to comply with, but the expression of the fact that the order which we experience is the order that exists. We are not to be like the elitist world citizens of the eighteenth century, but just simply everyday cosmopolitans like the children in Newcomer High School in San Francisco. The former, says Beck, cultivate cosmopolitanism, the latter live as everyday globalists in the actually existing cosmopolitization. The universal principles of the eighteenth century are not ideas that are to be used to overcome all the differences that globalization creates, but are practical tools that are constantly necessary in order to handle the differences of globalization across existing borders to enable us to live with them.

The utopian cosmopolitans who stand rejoicing in Paris or keep company with Goldsmith in the pub in London dream of being cosmopolitans in particularly highly developed locations. Beck claims that they do not need to travel anywhere. The cosmopolitan outlook has something to gaze at everywhere, in Nuuk, Tokyo, Manila, Middletown and a spot in the Amazon rainforests. And all of these places can be concretely present at the same location, in a TV broadcast, in my photos on the hard disk, in the involvement of the Tokyo millionaire in the rainforests of the Amazon via the New York stock exchange or in the gaze of the inhabitants of Nuuk at the incredibly beautiful colours of the northern lights caused by the ash from a volcanic eruption in the Philippines, that is if they have understood newspapers and television correctly. And we must also not forget the co-op in any small godforsaken town with its commodities from all over the world, its contribution to CO_2 emissions from the frozen food counters, or its organic produce from at home or flown in from abroad. Now, we don't have to go to either Paris or San Francisco to be globalists.

What is one to call a place where we experience something like this? It was at any rate not that which Campe saw in Paris. He probably overlooked a great many details, as we all do when we have fallen in love. But there were also relations which he was unable to see. They were as yet not possible to experience, but later I happened to experience them in the classroom in San Francisco. Globalized places are not clearly demarcated spaces with uniform traits or a clear common characteristic that enables one to collect them together with one common denominator. Cities such as Paris were also even then a dynamic myriad of people and humming with culture, to put it politely, and also a complete and utter mess topped with power and lustre, to pass a more sober judgement. Campe, however, was able to find one common denominator that allowed him to ignore everything else. Paris was the centre of everything. But Beck's cosmopolitan outlook does not look aside. It sees what is there, there where it is.

Mary Louise Pratt suggests in *Imperial Eyes* (1992) *contact zone* as a globalized term for that type of place experience. I prefer the more straightforward *meeting place*. She is mainly thinking of colonial or postcolonial locations, but they are structurally related to the places of globalization. Both *place* and *meeting* have several dimensions. At such places, people cross who otherwise are separated geographically and historically. Perhaps they are present together relatively by chance, but they have binding relations to each other while they are there, temporarily or for the rest of their lives. Such places are not necessarily sought out, as Campe does in Paris. The places are meeting places because of those who are meeting there, not because they are specially chosen places. Therefore, the meetings do not only comprise the concrete individuals involved but also the relations that have brought them together – power, inequality, coercion, conflict and various values. The own local prerequisites of the place are only one component among others – perhaps not always the most important one.

Meeting places have a horizontal dimension, made up of those who concretely meet there at street level. Horizontality here means coexistence within the same time frame. But meeting places also have a vertical dimension. They contain traces of all the meetings that have already taken place there previously, and of the meetings in other places that have supplied the cultural baggage for the people now meeting. Verticality here refers to a combination of phenomena existing in different time frames, one preceding and maybe determining the other, like the past in relation to the present.

The horizontal dimension may have a centre, such as Paris, or several centres, such as the medieval trade routes. The vertical does not. Local tradition alone does not determine either the real past of the meeting place or the network of cultural prerequisites that are brought into the actual meetings. Local relations cannot decide which traditions people bring along with them, or what parts of local tradition they choose to rely on. For that reason, a meeting place as a whole cannot have a permanent centre.

Meeting places are therefore places where meetings are improvised to become durable, Pratt says. No one can predict who 'is on', no one knows completely the sides of his or her own background that other people perceive.

One is perhaps personally not completely aware of the fact that one's background contains the aspects that are visible to others, and no one can predict where the assembled collectivity is heading, and of how and when people are replaced as they go along. There was no Chinese central committee that said what was to happen with the Chinese Peruvians going to San Francisco, but they found out themselves when their Chinese and Spanish backgrounds were mixed with their American possibilities. The borders of the meeting place shift as a result of our activities. But for those who do not take part in the diversities and conflicts of the place, Pratt says, things remain chaotic.

Meeting places are then not empty rooms we walk into, like a freshly painted school class after the summer holidays, such as the eighteenth-century utopians dreamt of. The new world was admittedly new for the settlers back then, but old for the native Americans and other indigenous peoples elsewhere. Meeting places are first and foremost places where we cannot avoid taking part in the meetings that have already taken place – between people, cultures, customs, memories, conflicts, physical structures and languages. Those who wish to have a neutral meeting place, or a place that does not have to be regulated by improvisations but by known norms, become homeless. Like native nationals who would prefer to live in a remote village without foreign intruders, but actually reside in an ethnically mixed neighbourhood in a major city, or migrant families that arrange things as if they lived in Kabul, but forget that they are living on a third floor in major Western city with church bells taking them by surprise every Sunday morning. Meeting places do not make us homeless if we participate. But they are a challenge to our patterns of experience.

In a global living room

Literature has always dealt with meeting places, also before they became global. They have often concentrated on one or two events: a young man sets out, or a stranger knocks on the door. The one who is in search of something new becomes a stranger in the new places he comes to, but he brings his old experiences along with him. The stranger at the door where the first person has set out from is exposed to the same fate, but in the reverse order. Sometimes literature does this humorously, at other times tragically, but never indifferently. The meeting places of literature confront concrete experiences with patterns of experience that do not have room for the new experiences.

In Isak Dinesen/Karen Blixen's *Out of Africa* (1937), we can see one example of how literature adopts Beck's cosmopolitan outlook in a concrete experiential context. One of the small sections in the book is called 'Farah and the Merchant of Venice' (Blixen 2013: 139–140).[2] From the very outset, concrete experiences are seen through different eyes: the title places the real-life figure of Farah, Blixen's steward, on an equal footing with an imagined person, the merchant of Venice from Shakespeare's comedy of the same name. Blixen entangles us in a series of tales organized as links in a chain before the impact of the unexpected experience strikes all the harder when it takes place at the end. She has received a letter that tells of a performance of the comedy in Copenhagen, and she is so seized by her memory of the Shakespeare play that she simply *has* to tell someone about it. And that someone turns out to be Farah. The first link, then, is Shakespeare's narrative in Renaissance English, the second the Danish performance that tells the story to a new audience and the third one a Danish letter that relates this event.

After this, Blixen herself takes the stage. She tells Farah about Shakespeare's narrative, orally of course, in English, Swahili or both. *We* on the other hand read yet another narrative, namely, about the entire situation when she told him about the comedy, that is, not the content of what she said, but the actual event while it was taking place. That event she relates to us in English, and later in Danish and in many other languages into which Blixen's book is translated. There are concrete events at both ends of the narrative chain, a performance in Copenhagen and a meeting between Blixen and Farah on the farm. It is the latter event that breaks the chain and unravels all the various stages backwards, along with the pattern of experience they contain. It is this unravelling we witness in the narrative that *we* read.

The two meet in Blixen's living room on the farm. The impression it conveys is of colonial condescension in the everyday life at the farm. If one happened to pass by and looked in through the window, one would think they were organizing household matters, Blixen writes. That is the pattern of experience that normally frames their meetings in the living room. The narrative we read emerges, because things did not go as expected. She 'called in Farah to talk with him about [the play], and explained the plot of the comedy to him' and this trivial everyday event could be the end of it. But it is not.

The first half of the sentence 'to talk with him' points forward, that is, what is shortly going to happen, then a comma. Surprisingly, she does not continue by 'and explain to him' but uses the past tense: 'and explain*ed*'. The whole thing has, then, already taken place, and she has got the breath of fresh air she needed. In spite of this, she goes on. So the actual course of events has clearly made the original intention irrelevant. It disappears behind a comma.

Blixen has probably told Farah about the plot and the characters. Bassanio with an empty purse and a full heart loans money from Antonio in order to propose to Portia. Antonio waits for money just round the corner and has recourse to the Jew, Shylock, for a temporary loan. The Jew does not want any guarantee, only the right to cut a pound of flesh out of Antonio's body, roughly the weight of a full heart. The proposal goes off well and results in a marriage, but Antonio's money has not come round the corner. The Jew refuses to take Bassanio's money from Portia instead, even when tripled, but insists on his pound of flesh, as stated in the contract. The shrewd Portia organizes a fake trial before Venice's most prominent judge, the Doge, and stipulates that the Jew must only take one single pound of flesh, neither more nor less. And only flesh, no blood is permitted. And that of course is impossible. So the Doge sentences Shylock to give up his faith and his house. He becomes homeless among both Jews and Venetians, while Antonio's money after all manages to get round the corner before the curtain falls.

The rest of Blixen's narrative shows us how the meeting with Farah via Shakespeare becomes an unexpected new experience in the living room, *her* home ground, where they normally meet on her conditions to deal with routine matters. The situation is a new one for him, and it eventually becomes a new one for her too. She tells the story twice. First, she describes Farah's reaction, packaging it in her knowledge of his Somali and Moslem background. She still has an imaginary schoolmistress's bun at the back of her neck and explains to him the rules that then applied for loaning money, contracts and legal principles. He is ignorant of them. And also she explains to us how Somalis think, respectfully but also slightly condescendingly. We are ignorant of that. The complicated affair with money, marriage and expensive loans is 'somewhat on the verge of the law, the real thing to the heart of a Somali'. Portia makes Farah open his eyes: 'I imagined that he saw her as a woman of his own tribe, Fathima with all sails set, crafty and insinuating, out to outman man.' And she sums up: 'Coloured people do not take sides in a tale ... the Somali, who in real life have a strong sense of values, and a gift for moral indignation, give these a rest in their fiction.'

And it is here, while both of them are taking a holiday from their everyday lives, that narratives, overview, colonial power structures, their usual everyday relations are insufficient, and a different experience breaks through. Blixen has also taken a holiday from real life, brought about by the memory of her reading of Shakespeare. But there is no escape to a different place than the living room where they usually discuss household matters. She has a need to relate, but he does not have any need to listen. Her need outside her daily life is thus realized within the power structures of the everyday. She calls him in.

Until now, the living room has seemed to be a clearly divided, well-defined space, with her, Shakespeare and European culture, legal system and rules for loaning money on the one hand, and Farah, Somali culture, Islam, Kenya on the other, in a respectful, but distanced exchange. Now it becomes a meeting place where the two opposites intertwine, and Farah and Blixen have to improvise to get things to hang together. They both take 'a rest' outside their everyday lives and thus also outside their normal patterns of experience, pushed out there by Shakespeare. Here, she and Farah find themselves under identical conditions. She is thus indirectly describing herself by describing things to him: they are both on holiday from their usual lives. The one who has a need to listen or to tell, the one who has something to tell and the one who does not, is reversed. Her schoolmistress role, instructing Farah and us, is no longer valid. It is this new experience that intrudes towards the end.

In the final section, Farah takes over control. Not by trying to instruct her or us but by asking questions that she is unable to answer and unable to explain, but which are just as genuine reactions to Shakespeare as the standard interpretation she wants to unfold to him. The place changes character, and so does the text. The story is now no longer told with Blixen as the fixed narrator, but it is conducted as a dialogue with lines, just as at the theatre in

Copenhagen. Blixen only inserts the obligatory *inquit* 'he said' and 'I said' and a couple of lines that describe the figure of Farah while he speaks. There is no longer anything about what all Somalis think and feel, only what he looks like. It is Farah here and now, seen from the outside while he performs like an actor on stage. There is nothing lacking as regards Farah's own understanding. He immediately pinpoints what everyone who sees the play is disturbed by: the role of the Jew. Shylock is right, but he is cheated, pure and simple. Yet, his demand is unreasonable and beyond all accepted norms. He is both right and wrong at the same time.

And Blixen's introductory short remark that she explained everything to Farah is a lie, pure and simple. His reactions show that she has actually not explained anything to him at all, but set alternative thoughts in motion in him. He asks: Why did nobody help the Jew? Why did he give up – he could have used a red-hot knife that brought out no blood? Why didn't he take small lumps of flesh one at a time and weigh them? He does not expect any answer, though, for he concludes himself: 'He could have done that man a lot of harm.' Blixen's only answer is no answer at all. No teacher of literature would accept such an answer at an examination: 'But in the story the Jew gave it up' – A pupil asked to explain the formula for the circumference of a circle, $2\pi r$, who replies that this is just the way circles are, is also not going to be wildly applauded by a maths teacher. Blixen's answer shows that she is floored, just as Shylock floors the onlooker with his indissoluble mixture of right and wrong. Shakespeare's openness is thus explained to Blixen by Farah, not in didactic terms but by the fact that he, through his concrete and surprisingly acute reaction and strong involvement, has transformed the living room into a meeting place beyond her small-minded need to get some air and instruct Farah and us.

There is no conclusion apart from this concrete experience. Blixen cannot sum the experience up in a conclusion; she is still in the midst of it. Farah has got a new angle on the way Blixen and Europeans think, and she has got a new view of herself, Farah and the contrast between them. *He* was the one who was able to see Shakespeare with new eyes and show this to her. He was better at placing himself in Shylock's position than she was able, in a generalizing and slightly condescending way, to understand the way Somalis think. And Shylock is, even so, thrice more alien to him: a Jew, a European and a figure from the European Renaissance, whereas Farah is a contemporary African Moslem.

Both Blixen and Farah have improvised their way through a dialogue in a concrete experience of mutual dependence. This became visible when the scope was expanded beyond everyday routines and came to include the personal and cultural meetings that structure the pattern of experience. The horizontal and vertical meetings at the location have intersected each other, outside their own conscious control. She showed an intention and a will and used her power to call him in without asking him if it was convenient. But her will did not control the course of events. The colonial space, the Danish and the Somali, that of the Renaissance and the present day, what can be said in Danish in a letter and the narrative we read, in broken Swahili and broken English between the two characters, and Shakespeare's Renaissance English – all of this has created a meeting place beyond plans and intentions, but determined by the experience of place in the concrete situation. Their experience has acquired a new pattern.

The text does not deal with globalization just because it takes place in Kenya. But it deals with the breaking away from set-routine local experience that is fostered by globalization. Ulrich Beck himself is on the lookout for concrete examples of how the cosmopolitan outlook is directed towards the less direct but highly concrete everyday experiences of globalization:

> What do we mean, then, by 'the cosmopolitan outlook'? Global sense is a sense of boundarylessness: an everyday, historically alert, reflexive awareness of ambivalences in a milieu of blurring differentiations and cultural contradictions. It reveals not just the 'anguish' but also the possibility of shaping one's life and social relations under conditions of cultural mixture. It is simultaneously a sceptical, disillusioned, self-critical outlook. (Beck 2006: 3)

It is such a vision that enables Blixen's text to show us her meeting with Farah – a possibility to form their lives on the multicultural conditions they have, with a sense of history and self-awareness, at the place where they meet. Their patterns of experience of the colonial reality have been shaken. Literature contains some of the examples Beck is in search of, also in relation to *models of knowledge*.

Models of knowledge

Risky knowledge

Most people use the terms 'danger', 'risk' or 'threat' at random for something overwhelming we are exposed to. Perhaps slightly fewer now after the expression 'risk society' has slipped into the language. If one takes one's precautions, one can avoid danger, risks and threats. It calls for a special type of knowledge which by definition is uncertain: knowledge about the future. Yet, we can try to avert even the uncertainty by making our knowledge more certain. This takes place in science and in the general expansion of the knowledge we gain from practical experience when we learn things the hard way. All cultures seek to know enough about the future in order to control it as much as possible. Science and spurious prophecies do not have anything to do with each other as far as content is concerned. Although complementary in relation to each other, they are identical in their cultural function: to satisfy the basic need for reliable knowledge about the future.

There is a tendency for us to talk mostly about risk and threat when there is a human will behind something, with dangers mostly related to the more undefined moods of nature. All we need is knowledge about the origins of risks, and then we can react. Perhaps, there are particular persons we can hold responsible and judge, or insecticides we can use, trees we can fell, or water that can be dammed. And if we do not possess the necessary knowledge to act proactively, then we set out to get hold of it. The mystery of cancer or Alzheimer's disease is still unsolved; it constitutes an ongoing knowledge project of precisely that kind, but not finished – yet. However, we cannot acquire special knowledge about our death and other fundamental natural conditions in that way. Here, we only know that we have to know how to face the facts, no matter how many life insurances we take out for our surviving relatives. Literature has always dealt with the disparity between our grip on the future and our precautions when the concrete experience turns a planned future into an unplanned present, and also when impossible knowledge about life after death turns into faith. Not always with the same prominent position in all periods, but never absent.

In his book *Risk Society* (1986) [Die Risikogesellschaft], Ulrich Beck shows us how this primeval conception of the relation between danger and risk, nature and culture, human responsibility and non-human processes does not apply in globalization.[3] First, the effects of human social activities are on a par with even the greatest of natural disasters. The nuclear disaster at Chernobyl in 1986 or in Fukushima in 2012 was on the same scale as any major natural disaster, and oil pollution in Alaska or in the Mexican Gulf is no less potent than any natural disease of the area's flora and fauna. Second, and more importantly, Beck claims that risks have become visibly different over the past fifty years and are an integral part of globalization. Climate change, holes in the ozone layer and lifestyle illnesses are not isolated side-effects of our way of maintaining normal Western culture, but are preassumptions for the existence of present society. To remove, for example, lifestyle illnesses would change the entire social organization of work and leisure, commuting, family structure and patterns of consumption that all contribute to keeping the entire machinery of society going. We create risks, because we create welfare, and we create welfare, because we create risks, according to Beck. There the production of risks is one of the preassumptions of the late industrial society. 'If you hang yourself or you do not hang yourself, you will regret both', was how Søren Kierkegaard put it (1992: 54).

Do not hang yourself

Beck does not go along with this formulation. New forms of knowledge about the future must be used, forms that include more factors than those we normally have recourse to, and a new knowledge must be formulated about the society that already exists. We reacted to the old, isolated risks as if one ought to turn a screw here and adjust a cog there in the machinery of society. This way of controlling the future was directly transferred to our political systems and their solutions. The entire mode of thought is based on a belief in the future where the world can be controlled with a reasonable degree of predictability, as a set of clear causes and effects fostering controllable and man-made progress. This is a model of knowledge in continuation of the world citizens to which Campe belonged in Paris in 1789.

Beck's main point is that this model is not what we are in need of. When risky effects are also one of society's basic products, and when the relation of the risk society to its natural foundation is not an isolated issue of resources, waste and conservation, but has to do with the total organization and underlying values of society, this reflects back on our entire way of thinking and organizing things. There is a totality that is at stake, not single factors or events. It is not only knowledge about economics, politics or technology Beck has in mind, but also the knowledge models that comprise our cultural basis.

Knowledge about the future has always been uncertain and has to be accompanied by credibility, beyond the concrete instances of uncertainty. This still holds, but within a new knowledge model where both uncertainty and credibility is of predominantly human origin and has a global outreach. The knowledge project of globalization is therefore a broad cultural project, not only one about particular new knowledge. This openness challenges our very ability to keep alive the necessary future orientation and its credibility that make people engage in their lives of view of its future possibilities on changing conditions, today conditions of a more complex and translocal nature than before.

Literature can deal with death, with natural disasters or overwhelming dangers we do not know enough about. It can on a large or a small scale show the disastrous limitation and naivety in humanity's use of knowledge about the future. It portrays how knowledge, belief and illusions are mixed up in the actual culture people live in. It can dish up incredible feel-good stories about everything eventually turning out all right, just as in slimming pill commercials, which are more fictive than literature has ever allowed itself to be. The crucial thing is that literature cannot refrain from transforming all experiences, so that they acquire a direction towards the unknown – on a large scale in utopias, on a small scale in the fragile and transient hope we have to renew every day to get along, or simply in the trivial reading experience when we laugh, are moved or scared, and thus cannot avoid moving forward towards what we are going to experience on the following pages.

When literature deconstructs models of knowledge, the future-orientation always still remains as the fundamental task, maintenance of the ability to direct ourselves towards the unknown. Without that ability, we and our culture cannot survive. And even without dealing directly with the actual dilemmas of nature and society, literature always holds a crack in language open, so it is always ready, despite everything, to formulate a knowledge that points towards the unknown. Even the writer who only throws sand in our eyes, places shards of glass in our mouth and images of the total cultural meltdown in our imagination has, despite everything, found it worth the trouble to find words, join them together and arouse someone's future attention. Literature always says: Do not hang yourself.

The future is now

Once again, I intend to use a passage from *Out of Africa* to demonstrate this transformation from a past that is breaking down and a deadlocked present to an open orientation towards the future. It is the introduction to the book on the first page (Blixen 2013: 3).[4] On the surface, the passage does not have anything to do with globalization but precisely with this attention to a foundational future-orientation that globalization requires us to maintain, even when it is not supported by any precise content. Beck speaks in this context, although mostly negatively, about an unconscious cosmopolitanism (Beck 2006: 19–21). What he has in mind is the negative mental impact of the dissolution of local traditions, the immediate experience of the blurred boundaries between oneself and other ethnic and social groups and the ambivalent emotions of empathy and aggressions this situation creates. At the same time, close personal relationships are being recreated in electronic and open social networks or global news fora. But unconscious cosmopolitanism is also a positive resource, because the strong mediation makes possible an awareness that opens for a reflexive and self-reflexive approach to an unconsciously grasped new reality which hides the potential for a radical breaking away from the past and a disorientation of the present into an orientation towards the future. Here, Beck envisions a new sociology, but the practice of literature is already active in this reconfiguration as in Blixen's opening to her book on Africa.

She portrays the wonderful, almost paradise-like landscape around her farm in Kenya near the Ngong Hills, both in concrete descriptions with colours, scents, shapes and movements and in relation to a particular situation where her 'individual existence becomes part of another world' (Beck 2006: 19). She is waking up in the morning and provides us with an elementary knowledge of the concrete details of the outside world: this is what it looks like. But it is not completely matter-of-fact. She sounds like a Romantic, far from all the noise of the world, more universal than global, more uplifted than affected:

> The geographical position, and the height of the land combined to create a landscape that had not its like in all the world … Up in this high air you breathed easily, drawing in a vital assurance and lightness of heart. In the high-lands you woke up in the morning and thought: Here I am, where I ought to be.

But the way in which she works on this basic mood has larger perspectives. She opens the description with the first sentence of the book: 'I *had* a farm in Africa, at the foot of the Ngong Hills.' She is writing about the past, something that inevitably has disappeared, yet still fills her completely.

The very last sentence of the book shows the background. She is now looking on the landscape soon to be lost as she sails away: 'But is was so far away that the four peaks looked trifling, hardly distinguishable, and different from the way they looked from the farm. The outline of the mountain was slowly smoothed and levelled out by the hand of distance'. (Blixen 2013: 212). First, the hills seem no longer hers, and finally, they disappear, also physically. It is that disappearing that ignites the first sentence of the book: Once I *had* those hills and the farm, personally and physically. It is a whole world that vanishes, for the landscape existed, and still stands there, unparalleled anywhere on earth. The present is only a past that has disappeared, and the future is just as empty as promises in commercials. But when she reshapes this situation, first into an independent experience of the present and then into an orientation towards the future, it becomes fundamentally like a cultural process that goes beyond Blixen herself. She transforms her knowledge of the landscape and the loss of it into a general model of knowledge about an open future.

The description is in the past tense, even though the landscape still lies there in Kenya. It is *her* landscape that is in the past, and it is *that* which we learn something about, like a thin membrane drawn over its disappearance:

> The colours were dry and burnt, like the colours in pottery. The trees had a light delicate foliage, the structure of which was different from that of the trees in Europe; it did not grow in bows or cupolas, but in horizontal layers, and the formation gave to the tall solitary trees a likeness to the palms, or a heroic and romantic air like full-rigged ships with their sails clewed up,

and to the edge of a wood a strange appearance as if the whole wood were faintly vibrating.

By virtue of her very description, still in the past tense, she makes her lost landscape become much more than her own. It can now be understood against a general cultural background, Europe, in relation to images from European culture: the Romantic attitude, a full-rigged ship with its sails furled. The distance that she talks about at the end of the book is not only a personal and physical distance but also a cultural distance between Africa and Europe. She transcends it here by using it to give the landscape significance. With the images, the reader gains certain associations with which to understand the alien place to activate supplementary experiences, even though it is unique in the world.

She manages to inscribe the European images into the African landscape itself, so that it can even so become hers at a distance. This is done via images that include technology, gardening and art craft – ships, trimmed hedges and pottery. All of which are a visible result of human activity. In that way, she starts to draw closer to the present, for it is that sort of work she is engaged in while she writes. She transforms the landscape into a piece of linguistic handicraft via images, associations, a rhythm we can see and hear in the text we read. But, she assures us, the potential is already there in the landscape. It resembles those sorts of things itself. Here, description then does not in the first instance provide us with knowledge about what the lost landscape is like, despite sharp details that appeal to our senses. She first and foremost emphasizes the aesthetic details that show its potential for being transformed, so that she can come close to it once more in the present.

She marks this present in the middle of the description. 'Looking back on a sojourn in the African highlands, you *are* struck by your feeling of having lived for a time up in the air.' Here, she finally comes forward as the person sitting at a distance with her linguistic potter's wheel throwing a potter's text. But although the landscape itself invites one to reconstruct it in this way, it is no longer the same. It becomes 'a strange appearance', she says, and one feels 'struck'. Just as the landscape has become strange and is now at a distance, she too is at a distance from herself as she sits there writing. She writes 'you' in the meaning of the impersonal 'one', and not 'I'. The present is an impersonal present tense. The airborne feeling she mentions runs contrary to experience and nature and thereby makes her as strange as the landscape has become. The present, while the landscape once more becomes hers, is turned upside-down and floats between the real and the unreal – 'The air ... created great Fata Morgana'. The present is not objectively anchored in the landscape. She recreates the landscape as a mirage for us in the text, so that we float in the images that she creates, without setting foot in the landscape.

Last, the text goes off in a new direction. 'Up in this high air you breathed easily, drawing in a vital assurance and lightness of heart. In the high-lands you woke up in the morning and thought: Here I am, where I ought to be.' In these lines, the present finally breaks through as a personal present. She steps forward and says 'I' and not 'you'. It is this I that, as the first word in the book, assumes responsibility for the entire book in front of the reader: 'I had a farm ...' Now we know that we are not going to hear about a Romantic who is unable to rise up out of the quagmire of nostalgia, nor about an acrobatic existentialist exercise in tying oneself in knots out of sheer misery. Although it says, 'I *had*', the 'I' that emerges out of the introduction directs the attention of the narrator and reader forward towards the open life that lies right in front of her. The description is not turned backward towards the landscape or downward towards the potter's wheel on which the text is being thrown. It is a hope which, by being a hope, is future oriented, 'a vital assurance and lightness of heart'. Her body, life and individual existence – in Ulrich Beck's words quoted above – is through her self-awareness of participating in a translocal reality turned towards the future.

Responsibility for the future is a recurring theme in *Out of Africa*, even though it is a memoir: responsibility in relation to the hopeless economy of the farm, to the family back home, to the culture of the Masai and the Kikuyu under the yoke of colonialism, also after her departure, and in general an elementary responsibility to move forward every time all exits would seem to be blocked on the farm because of death, fire or impending bankruptcy. To be responsible is to improvise in order to be able to move forward. The past represents a whole world and it cannot be repeated, extended or altered. The present is both concrete and real, while she is working, as a farmer or a writer, and yet unreal and strange. She reshapes past and present in language, memory and improvisations with pictorial associations. Thereby, she creates an orientation towards the future that gives her identity and an inner readiness to move on, make the loss a 'liveable' reality, again exemplifying Ulrich Beck's words above. She gains identity in the very process of looking forward.

In agreement, Ulrich Beck quotes Imre Kertész, whose Nobel Prize winning novel *Fateless* (1975) from the German concentration camps I will return to later: 'The holocaust does not have to be made an explicit theme for us to sense the under-current of trauma that has haunted modern European art for decades'. (Beck 2006: 3). The same applies to globalization. To avoid direct thematization does not mean that for our own convenience, we are to think of something else than the experience of globalization. It is instead an invitation to find other concretizations than the obvious themes. Blixen's text does not deal with a trauma on the scale of the holocaust, but structurally it is the same experience: a whole world of coherence and identity, bound to her experience, gets completely lost. And, according to Beck, that is the situation of many people faced with globalization, both in the details of the everyday and in major contexts.

In his speech of thanks at the Nobel Prize-giving ceremony, Kertész states that he read in a report from Buchenwald that he died on 18 February 1945, with an incorrect date of birth, 1927, which he had lied about himself. 'In short, I died once so that I could live. Perhaps that is my real story' (Kertész 2002: s.p.). This is completely in accordance with Blixen's description of her departure from Kenya. She was 'through death, – a passage outside the range of imagination, but within the range of experience' (Blixen 2013: 210). It is not the scope of the trauma or the loss that in itself determines its importance to us, nor the loss of reliable models of knowledge that risk society represents. This would only display a sentimental or nostalgic longing for a time before the world was out of joint. Knowledge about the loss becomes important to the extent we are capable of integrating it in a future-oriented model of knowledge the concrete knowledge of what has been lost and of the inevitability of the loss.

In another essay, 'Who Owns Auschwitz?' (2001), Kertész points out that knowledge about that type of experience is not covered by any number of truthful descriptions of realistic details: 'The concentration camp is imaginable only and exclusively as literature, never as reality' – and why? Because the details do not say anything about 'the PERSON (and thereby about the idea of the Human as such) who emerges from the camps healthy and unharmed' (Kertész 2001: 268, 270). It is that formation of identity that Blixen's text depicts: She becomes an 'I' via the collapse of the farm. In his Nobel speech, Kertész characterizes the situation as precisely future oriented, with a quotation that is also used by Beck: 'Whenever I think of the traumatic impact of Auschwitz, I end up dwelling on the vitality and creativity of those living today. Thus, in thinking about Auschwitz, I reflect, paradoxically, not on the past but the future'. (Kertész 2002: s.p.).

This reflection Kertész practises in literature. Reflection is the subject of this chapter's final subsection. Beck redefines reflection as reflexivity and makes this concept his trademark in the analysis of globalization as a broad social phenomenon. Reflection is at the same time an important concept for the concrete practice of literature, its self-aware, aesthetic potter's work. In this conceptualization, the analysis of globalization and aesthetics meet as an answer to globalization's challenge to *the forms of communication*.

Forms of communication

Reflection and communication

Reflectors are safety equipment on a bicycle, reflections can be the mirror image of a tree on the surface of the water, and reflexes can, for example, be the salivating of Pavlov's dog at the sound of a food bell. But reflection is also a process of the mind. Yet, all these terms have something in common.

For thousands of years, the basic idea has existed that the capacity to think, and in particular to think things over, is a specifically human talent, since we are beings with both language and consciousness. When we translate reflection into arguments or express it in literature, science or other concentrated forms of expression, we become more knowledgeable about the world around us and about the fundamental characteristics of existence. When we reflect, we ignore the immediate experience in order to gain an overview that is larger than our individual horizon. Universities and think tanks are institutions for more broadly organized reflection on behalf of the community. Individual or institutionalized reflection is always a general mental activity – I am not just thinking my own thoughts but always thoughts that can be communicated to others.

In that way, it is possible for us via reflection to shift the boundaries of what we know in common about the world and ourselves. Reflection is therefore always connected to certain media through which it can be communicated, especially language, and it is therefore indissolubly linked to forms of communication. In Chapter 2, I briefly characterized forms of communication as a totality of all the factors that determine a communication – media, content, recipients, cultural preassumptions and so on. Reflection is never just an internal process of consciousness. It coheres with the world around us, both prior to reflection and when it later is included in a form of communication.

No one will presumably suspect Pavlov's dogs of thinking things over thoroughly before their mouths salivate or of considering a particular form of communication. Their reflex, just like the reflector on a bicycle and the reflection of a tree on the surface of the water, is a piece of automatized reality. Even so, that type of phenomena contains certain characteristics that also typify thoughtful reflection. The word 'reflection' literally means 'bending back' or, more broadly, 'mirroring' or 'doubling'. Something outside the bicycle, the tree or the dog causes attention to be 'bent back' towards the cycle, the tree or the animal so that we can catch sight of it, perhaps in a new way: the bike in a dangerous situation, the tree as an aesthetic nature experience and the dog as being hungry. The things are being mirrored or doubled into a different medium than the reflected object: car lights, water or the ringing of bells, and becomes a specific bike, pond or dog.

For that reason, the word 'reflection' has often also been used to describe the human activity. For via reflection, we double or mirror the things we wish to know something about. We look at something from a different position, and our attention can be 'bent back' towards it, so that we can understand it in a different way than at first glance. While the automatic mirroring only reflects a surface, our reflection is a construction we ourselves have chosen in order to get behind the surface. There is a difference between things that reflect and reflection.

However, they share the characteristic of being able to be repeated. Cycle reflectors do not only work every other day, or when we are in the mood. Water does not only reflect between 8 am and 10 am during the month of May, but each and every time. They are not random and, hence, they can help us to understand the world. Something takes place by itself, as with the plastic thingummy on a bicycle: it is the property of the materials that causes them to reflect. Others are the results of experiments, as in laboratories using measuring instruments. It can also be Pavlov's dogs, or the roses that stand at the end of a field of vines to reflect attacks by phylloxera.

But when experiments are constructed using certain methods and theories, they always intertwine with human reflection. The mirror that we hold up to things in the form of an experimental arrangement, a theory or an argument is something we ourselves have defined. That is how we conduct research, but also how we attempt every day to inch forward in search of a good way of tackling something. This form of reflection always follows two tracks at the same time. It is directed towards the things we are reflecting about, but also, in a self-aware and self-critical way, towards the medium, methods, forms of expression and forms of communication we have chosen to implement the reflection. Irrespective of whether the reflection takes place in literature, science, art or daily speech, we must at all times be self-aware in order to be able to assess and justify the choices that shape the reflection.

Literature has always been very interested in this double reflection we carry out, while Ulrich Beck is interested first and foremost in the reflections we meet in the world around us. Using the term *reflexivity*, he attempts to point out certain characteristics in the social and natural world around us, where the conditions and processes of globalization are reflected in a fundamental way, independently of us. We can close in on them in order to understand globalization and adopt an active stance towards it. Beck, however, points out that the special manner in which globalization mirrors itself in the social and natural realities is so contradictory that we cannot without more ado convert this reflexivity into practice. So it is therefore not enough just to observe them in order to become wiser, as when the car driver registers the cycle reflector and immediately acts so as to avoid an accident.

Reflexivity in the world thus of necessity triggers a need for reflection as an activity of our consciousness that enables us to cut across the models of knowledge and forms of communication on which we normally rely when studying society and nature. It calls for an alternative human imaginativeness and richness of ideas, one where we at the same time reflect on what experiences globalization confronts us with and how we ourselves are to deal with the reflection and communicate it. It is this form of double reflection which literature cannot avoid undertaking, and which it initiates via the aesthetic self-awareness I drew attention to in Chapter 1.

It is not, however, completely straightforward if one wishes to connect the reflection of literature with Beck's reflexivity. Beck is a tricky dancing partner. His way of presenting most of his considerations offers a wide range of uneven dance rhythms that do not always keep time with the music. On the other hand, reflexivity is at the heart of his theoretical thinking. The complex, convoluted and hidden processes of globalization *are* difficult to set to music for us to keep in time with. Such an attempt is rarely immediately successful. Beck's books are such continued attempts. Before we read the final Blixen text in this chapter, I therefore intend to make a slight detour and take a look at the basis, the perspectives and the limitations that typify Beck's reflections concerning *reflexivity*.

Reflection becomes reflexivity

Beck is best known for his concept of risk society as a codeword for the globalized society. But it is framed by highly convoluted concepts to do with reflexivity. He presents these, for example, in his contribution to *Reflexive Modernization* (Beck et al. 1994: esp. 1–13; Beck and Bonß 2001: 11–63). His point of departure, here as everywhere else, is the Europe of the Enlightenment. It is here the form of modern society begins that triggers globalization in a broad sense, in politics, economics, culture and communication. It is also here that Beck finds a starting point from which he can distance himself so that his own profile stands out. He mainly views the reflection of the Enlightenment as a concept of intellectual reflection – the individual's emancipation from self-imposed deprivation of autonomy, as Immanuel Kant formulated it in the first lines of his article on Enlightenment from 1783, 'What is Enlightenment?' [Was heist Aufklärung?] (Kant 2006: 17). The underlying assumption of Kant's position is that reality can be controlled by human will and intention, as long as we simply think things over. This helps us to turn a development in the direction of positive progress as does the world citizen when he uses the principles of human rights, freedom of speech and so on for permanent ideological and political self-criticism of his actions, with the ideal principles as a guideline. Reflection starts and ends in the person carrying it out, not in the world that makes it necessary. This form of responsible reflection started to appear on a massive scale in all forms of written communication in the eighteenth century with the French Encyclopedia as the most prominent example.

The society that emerged at that time is also the beginning of the real, contrast-filled social reality of today, a totality where certain predominant traits determine more and more particulars thus producing global conditions of local lives. These features, like economy, media, global markets and institutions, do not express separate sub-problems but mirror or *reflect* in their built-up the contrast-filled totality. It is this self-mirroring effect embedded in reality's own processes that Beck refers to as the reflexivity of globalization.

To explain this complex idea, Beck points out that reflexivity has four stages in its development since the eighteenth century which do not place thoughtful and responsible people as its starting point, but an outside world that triggers the need for reflection. He describes it as the process of modernization. The first modernization took place when the existing traditions, forms of organization, forms of production, view of humanity and values in the former static feudal society or absolute monarchy dissolved, while the eighteenth century began to open the gates to the urbanized industrial society of the next century. This process is repeated in the modern globalization of the twentieth century, although now directed towards the basic ideas and structures of industrialized society itself. They break up, and a new societal process imposes itself on early modern society. Outsourcing from the old industrialized countries is just one example – lifelong learning, management as network management, interdisciplinary knowledge acquisition are others. The new society turns the very establishing process of industrial society against itself and breaks down the structures and basic ideas that it itself has gradually established. This *radicalization*, as Beck calls it, is the first stage of reflexivity, evaluated by Beck as a positive force.

Further on, the so-called developed late industrial society, which we are still living in, is confronted by its own built-in problems, not as moral or political boundaries but as problems in its own practical activity. That is the development of risk society over the past fifty years. We create wealth and progress, and we create risks and limits to progress in one and the same process. The process is confronted by its own limitation. It is not a process that is intentional or controlled, or that can be altered by us, as in the industrial society, where we think things over and find an overall solution, after which we eradicate risks as unintentional side-effects. Society's *confrontation with its own productive limitations* is the second stage of reflexivity. It is here that the negative side of reflexivity is felt.

The next stage comes when this built-in dilemma spreads from industrial production in the strict sense to the rest of society, its institutions and life-forms. Risk is then not primarily linked to particular phenomena, such as energy, transport, edible commodities but to the totality of production, technology, social structure and basic values that hold all of our society together. Therefore, we are confronted with cultural boundaries for what we are capable to imagine as a future social practice, based in the values, forms of organization and conceptions of humanity we adhere to. The whole discussion in parts of Europe concerning the future of the welfare society and the European Union and all the contradictions in expectations, demands and possibilities that thereby appear show what this stage is all about. *The confrontation of society with its cultural boundaries* is the third stage of reflexivity. It is here that the boundaries for innovative thought, imaginativeness and creativity in relation to the dilemma of risk as the immanent feature of the very unfolding of society catch us by the scruff of the neck. It is here that reflexivity becomes a challenge by taking the form of risk.

The fourth and final stage is a new form of critical self-reflection what Beck also calls a meta-transformation of modernity into modern globalization (Beck and Bonß 2001: 31–53). It is to lead to a new understanding of how one can live with risk society's built-in uncertainty about the future with regard to knowledge, education, identity, organization, relation to nature, global networking and so on. It is not a reflection on our unfortunate practice but on our total cultural ability to establish future-oriented sustainable conditions for humanity on all levels, from individual experience via cultural patterns and global connections to relations to the natural foundations of human life. How do we avoid being caught up in the dilemmas of risk society in a self-defeating process? How can we continue to use critical self-reflection to challenge our cultural boundaries for innovative thinking? For Beck, a human is still a rational being that can develop relevant knowledge and direct it towards the future and that can use the public debate in all the media and institutions to that end, as he did himself. But the reflection is not, as in the eighteenth century, mainly directed towards the boundaries of nature and mankind's endless ability to adjust them. It is directed towards how we are constrained by certain boundaries we have brought about ourselves in society and the entire surrounding world, at the same time as we must understand the possibilities for changing the world as being if not inexhaustible, then nevertheless open. A bit like playing a piano – the number of keys is limited, but the potential for creating new music is endless. *Critical reflection on how to move common cultural constraints* is the fourth stage of reflexivity and at the core of globalization as a cultural process. It is as part of that reflection that literature takes up the challenge of reflexivity.

But Beck has no solution to how we communicate modern reflexivity so that we can observe it in things around us to make it a common condition of life embedded in concrete individual experience. Nevertheless, that is what he attempts to achieve. The aim is to make the confrontation of social reality with itself in the overall structures of globalization 'visible, comprehensible and even liveable', so it can be registered by a 'self-critical outlook' on the everyday world (Beck 2006: 3).

On the other hand, he has a feeling of complete solidarity with the self-critical project of the Enlightenment. It is a human responsibility to look self-critically, to the best of one's ability, at one's actual society and to develop knowledge that can shift it, discuss it with others in order to have knowledge be translated into common insight. He has, however, no solutions, only diagnoses of the deadlocked situation. This is partly due to Beck's own limitations. First, his history only starts with the eighteenth century. This blinds him to the fact that considering also earlier periods could give his concept of reflexivity more scope. Second, his view of the eighteenth-century conception of reflection as an intellectual, self-critical form of thinking is too narrow. An example can serve to illustrate this narrowness and then lead us on to a historical perspective Beck seems unable to catch sight of.

More than an earthquake

Alongside the French Revolution in 1789, the Lisbon earthquake of 1755 is the one single event that proved to be of the greatest significance in changing the eighteenth-century conception of society, religion, nature and humanity.[5]

In the morning of 1 November 1755, large parts of Lisbon were destroyed by fire and water. Lisbon lies slightly up the river Tejo, close to the Atlantic Ocean. A submarine quake started a huge underwater wave, a tsunami, to surge in towards the coast and up the river, where it battered the central part of Lisbon with full force. Naturally, the earthquake had to be of a certain size and effect to at all be able to form a basis for broader cultural consequences. This it had. It is estimated that it corresponded to nine on the Richter scale, on a par with the tsunami that hit Thailand and neighbouring countries just after Christmas in 2004. The present estimate is that between 35,000 and 50,000 people died. Just for purposes of comparison: in 1755, Copenhagen had about 25,000 people, all living inside the ramparts. The earthquake occurred just when churches were holding religious services for the most important Catholic festival of All Saints Day, 1 November. And this took place right in the middle of Lisbon's power centre, where monasteries, castles and palaces, some quite recent in date, were razed to the ground and many of the central prominent figures of society also perished. There was a host of religious and moral interpretations of God's punishment on mankind's sins, a reappearance of the Flood. Omens, the beginning of the end and God's judgement, were the interpretative framework used to understand the event.

The Marquis of Pombal was appointed to lead the reconstruction of Lisbon. And he did not care a damn about fate, Flood, prayers and omens. He looked at everything from a societal context, as a problem of new knowledge, dissemination and organization. The disaster held a mirror up to society with all its strengths and weaknesses, and was not a reflection of God's will or the expression of God's mercy and punishment. How can we develop a new city? How can we maintain Lisbon's initiative? Make use of the media, is what we would answer today. Pombal was aware of this back then, even though the first regular newspapers had only just started to appear. His use of the new form of communication became part of the reflexivity.

The earthquake could be felt throughout Europe. There were reports of tremors elsewhere, movements in meadows and wetlands, ripples in hot springs in Bohemia and changes to the water level in waters and harbours all the way up to the Gulf of Bothnia. Lisbon needed the rich foreign commercial houses remained in the city and did not move further north to Rotterdam or elsewhere. For that reason, Pombal ensured that Lisbon's local newspaper, the weekly *Gazeta de Lisboa*, came out on time, as early as 5 November, and continued to appear without a single issue being cancelled. We've got our act together, was the signal to international commerce. For that reason, this paper was an important source not only for knowledge about the disaster but also for a European debate about a common understanding of a societal relation to itself, nature and God. So the news spread with what was at the time the speed of lightning. It reached Berlin on 11 November, Paris on 22 November, London on 26 November, Hamburg on 29 November and Vienna, Rome and even Bergen at some point as well as Copenhagen on 15 December, in *Kiøbenhavns Post-Rytter*. The far corners of Europe were also in the loop.

At the same time, Pombal had to have precise statistical knowledge that could be converted into preventive forecasts in a different way from omens and prophecies. He sent out questionnaires to all the parishes regarding concrete, factual details: weather, pre-tremors, animals' reactions and so on. The material still exists. And he conceived the structure of the city in a new way, since they were virtually starting from scratch anyway: straight streets down to the harbour forming a right angle with the river, practical for leading the water elsewhere on any other occasion, and practical for personal transport and the transportation of goods. They still lie there. Nature or not, the natural hazard was reflected as a social risk, as yet not at a modern level, but well on its way. The reaction to the disaster took it first of all to be a reflection of the way the city has been constructed and managed. This took place on the basis of a modern applied knowledge that was empirically based, and a type of knowledge that thereby became an active part of the reflexivity.

But it is only possible to pursue such a course of action if two general principles are accepted. The first is ideological: society is not a model of the universe, crowned by God and his intentions, but an area of human responsibility. The second is scientific: the best knowledge concerning the world of human experience derives from observations and the resulting theories, not omens, speculation or reading the Holy Scripture. These fundamental meta-perspectives were too diffuse for the rude and practical Pombal, but they led to an important cultural European shift, and like all important shifts or turns, it was a common although uncoordinated movement that took place in many different locations where it ran parallel rather than intersecting. Just as today there are parallel developments arising out of information about climatic issues that are to be seen everywhere and are described everywhere in the media.

The most widely disseminated ideological contribution came from François Voltaire. On the basis of knowledge acquired from the new medium-borne information, he published already before the Christmas of 1755 his *Poem on the Lisbon Disaster* [*Poème sur le désastre de Lisbonne*]. With biting irony and also strongly affected, he attacked the religious interpretations, which aggressively confirmed the world order and thereby the concomitant social order. Many people believed that the disaster was clear proof of God's governing of the world, the so-called *theodicé* argument (*theos* = God, *dike* = justice), as the best of all possible worlds. Now, humanity had sinned and deserved a good box on the ears. Whatever God does is always good in the last resort, even though this is not always so obviously apparent to humanity.

To Voltaire this argument seemed self-contradictory. Why should so many innocent women and children and chance visitors be cannon-fodder in order for God to make his message clear. Rather, the conclusion must be that whether God has created the world or not, its creation is now a finished chapter. From now on, it must be clear to everyone that people themselves are responsible for the present and the future as well as the organization of society. The world is neither good nor evil in advance, but an open challenge. This responsibility means both a future orientation on man's conditions – hope, says Voltaire – and a demand that we should acquire knowledge ourselves and also ensure that we communicate it to others. God does not send us any signs, humans do. The traditional relation between patterns of experience, models of knowledge and forms of communication has been broken and must be reassembled in a new way.

A distinct sign of a turning point comes with the German philosopher Immanuel Kant. Until 1755, he had been a strong member of the club of *theodicé* supporters. He wanted to become a geologist, but the only stones he had ever seen had been the cobblestones of Königsberg and the gravel on the paths in the city gardens. For many, natural science was just as much abstract philosophy as empirical methods. Either nothing comes out of that, or vast systems. Kant devised vast systems about the divine order of the universe. But the earthquake transported away his systems along with it, and Kant changed course. In a couple of small articles, he collected empirical material, like Voltaire, from the newspapers and magazines of the time about the quake and its continuation across the European continent, and he came up with experimental material explanations (Kant 1994). They are admittedly antiquated today, but he saw science as a way in which we relate to experience, both practically and cognitively, and saw it as an ethical task for science to be able to substantiate predictions and warnings. He published his articles in a public magazine, not an academic book.

Experience, knowledge and ethics became the hub of Kant's later writings, which to this day is still part of the basis for our thinking about nature and society and human life, even for those who have never read them. Nature is not a challenge because it has a hidden teleological order greater than man, Kant indicates, but because as a material reality it gives us a concrete, experienced uncertainty that is greater than our mental capacity, but from which we cannot escape. And society ought to be understood as a world society, in Kant's opinion, as a consequence of the development he could see then and what we call globalization today. Voltaire, Kant and Pombal belonged to the world citizens of the Enlightenment, in literature, in the cultural debate, in philosophy and science and in practical politics. In the mirror of the disaster, Voltaire saw man emerge from the shadow of providence, Kant saw new demands made of the relation between experience and knowledge with an ethical view of our use of the globe, and Pombal saw the social demands and possibilities that followed from the link between practical experience, concrete knowledge and its communication. Taken together, they prepared us for living in globalization via a reflection that has many more dimensions than Beck is prepared to grant the Enlightenment.

Speculation

With the earthquake, we are in the midst of a new Europe that is beginning to emerge, a process we look back on in order to get a better grasp of our own age and its future. Those living then could only look forward in the same way that we do today when we try to orientate ourselves in an unknown globalized future. But they also took as their point of departure a historical past they were familiar with so as to orientate themselves in a world that was starting to become uncertain in a new way. The whole debate about the conception of the earthquake and the great change in Kant's writing is thus based on a showdown with the medieval and parts of the renaissance organization of society and their conception of knowledge and their view of man's relation to nature and God, in the same way as Beck takes his starting point in the Enlightenment he is familiar with.

For him, the eighteenth century is a sufficient starting point for an understanding of reflexivity in the general social processes of globalization. But if we also want to understand it in relation to reflection and its connection with forms of communication in all their cultural breadth as they developed after Lisbon, it would also be useful to look at what the period before the eighteenth century has to offer. The core concept used in the Middle Ages to describe relations similar to Beck's reflexivity is what was called *speculation*. We seldom tend to associate this with anything positive. It is either used to describe an abstract ticking-over of the brain, detached from any experience, or risky economic measures on the border of the legally and morally acceptable. This is perhaps why Beck, unwisely, does not deal with it.

The sharp brains of the Middle Ages had a slightly different view of speculation. 'Speculation', 'to speculate' and 'speculative' come from the Latin word for 'mirror', *speculum*. The concept thereby covers a different period's discussion of reflection and reflexivity. It refers to the aim set for all thinking, political and moral at that time: it was to mirror the real world. So speculation is not regarded as mere figments of the imagination. But the real world that was to be mirrored looked very different from the modern material world that became visible in the ruins of Lisbon, and that Beck encounters in its later phases. What speculation was to mirror was the inner order of the universe that was controlled by God on top of the hierarchical universe, from where his will determines all the descending rings, right the way down to the tiniest bits and pieces.

From top to bottom, from great to small, the basic structure of society mirrored the immovable order of nature and the universe. In this universe, God sat uppermost, in society the king did so, on the great estates the nobleman, in the family the father, among the children the eldest son, and man was above woman. Children, peasants and pedlars were simply necessarily filling, and small infants were not counted at all. If one of the top figures lost his head, the whole system was threatened. Worst of all if it was God, next worst if it was the king. Charles I of England lost his head in 1640. The system got over that. Next time was during the French Revolution, shortly after Campe had called himself a world citizen in Paris. Here Louis XVI lost his. That the system did not recover from, for in the meantime God's head had also started to dangle, shaken loose by, among other things, the Lisbon earthquake.

Beck's concept of risk society was released at the point when the news of the meltdown of the nuclear plant at Chernobyl in 1986 was released on the world as a man-made disaster of global proportion. With a similar effect, the eighteenth century, the earthquake in Lisbon in 1755 and the French Revolution in 1789 provided some powerful shoves towards ideas about the modern society when the news spread out via the media of the age. Such events gave rise to greater tremors in our conception of humanity, society and nature than many of the wars that ravaged Europe at the time. It was here that science in the modern sense became a crucial part of the reflection on the organization of society. Here, the challenges which globalization makes of the relation between patterns of experience, models of knowledge and forms of communication became clear for the first time.

At this point, speculation was greatly different. It did not need much empirical material at all, for the order one was searching for was after all already known from the Bible and philosophy, so it was merely a question of finding the order once again in phenomena and nature around us. The Bible and the things themselves in nature and society were the two basic forms of communication in speculation, the book of God and the so-called book of nature. To merge those two books into one was the task of speculative thinking, no matter whether it dealt with grammar, music, astrology, medicine, politics or anything else whatsoever. The total universe was mirrored in all the phenomena of nature, and at the same time in the thinking of philosophy, art and literature, which explained the divine order of the created world.

For that reason, literature is an integral part of speculation, both one of its examples and also one of its forms of communication, all kept together by the idea of the book of nature. Nature in itself is seen as a book, and the reading of it finds its interpretative models in the Bible and in literature. In an unbroken totality, speculation comprises creative as well as dogmatic thinking and the things in the real world. Kant's works prior to 1755 were speculative in that sense, just as the *theodicé* disciples at whose heels Voltaire snapped, and the view of society that Pombal tried to turn around.

The relation between reflection and reflexivity is problematic in a different way. Reflection is an attempt, from the inside, to understand the unclear world outside, the form and development of which we do not have any clear picture. We are never completely sure that our reflection and the forms of communication we use are enough for us to assume our responsibility for how the world is organized. That responsibility the speculative minds of the Middle Ages had no need to take upon themselves. They did not have to organize the world themselves, but adjust themselves to fit it as it had been created by God. The role of literature, as well as of other similar texts, was clear and fixed: to confirm that order. So speculation aimed at trying to understand the stable order of the world, and was not, as is reflection, a method of intervening in an ongoing process of change in order to shape it. Based on medieval conditions, it was an ambitious attempt to allow reality to reflect itself at all levels. In practice, this mode of thinking kept culture alive under various religions and at all levels for more centuries than industrial society and existed well into the nineteenth century. So it is no idle talk.

Literature as the mirror of nature

With speculation as the model of knowledge, literature became an imitation of nature, a *speculum* of nature: not nature as a physical landscape, but the hidden order of nature. The imitation did not lie in concrete details but in the form. All details had to be ordered in relation to contrasts, symmetry, forward-moving action and hierarchies, organized around a clear centre. The form reactivated nature's creative principles. This led to literature being grouped in various forms that were collected together in the classical genres, later also called the natural genres like tragedy, with subgenres like tragico-comedies.

The most ideal forms in nature were the square and the circle. It was thought that they united all the fundamental characteristics of nature and were visible in the outline of the Earth, flat or round, and in the orbits of the planets. Literature was to exemplify that order in its physical appearance, its aesthetic form. A crown of sonnets, for example, was a particularly fine genre from the Middle Ages. In its form, the sonnet sequence imitates the ideal circle of nature, and it shows that man himself can contribute to and participate in the order of nature by creating something that itself resembles divine nature.

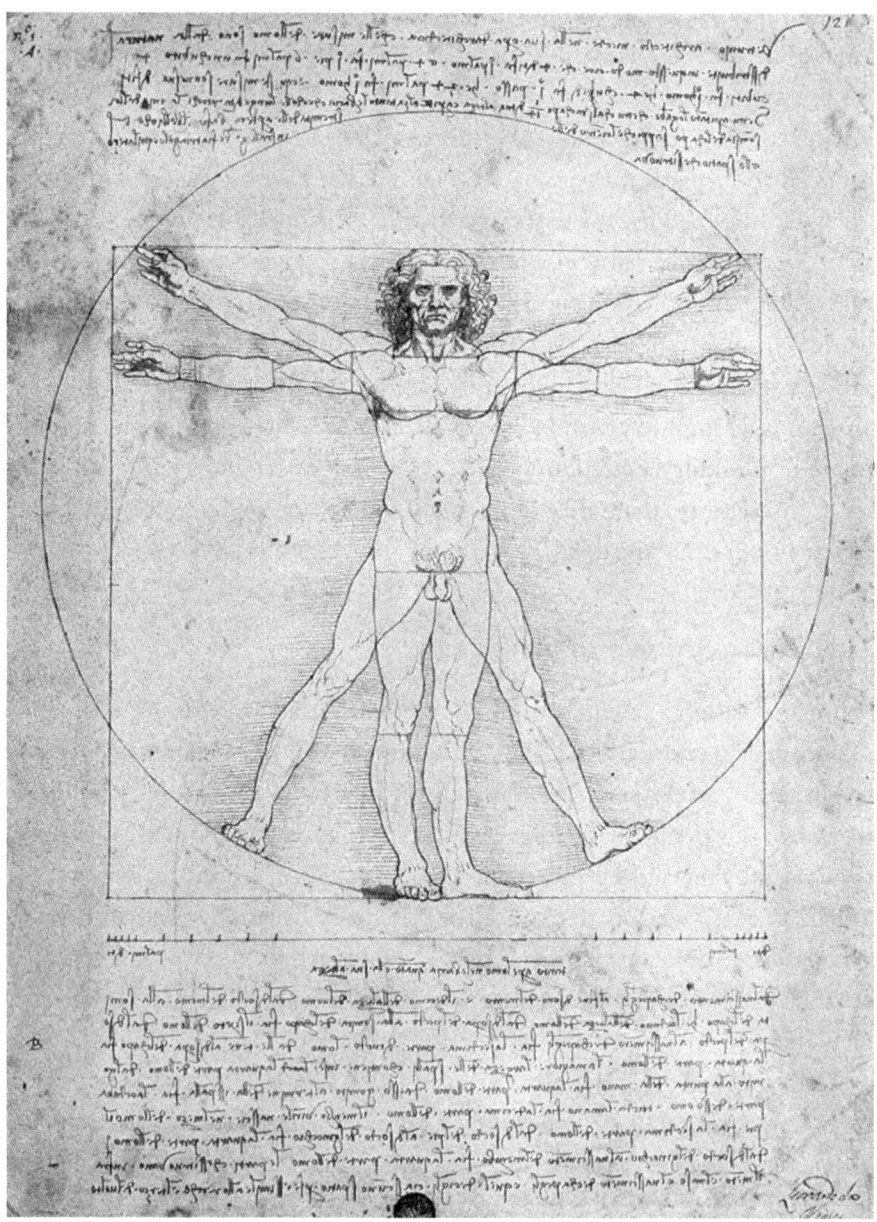

Figure 3.1 Vitruvian Man, 1493 (Vinci 1998).

We are all familiar with Leonardo's enviably fine fellow, the Vitruvian Man, who looks as if he, *contra naturam,* is about to learn to fly. The drawing is not a realistic reproduction of a muscular male body. It is speculation in the medieval sense. Here, the man is positioned within nature's ideal forms, the circle and the square, so that one can see that the form of his body corresponds to the order of nature – an idea also found in many cultures outside Europe (Kurdziałek 1971; Kiddel and Rowe-Leete 1989). There are small strokes on his body. They mark all the ideal proportions that are hidden in the square and the circle and reflected in the proportions of the body: between length of head and length of body, arm length and finger length and so on. Leonardo's accompanying text comprises quotations from the Roman architect Vitruvius' *On Architecture* from the first century BCE (153, 154), which became very popular in the Renaissance as a precept for urban and social planning (Eaton 2002). The text says which fractions correspond to the ideal order of nature – the relations 1:3, 1:2, 1:4 and so on. That the muscles, sex and magnificent hair resemble an actual body is of secondary importance.

Although no one in reality looks like Leonardo's man without pumping iron and using forbidden substances, it is not the slightest bit abstract. Put to practical use, the principles of ideal order could be converted into a physical space. These proportions were used to construct ideal buildings and cities, so that humans in their wretched mortal frames could move around in surroundings which in the *speculum* of nature mirrored the ideal forms that our lifestyle neglected bodies also have. We can still see this in many buildings and building complexes from Antiquity via the Renaissance right up to the functionalism of the twentieth century. In addition, literature and art also have a long tradition of working with reflection, though not for contemplating their navel. The aim is instead to get literature, and thereby the people who create and use it, to take part concretely in the reality which one regards as being the most real. In that reflection, it is the sense-related side of literature and art, its aesthetic form that becomes its anchor in reality, not its content.

Apparently without knowing it, with his notion of reflexivity Beck is attempting to repeat the speculation of the Middle Ages on new conditions. Back then, reality was also confronted with itself in everything, from the greatest to the smallest, but as a harmony that rested in the heart of nature. Today, it is the man-made reality that is being confronted with itself in everything, also nature in a conflict with disorder in society. This is the reflexivity of reality. The Middle Ages possessed the means of an aesthetic practice that communicated this confrontation to the individual in the smallest things: look, here in the tiniest flower you can see an imprint of the great inaccessible world order. At the same time, it could be reproduced by the individual and shared with others: 'If you tell what you see by imitating the order of nature, then you yourself take part in it.' Speculation and reflexivity both conceive the Earth as a totality, but in entirely different ways. Speculation makes it into a total picture of the universe of which humans are an integral, but not an interfering part. Reflexivity makes the Earth into a globe: a special material totality, where we have developed in such a way that we, for the better or worse, actively take part in its processes everywhere. That is globalization's starting point.

How do we communicate globalization in its omnipresent forms of expression as a concrete experience, so that everyone can see the reality of the experience? There are no model solutions to pass on to anyone, as when authors of the past could learn to imitate nature by looking at their canonical classical predecessors. Now, all we have is the reality of the actual experience. No pattern of experience, model of knowledge or form of communication is excluded in advance. To turn comprehensive and complex conceptions into a concrete reality for the individual person – that is a requirement which appeals to literature's aesthetic self-reflection, which turns its works into a concrete reality for the person reading, listening or watching. Its history goes further back than to the Enlightenment. Literature is a historical reservoir of experience and experiments with that type of aesthetic forms of communication.

'Speak like rain'

A small narrative of only one page in *Out of Africa* belongs to this reservoir. In 'Natives and Verse' (Blixen 2013: 150),[6] Blixen shows how the concentration of literature's own aesthetic effects moves the reader's focus from the individual work to the actual communication situation. It becomes a concrete collective experience with those who receive, read, hear or use the text placed at the centre, even if there is no unambiguous message. Aesthetic self-reflection is first and foremost an experiment with forms of communication.

The situation is a simple game with words, just like the children's game at Newcomer High School with the figures of the gods where they click with the mouse. Blixen relates that she is out harvesting maize with some of her young native workers. She knows that they have a strong sense of rhythm, but are not acquainted with rhyme. Not, at least, she teaches the reader from her superior position, 'before the times of the schools, where they were taught hymns', that is to say before colonization and Christianity. As at Newcomer High School, even the most innocent parlour game is framed by its place of action when it is enlarged as a cultural meeting place between religions, social powers and traditions for child-raising and language learning. The nature of the place as a meeting place is made concrete in the playing with words. Karen clomps into the language of the natives in her European clogs and starts to rhyme in Swahili:

> There was no sense in the verse, and it was made for the sake of rhyme:
>
> Ngumbe
> Na penda chumbe
> Malaya
> Mbaia.
> Wakamba
> Na kula mamba.
>
> '...The oxen like salt. Whores are bad. The Wakamba do eat snakes'. It caught the interest of the boys, and they formed a ring round me. They were quick to understand that the meaning of poetry is of no consequence, and they did not question the thesis of the verse.

Just as well. For it would be an insult for the Wakamba boys present to accuse them of eating snakes, Blixen says. We are not told why. The content is of no consequence, she thereby demonstrates to us. But all workers are standing round her in an unbroken circle and know what all that about snakes means. We are only present as guest listeners and onlookers. By not having any meaning and only being sounds, the focus shifts from the words to the situation in which they come into existence, and Blixen and the boys are all turned into members of a kind of improvised community. The text is only something because it is performed with someone, just like nonsense verse. Precisely because the meaning is of no consequence, this circle becomes a concrete and living community for those who are in it, while the game is taking place.

The little Swahili poem does not reflect on the situation with its meaning but, to use Beck's expression, it is confronted with itself in the situation it creates. It refers to its own rhyming, but in doing so also actively reshapes the situation. The natives stand eagerly waiting for the rhyme and laugh when it comes, Blixen tells us. They know it is for fun. But then Blixen expands the game, since things are going so well. She also tries to get them to rhyme and tempts them by serving them the first rhyme word, as when a teacher asks a rhetorical question. But the natives do not want to join in. They turn their heads away from the circle, without her understanding why – 'but they could not, or would not'. The intimacy is broken, and she does not know the reason why. And so they continue, until she finishes the story:

> As they had become used to the idea of poetry, they begged: 'Speak again. Speak like rain'. Why they should feel verse to be like rain I do not know. It must have been, however, an expression of applause, since in Africa rain is always longed for and welcomed.

Here, the young workers are the ones to take the initiative and poach on her preserves with a request, almost a challenge. She translates for us readers, she can still manage that. But it is of no use. She cannot react, for she does not know what they are thinking of. She only interprets it as acclamation, as if she is still at the real centre of the circle.

But of course she is not, for they now challenge her to join in on their terms, just as she earlier urged them on with a rhyme when they turned their heads away. She reacts by turning against the very game she has started herself. For now she interprets references to reality and meanings into the reaction of the natives, in which they use 'rain' as an image. Yet, the condition for the game and its success was precisely the absence of any meaning. The entire situation is confronted with itself through the actual playing with words. Precisely, because the game is a success, it rolls on and expands, but in doing so breaks up the situation the game itself has created, and the game becomes something else. It is this break up that the last section of this little story deals with.

The actual poem has turned her intentions upside-down: poems that are anchored in a shared situation cannot avoid acquiring meaning *there*, a meaning that cannot be controlled by just one of the participants, not even the initiator. And the poem has also inverted the mutual relationship of the participants: she starts out and continues her role as the colonial boss, but something unexpected hands the initiative over to the others, and they are still in command of the situation when the story ends. For that reason, there is no real conclusion, only a final remark about the meaning of rain which contradicts everything that has happened before. The text meant something after all, in spite of everything, and was not just a game. But what was it then? The answer disappears in the rain. Blixen's text thus also turns into a word game with us readers. Is she at the centre of the story or not? Does the text mean anything or not? The responsibility for interpreting rests with us, as it did when the natives took it over from her.

A game is a serious thing, as we know since childhood. It can really give rise to fights and tears, or friendships for life. So are schoolchildren's games with the gods on the computer screen, too. And it is also the case with this word game. It actively uses the aesthetic self-awareness of language, as here in the rhymes, or slightly more subtly, when the story contradicts what it has just said, and in doing so refers precisely to the text as a troubled cultural product that turns the situation into a power play with wider implications. It is the same kind of contradictory rethoric used by politicians claiming that they will not call their opponent a blockhead, and have now *de facto* just used the forbidden word. The situation is a concrete mini-model of the general and abstract cultural confrontation mechanism that Beck calls reflexivity. But here it is turned into an actual experience in an actual situation with actual people through the way in which language orchestrates the confrontation. Beck cannot do that, but Blixen and literature can.

The overall outcome of the situation is that reflexivity, also in the aesthetic form in which we meet it here, is a precondition for us to catch sight of ourselves as interacting and responsible individuals, also with regard to relations that are otherwise general and abstract. The young natives act on their own initiative when they ask her to continue in *their* way of asking. She has not requested them to press her to 'speak like rain', but to come up with the rhymes *she* has ordered. They do not criticize her with critical-theoretical reflection.

But in practice, they do, when the poem has first made the possibilities real for them. The entire abstract power structure with the Europeans and the 'others' is set in motion in a different concrete and manageable context.

Here, again, Beck's cosmopolitan outlook is activated with 'a dialogical view of ambiguities in a milieu of blurring differentiations and cultural contradictions. It reveals not just the "anguish" but also the possibility of shaping one's life and social relations under conditions of social mixture'. (Beck 2006: 3). Or, if not shaping one's life, a least shaping a concrete situation in which they live – that is what takes place in the maize-field. It is a communicative situation like that Beck just characterized as 'a dialogical view of ambiguities in a milieu of blurring differentiations'; and the balance between material manifestation and meaning production occurring in the field is an example of the forms of communication towards which Beck's understanding of globalization points, but which he himself is unable to encompass. This, on the other hand, literature is able to do by means of its aesthetic self-awareness and thus by actively including the participants. Literature here functions as a form of communication about dissolution of power relation, a specific manifestation of abstract reflexivity on a concrete, everyday micro-level.

People with other eyes

Both the theorist Beck and the aesthetician Blixen have the same aim. Beck's aim is to get us to understand risk society's confrontation with itself in the light of globalization. His expression for this new view is the cosmopolitan outlook, which must 'succeed in opening the iron conceptual cage of methodological nationalism and reveal how, and to what extent, global reality can become cosmopolitan, thereby rendering it visible, comprehensible and even liveable'. (Beck 2006: 3). As a child of the Enlightenment, his attitude has been expressed by Immanuel Kant. In 1786, he wrote in an article 'Conjectural Beginning of Human History' [Mutmaßlicher Anfang der Menschengeschichte] in his compact language:

> Such a portrayal of [human] history is fruitful for the human being and serves to teach and improve him when it shows him the following: that he may attribute no blame to providence for the ills that afflict him; that

he is not justified in attributing his own trespass to an original sin of his ancestors; ... it shows him rather that he ought to acknowledge fully that which they made happen as if he had done it himself, and that he ought to attribute completely the blame for all the ills that arise from the misuse of his reason to himself. (Kant 2006: 36)

The misuse of reason involved in refusing to recognize the radical effects of globalization is Beck's battleground.

As far as Blixen was concerned, coming to Africa was an experience that had the same effect, but as a concrete, personal experience, not in theory and analysis. In her essay 'Blacks and Whites in Africa' (1939) [Sorte og Hvide i Afrika] she declares that coming to Africa

> ... the whole world, and life, expanded for me; a reciprocal interaction came into being ... We had not sought each other, we had not come to the land in order to study the Blacks, and they would have preferred us not to have come there at all. But joined by fate, we now came to belong together in our daily lives. (Blixen 1985: 57)

Her knowledge of Shakespeare, of the details in the landscape, of what the Somalis usually think and believe, of the use of verse against local traditions, all this becomes a new, concrete expansion of her experience. It is transmuted into a personal human identity that is forward looking, despite everything, even though it points to an open future beyond what she actually writes about. Her whole experience of loss of social and cultural anchoring is changed into a new view of place, environment and herself.

She comes to 'a people that has other eyes to see us with' (Blixen 1985: 67). Her texts show that she does not completely understand that look. But she is well aware that it is important to expose oneself to it, and to understand and use the experience of being exposed to it. In that uncertainty, she sees herself for the first time: 'Here I am, where I ought to be', as we heard her exclaim in *Out of Africa*. It is a concrete version of Beck's cosmopolitan outlook. It is not a look one simply has or freely chooses, but it is shaped by what one is exposed to from other people's eyes. The cosmopolitan outlook is not a piercing look from superior Norse god Odin's single eye, governed by the highest wisdom for which he has paid with the sight of his other eye. It is a fly's eye that sees from many different angles at the same time and can change focus while doing so. The cosmopolitan outlook is multifocal for Blixen and also for Beck:

> My life, my body, my 'individual existence' become part of another world, of foreign cultures, religions, histories and global interdependencies, without my realising or expressly wishing it. (Beck 2006: 19)

Blixen is an example of how literature can enable us to see things for the first time by looking at them with several eyes at the same time. It is a fundamental cultural need, also from Beck's point of view, when our everyday experience is to be viewed with a cosmopolitan outlook. Beck approaches individual experience from the helicopter perspective of his theoretical considerations. Blixen starts at maize-field height with the open, searching nature of individual experience, so that a larger perspective opens up in the midst of random single events and concrete individual experiences. Literature builds on fundamental features of experience, knowledge and communication, so that they become concrete experiences, both in the meanings of the texts and in their linguistic presence while we read. Literature turns our gaze away from the concrete, immediate global issues and points it towards the basic conditions that make a person a participant in cultural processes. The attempts made by Beck and Blixen to see things for the first time do not yet meet. They still appear to belong to complementary domains of knowledge. Yet, it is one of the major cultural projects of globalization to make them engage in a close dialogue. This book tries to to do so.

This chapter has exemplified how literature offers a more profound approach to the break-up of each of the three cultural building blocks, the patterns of experience, the models of knowledge and the forms of communication, than theories on globalization and domain-specific understandings of it can present. In this chapter, they have been looked at separately. The agenda of the next chapter is set by the questions: How can literature combine them when its basic nature is to lie? And why is literature's potential to do so relevant for the link between literature and globalization?

4

Knowledge as Creative Lying

Truth and lies

That 'literature's a pack of lies' is nothing new. That's why some dismiss it, others grab it. If instead we say 'fiction', that is only a more presentable way of packaging the unpalatable fact as a captivating creative challenge. Fiction comes from the Latin *fingo*, which means: I feign, pretend, imagine or invent. The Greek noun *pseudos* covers roughly the same meaning, both invention and lie. Literature is pseudo-truth that not only ends up lying but doing it creatively and deliberately. Despite this, its readers seldom take it to court to demand their money back, for the lies of literature are a necessary way of dealing with knowledge and truth different from the incarnate truth. Lying with purpose and talent is how literature makes readers accept the literary form of communication and to personally situate its imaginary creation in lived reality where their patterns of experience are active and their models of knowledge are challenged.

One of the most provocative examples in European literature of the relation between true knowledge, lies and literature is Ludvig Holberg's Danish comedy *Erasmus Montanus* (1723). Holberg's comedies and other writings were widely translated, read and performed in Europe of his time, and this comedy was also turned into a film in the twentieth century.[1] Rasmus Berg is a farmer's son from a small village who has made it to the university and returns to brag about his erudition. To make matters worse, he has Latinized his name to Erasmus Montanus and now wants to prove that the Earth is round and not flat, that his Mother is a piece of rock and that Peer the Deacon is not a man but a crowing cock (Holberg 1990: 162, 163, 179, 180). All this is done by skewed syllogisms, arrogance and self-sufficiency that first make the parents proud of their learned offspring, but later turn the whole village against him when he attacks their unquestioned commonsensical take on reality and reduces his local fiancée Lisbed to tearful despair and her father to a rage. The comedy revolves around questions such as: Where does the border go between logical argument, true knowledge, superstition and common sense? Where recedes the power and authority to monopolize the definition of models of knowledge?

When Monsieur Montanus on returning to his village attempts with eloquence and logical conjuring tricks to prove that Peer the Deacon is a cock and Mother a rock, his arguments do not actually hold water according to formal logic. After all, he is nothing but a half-learned sophomore but nevertheless able to seduce most of the stunned local audience, not least his two targets: everyone knows that a Deacon's natural characteristics is to use his voice at a high level of decibels, and that a mother is not able to fly. The shouting Deacon is deeply offended and Mother solidly tied to the ground bursts into tears. But it is still all lies.

On the other hand, Erasmus is unable to either prove or convince anyone that the Earth is round and revolves around the sun; the best he can do is to refer to established knowledge about nature among learned people. Yet, the statement is of course true, even though the just as well-established conviction in this neck of the woods is the opposite. The scientific assertion is furthermore directly insulting to people who are perfectly well able to use their own eyes, the village sceptics say, especially Erasmus' brother, Jacob, who clearly sees and lives from a perfectly flat earthly surface. From having been a source of admiration and provocation, Erasmus's knowledge becomes a matter of indifference, laughter and enmity: knowledge of man's relation to nature based on practical interaction with breeding and cultivation of the soil is all that one needs in this particular part of the world, irrespective of what is regarded as true knowledge in other quarters of society.

With an artful lack of respect, Holberg contrasts two firmly entrenched and unreconcilable convictions as to what comprises reliable experience and true knowledge, and the forms of communication that go with them. But Holberg allows them to clash without either being a clear winner. One refers to what we can see with our own eyes, and it is supported by the villagers' common sense. With Erasmus as its anything but modest spokesman, the other is based on what logic can shape into a correct but decontextualized argument, in this case based on true evidence which, however, he himself has no real grasp of.

The comedy is provokingly topical, because it does not decide what is *true, important, intelligible, acceptable* and *usable* knowledge in relation to reality, but implies that all these features will have to be taken into account whenever and wherever knowledge is discussed. These five dimensions could be called the necessary *social dimensions* of knowledge that binds a tight knot of patterns of experience, models of knowledge and forms of communication. Nor does the comedy say anything about how they ought to relate to each other. Ultimately, Erasmus is obliged, by way of a deceitful intrigue, a lie as it were, to renounce his knowledge that the Earth is round and give way to the flat earth of practical, commonsensical everyday life. Otherwise he cannot have his beloved Lisbed. Decontextualized truth, even when actually true, does not function as truth in a social and cultural context only because of empirical evidence.

In today's globalized reality, the relation between the five dimensions is still an open problem, also about subjects that directly influence the everyday lives of each of us. At a certain point, a *truth* may be appealed to that can scarcely be formulated: we know that climate change is a fact, although we cannot decide with 100 per cent certainty how the changes are caused and structured, and money, power and politics threaten to influence the evidence we use as the basis of our collective decision-making. In other situations, the *importance* argument may overshadow other aspects of the field of knowledge: it may be regarded as less important to explore the reasons for global warming when one country can buy CO_2 quotas from other countries. A lack of *intelligibility* can sidetrack the utilization of knowledge despite good arguments: although international guidelines concerning the combatting of pollution may be correct as regards content, they are not followed if they are too complex and thereby difficult to understand and implement. And taking stock of what people individually and locally can *accept* may dominate other dimensions of knowledge, even, as in Holberg's comedy, in blatant contradiction of established true knowledge: nature conservation regulations are felt to be unacceptable in many local communities, even though they may well be based on solid evidence. Finally, the *use* of knowledge is a separate controversial field: nuclear power does not itself tell us if it is for weapons or brewing coffee, but the dilemmas of use set a global agenda for international conflicts. True knowledge alone cannot do it, as tearful Erasmus was also forced to acknowledge. Knowledge always functions in a number of social dimensions and their interrelations change with the cultural and historical context in which they are embedded. The political compromises behind the global declaration on climate change, COP21, issued during the UN meeting in Paris in December 2015 show how all five social dimensions are interwoven in a global context and continue to be so in the still ongoing political debate on the ratification of the Paris protocol.

By knowledge, we normally mean a general insight into some matter or other that we can share with others and get them to accept in a combination of evidence and argument. This is what they are fighting about in all the hubbub of the comedy. Today, the hidden ideal of true knowledge is often taken to be scientific knowledge and its truth claim, thus serving as the basic model of knowledge. However, we all too often have to realize that, evidence or not, we are simply not able to communicate the fact to others to make it match their experience and thus make them accept it. Reasoning and documentation may be incontestable, but not even that kind of knowledge is simply self-evidently correct once it has been formulated. Hence, the comedy does not tell us who is right, or has the right to be right. It shows us that knowledge is not just a true or false cognition, but that it depends on certain conditions outside cognition in order to be efficient as true knowledge.

These conditions are what Erasmus and Jakob are arguing about: are the conditions defined by the experience of an argumentative training or everyday experience? Here, both combatants imply that there only exists one set of conditions and only one simple dichotomy of conditions. By letting the wrong knowledge about the shape and rotation of the Earth be victorious, the comedy shows us that such a paradigmatic monopoly always damages true knowledge and its use, even when it is based on evidence. Holberg's comedy is itself a creative lie that uses a final powerful lie to fool Erasmus back into the common-sensical world of wrong ideas about reality. But in doing so Holberg forces us to think about the conditions for how one attains and uses knowledge in a social context, with a laughter that makes us remember the complexity of it, combined with a disquieting irritation at the fact that the Earth ends up by being flat. Even more disturbing is the implication that Erasmus now subscribes to the pattern of experience and the model of knowledge promoted by the village where he is going to live with his Lisbed and has to give up logical argumentation as a form of communication. The village may become an early instance of a post-factual community.

Literature constructs its untruthfulness in such a way that the relationship between truth and lies is put to the test in and by its readers, challenging us to activate all the five social dimensions of knowledge without rushing into taking a decision. And perhaps the readers are unable to decide the matter, as in a crime novel without a clear ending – the guilty person behind it all, the spider, only casts a shadow, or disappears before the riddle itself is solved. Although the hidden ideal of knowledge may well be the truth of scientific knowledge, it too, like all other types of knowledge, is never pure but rests on certain conditions and contexts, theoretical, experimental and otherwise. Another kind of knowledge can build on practical experience or the 'it normally works' of familiar routines. The knowledge we normally make use of on our home ground emerges in a permanent commuting between knowledge ideals and the practical use of knowledge. Even the specialist in particle physics or in Indian languages has to rely on the body's knowledge when he wants to use a bicycle.

Also in a larger perspective, the treatment by the comedy of knowledge and its conditions is of topical relevance. When we do not always possess the knowledge we need, it is normally because we are in doubt about what its precise subject or content actually is. Hence, we are also unsure about the conditions for the best kind of knowledge. When asked why he knows the earth is round, Erasmus just sheepishly refers to the dogmatic authority of science beyond his own restricted knowledge. Thereby, the comedy topicalizes not only the social dimensions of knowledge but also its *cognitive dimensions*. It homes directly in on the uncertainty that now has become a fundamental and universal experience in a globalized reality. Is knowledge about globalization primarily based on economic conditions, or do we have to work with various kinds of knowledge relating to more complex conditions? Is knowledge about climate changes based first and foremost on sociological, economic, meteorological or biological conditions, or on some as yet unknown connection between various sets of conditions? Whatever the case may be, knowledge about global realities never rests on evidence we can fully experience and test ourselves, not even specialists. The amount of data is too large, and the interdisciplinary complexities require collaborations where scientists and decision-makers alike must rely on truths established by others and communicated by others to be made important, intelligible, acceptable and useful in new contexts. That evidence is never self-evident and is becoming a global fact covering an increasing range of forms of knowledge concerning areas which for centuries could be sufficiently grasped in a local setting.

Literature activates the entire problem of cognitive uncertainty in a refined mendacity which offers the necessary detour that reveals evidence in its full complexity and gives us a responsibility for it as more than just passive recipients. More than other media literature forces us to constantly keep all five social dimensions alive in our grasp of present-day globalized realities that shape our everyday lives. With Holberg, we find ourselves in the midst of the basic problems that globalization raises about knowledge beyond the parish border of the village. And the topicality of the comedy is determined by the fact that Holberg has lied to us with a twinkle in his eye. Thus, the problem is kept open as *our* problem when the theatre closes and we continue our lives.

Authentic knowledge

In such a situation, it is tempting to shift the point of view slightly. As long as we know that the events about which literature gives us knowledge are authentic and experienced by those who communicate it, we will gladly be indulgent towards lies and a subjective tampering with facts. Biographies and historical accounts about what has really happened are often based on a very selective truth, but are nevertheless read with an expectation of authenticity which underlines the fact that knowledge *that* an event is authentic is often more important than true knowledge *about* the event.

But when such works begin to question their own authenticity and the reliability of their knowledge content we enter a zone of complex doubt. And if what we cast doubt about is at the same time an authenticity and a truth beyond chance and personal interest, the uncertainty becomes a fundamental issue. This is the case in so-called *witness literature* (Engdahl 2002; Sanders 2007). This genre has appeared on the global scene over the past few decades. It applies in particular to recollections from German concentration camps during the Second World War, particularly those related to the holocaust. More recently, the term 'witness literature' has been broadened in two directions: on the one hand, to literature that processes individual and collective psychological traumas of every kind, although especially those linked to systematic suppression and persecution and, on the other hand, to memory-based depictions of genocide and ethnic cleansing over the entire globe. There is blood enough in which to dip your pen.[2]

This double orientation gives witness literature two cultural functions in its entire spectrum from poetry and fiction to reports and interviews. The one is therapeutic. Those who have been traumatized can by telling of their experiences regain some kind of control over their lives where their individual identity and their social identity have been made alien to each other. This division is clearly visible, for example, in cases of rape during times of war, when shame makes it impossible to speak of what has occurred. Individual identity is then linked to an indelible knowledge of what took place and social identity to an opposite public insistence that this must be kept concealed. Yet, by telling the story the victims may be able to bring their split individual and social identity closer to each other once more. They themselves put into words experiences whose full horror is beyond language, and can enable others to share in them. Blixen's *Out of Africa* belongs as a remote cousin to that family.

The other function is collective remembrance preventing us from stowing away as individual exceptions both social injustices and the direct and indirect complicity of the societies involved. This confrontation with the past, and also with our global present, is a boil that it is painful to lance: Germany's past, the South African apartheid regime, the Soviet Gulag camps, Greenland, Cambodia, the Balkans, Afghanistan, Rwanda and Argentina. And later, it will be the turn of Israel and Palestine and participants in the wars in the broader Middle East, situations that have already been dealt with in books and films. Syria in particular has now also been put on the global map of collective horrors. Witness literature has a global function. It is perhaps the genre the forms and issues of which cross most geographical and cultural boundaries, cutting across languages and media and exerting a strong pull on readers and viewers. Unlike classic war films, the knowledge such works pass on is not modelled on contrasts with a clear ideological profile and equally obvious positioning of heroes and villains, them and us, good and evil. The complexities and the grey zones of the contrasts, values and complicities and their afterlives in whole cultures and individuals are far greater in today's conflicts with various forms of global participation from the so-called international community beyond the local sites of the conflict.

But although truth concerning isolated facts can be woolly, authenticity stands out distinctly as an indubitable fact. The holocaust deniers are marginal fantasists. If both facts and authenticity are, however, questioned by those who themselves were witnesses, not as an individual contingency but as a fundamental condition for their testimony, readers and viewers are brought right to the edge of their seats. Indeed, even more provocatively, perhaps there is a doubt that *must* be kept open if one is to be able at all to bear witness, so that it can acquire its cultural functions beyond the direct context of the atrocities themselves and engage people outside the scene of atrocities, also later generations. There must be a need to constantly add something to the facts themselves for them to continue to have an impact on individual identity and collective recollection. It is not enough for the author to have the authenticity confirmed on the back cover – 'presents the author's own experience', as it says on the back of Jorge Semprún's memories of the journey to the concentration camp of Buchenwald in *The Long Voyage* [Le grand voyage] (1963). Authenticity is never a simple fact, but is always the author's open project in the text itself directly involving the reader's active engagement with the story, and not the publisher's information to the book market.

Imre Kertész asked in 2001 the provocative question 'Who owns Auschwitz?' in a review of Roberto Benigni's film *Life is Beautiful* [La vita è bella] from 1997. The film is a comedy à la Chaplin. Guido is in Auschwitz with his son Giosuè and the father dupes him into believing that the whole thing is a game and that there will finally be a prize – a real tank. His kind but deceptive translation to the boy of the concentration camp guards' rough words and behaviour and the participation in the game by the other prisoners turns the film into a comedy. It caused quite a commotion when it came out, because it removed the authenticity from the experience and changed the tragedy into a comedy. Moreover, although the son of a survivor, the director was born only in 1952. How could he have access to any reliable experience and truth about the historical events? And how could he show such disrespect?

Kertész, himself a survivor, writes however in his review: 'But doesn't this trick of "the game" correspond in essence to the experienced reality of

Auschwitz? One could smell the stench of burnt human flesh, but did not even so want to believe that it was true.' And when he continues, he plunges the knife deeper into the wound and claims that authenticity and factual truth in such situations directly oppose each other:

> There is something shockingly ambiguous about the jealous way in which survivors insist on their exclusive rights to the holocaust as intellectual property as though they'd come into possession of some great and unique secret. ... Only *they* are able to guard it from decay, through the strength of their memory. ... Is the representation plausible, the history exact? Did we really say that, feel that way? Is that really where the latrine stood, in precisely that corner of the barracks? ... But why are we so keenly interested in all the embarrassing and painful details, rather than just trying to forget them all as soon as possible? It seems that, with the dying-away of the living sensation of the holocaust, all the unimaginable pain and sorrow live on as a single, unified value – a value to which one not only clings more strongly than to any other, but which one will also see generally recognised and accepted. And herein lies the ambiguity. For the holocaust to become with time a real part of European (or at least western European) public consciousness, the price inevitably extracted in exchange for public notoriety had to be paid. Thus we immediately got a stylisation of the holocaust, a stylisation which has by now grown to nearly unbearable dimensions. ... Yes, the survivors watch helplessly as their only real possessions are done away with: authentic experiences. (Kertész 2005: 268, 270)

The intolerability for Kertész lies in the false authenticity that the details involve, for example, in Steven Spielberg's *Schindler's List* (1993). They become ethnografica, maybe even sentimentalized by being turned into a holocaust. Actually, the production of the film itself, in brief, shows that the global media reality doubles the problem of truth and authenticity. Spielberg's film is based on a novel that, with a reference to Noah's Ark, is called *Schindler's Ark* (1982). The Australian author Thomas Keneally was neither a Jew like Spielberg nor related to survivors as Benigni. But he found a gripping story concealed on the very border of reality and imagination: the impossible rescue of a group of Jewish children by a German. This novel, like his other ones, is an adaptation of real events, and the mixture of fact and fiction caused some trouble in 1982. But after the success of the film, the novel took over the name of the film and was effectively relaunched.

So, the basis of the film is *faction*, that is, a mixture of fact and fiction, and in addition to this mixed dish Spielberg's film makes a further rehash that mixes everything one more time. Retrospectively, it changes at the same time the book's status and shifts it into the globalized minefield of the media. Here, one forgets that it is a novel that gave rise to a debate in 1982 and was awarded the prestigious Booker Prize. Now, its status is that it forms the basis for a blockbuster film. One is tempted to say its authentic basis now that the concepts have begun to slide: the film recognizes the book as its actual basis, even though it is a faction. Incidentally, in mid-career, its author changed his name from the middle name Mick (Michael) to the first name Thomas. He is one and the same person, but perhaps a bit less of a journalist feature writer with the name of Thomas rather than Mick. Who knows what is truth and untruth here. Remember, this instance is merely a simple, transparent example of the general globalized conditions for the peregrinations of literature around the world in and out of languages and media, mixing evidence with complex mediation processes in an indissoluble blend of fact and fiction. A global form of communication based on creative lying.

So it is self-evident that Kertész is not interested in the authenticity in or behind the text, only in how it can be recreated in the text and live on in the reader: 'But, since we are talking about literature … that … is also a testimony, my work may yet serve a useful purpose in the future, and – this is my heart's desire – may even speak to the future,' Kertész says in his speech 'heureka!' at the Nobel Prize ceremony in 2002 (Kertész 2002: s.p.). The text must also deconstruct the sentimental or sensational stylizations that Kertész finds in Spielberg, but not in Benigni. And the deconstruction comes at a price: the reference to reality as the ambiguous basis of witness literature becomes irrelevant for its activating effect as a testimony for the readers. That is the keynote of *The Long Voyage*, written by the Spanish-French survivor from Buchenwald Jorge Semprún.

On the train to Buchenwald

'I was there myself' could have been the title of Semprún's memories from Buchenwald. That is how it really was during the transportation of prisoners.

On the back cover of my French copy of the book I read that it 'presents his own experience of the deportation', while the publisher, nevertheless, calls it a 'novel' in its list of works by the author on the penultimate page. Most of the hits on the internet under the name of the author or the book show at one moment that it is a novel based on personal experience, and at the next that it is authentic personal experiences processed using literary means. As always, the ball is in the reader's court.

Semprún puts Kertész's request into practice: forget knowledge of reality and authenticity, write in such a way that you place the responsibility for both of these with the reader. Then and only then, the experience will live on. The relation between reality and authenticity, truth and lies is not decided once and for all, but is a challenge each time something new comes to the surface throughout the novel. The necessary writing practice thus consists of four operations in groups of two. In the book they do not occur in a slavish order, but are repeated and turned round, isolated and mixed.

1. In the first group, one operation is to remove focus from the details of the camp and the journey.
2. Another is to focus sharply on the narrator's own take on the experience of them, no matter the details. Thus, a shift is made from supplying knowledge about the details to providing knowledge about the subjective authenticity of the experience.
3. In the second set of operations, a third operation consists in recreating in the reader's mind the experiences told in the book through the way it is written and composed.
4. A fourth operation homes in on what kind of knowledge or reflection the reader, under such conditions, may take with him or her – the way it speaks to the future, as Kertész just said. From the third to the fourth operation the movement runs from challenging the readers by literature to forcing them to anchor it in their own reality, where Semprún's experiences and the existence of Buchenwald then may live on transformed by being mediated by the novel.

The main plot of the book is the transportation of prisoners from the reception camp in Compiègne, close to Paris, until Semprún on the last pages enters the camp in Buchenwald, near Weimar. He left Spain in 1937 with his committed republican parents, who came from the diplomatic elite. After Franco took over power in the wake of the civil war of 1936–1939, they settled in Paris. Jorge went to an elitist high school, studied philosophy and entered the French resistance movement in the communist ranks. He was captured in 1943, twenty years old, and ended up in Buchenwald, but survived and returned to France in Spring 1945. This story is told in fragments, with sudden associations, leaps of memory, anticipation of future events in the camp, enhanced by historical and cultural perspectives. A simple basic situation forms the fixed central axis for these roundabout trips, so that readers are never flung off at a tangent: a group of prisoners is crammed together in a train carriage with two persons at the centre, Semprún and a guy from Semur. The two of them talk, eat, discuss, dream, disagree and encourage each other. This situation the book continually returns to as an authentic fact organizing his experience.

In the way he narrates, Semprún runs through the four operations I have just listed. That is the case in many places in this and other works by Semprún that are based on concentration camp experiences, deeply moving in their fluid transitions between life-assertion and horror, far beyond anything I can pass on here. Seven or so pages at the beginning of the book are a single concentrated example of Semprún's *modus operandi* (Semprún 2005: 18–25).[3]

Semprún and the guy from Semur are looking from the train at the winter landscape along the Moselle. They have just entered Germany. They look out and talk about the reception camp in Compiègne that they have left. The down-to-earth companion cannot imagine that there are other French camps. He is a patriot, and he has never seen any. Semprún explains the opposite to him. If the guy is like Erasmus' brother Jacob from Holberg's comedy, Semprún is Erasmus himself, the intellectual wise-guy lecturing on and over-interpreting everything. So apart from how things actually are when prisoners are being deported, in a couple of digressions we also get to know something about the French camps on the way, enlived by the two persons' different involvement with and knowledge about France's ambiguous relation to the Germans. Then, the focus shifts to the German winter landscape in front of them while the train whistles. The guy from Semur doesn't want to look at it. He is from the country and has seen enough countryside; and the wine of Moselle cannot beat the Chablis anyway or any other local French stuff. Once again, Semprún's thoughts drift off to his earlier life, called forth by hotels along the railway line while he remembers sleep in similar places interrupted by the whistle, and at the sight of German families with children out for a walk and looking at the train he recalls his own normal, uninformed everyday life back home. For them, it is just a freight train as it says on the outside. They cannot see any prisoners or personal life-stories.

Such are the narrow circles of associations linked to the experience during the trip. But they broaden out. Semprún recalls in short glimpses a sabotage action near Semur that coincidentally links his companion and the resistance movement together in one association. He makes a mental leap forward to the end of the journey: the guy from Semur 'died right next to me, at the end of this voyage, I finished this voyage with his body standing beside me'. And he looks forward in time to life at the camp after his arrival with the loudspeakers that broadcast soft music, and here too he sees a family of Germans taking a walk outside the fence. His thoughts move even further forward, till after he has been let out into freedom and walks outside himself and repeats the journey in reverse order on his way home. His imagined pleasure is overshadowed by his hatred of the Sunday Germans. But the first journey, the prisoner convoy he now sits writing about sixteen years later, has been forgotten and therefore cannot simply be reversed. Now, however, he sits in a new present and knows that the journey is waiting to be repeated, simply by being unravelled from forgotten memories. That is what he is doing at his desk, in order to integrate the journey into his life, and vice versa.

The prerequisite is that he can choose what he wants to write, so as to shape the journey himself and make it into *his* journey:

> Perhaps I ought to talk only of these people out walking and of this feeling [of being inside the train] the way it was then, in the Moselle valley, so as not to upset the order of the story. But I'm the one writing this story, I'll do as I like. I could have refrained from mentioning the guy from Semur. He was with me on this voyage, he died from it, that's a story which, actually, is nobody's concern. But I chose to talk about it. First of all because of Semur-en-Auxois, because of the coincidence of travelling with a guy from Semur. ... It's between the guy from Semur and me.

And from there we return again to the train, where he stands looking out of the window, while his matter-of-fact companion asks what he is looking at.

Nothing, Semprún replies. Stupid, comes the reply, to just stand there looking at nothing with open eyes.

The focus of what is related to us has been shifted. There is still a great deal about actual conditions and persons we meet. But they are the result of his choice, a freedom he first has gained sixteen years later while he writes. He chooses not to retrieve all the correct details out of their oblivion, but instead to raise himself above the demand for the most complete recollection possible. They are allowed to remain in oblivion. He stands looking at nothing, as he says. Instead, or rather therefore, he allows certain experiences to broaden out, especially about his companion and the untroubled Germans outside, with an authenticity that means he is totally free to organize the narrative with himself and his companion as the centre, even though the memory is fragmentary and selective. It is that form of narrative, not experiential authenticity he confirms and gives us knowledge about via his presentation of the journey.

By shifting the focus from knowledge about the content of things and the details of events to the narrator's experience, he acquires the opportunity to define himself what kind of narrative we are going to read: 'It's between the guy from Semur and me,' he writes. That is his focus. Back then he was unable to select anything at all from the situation. Now, he is able to and by selecting something and forgetting something else he highlights what he imposes on the reader as worth remembering. The reader is not supplied with any other information. Factual recollections or not, forgetting is a precondition for us to get to know anything essential about the experience together with his companion. The narrated trip creates that cohesion which was not there during the transport or in its immediate aftermath.

From text to reader

Semprún has now carried out the first set of two textual operations and moved from knowledge about the event to knowledge about the subjective authenticity of the experience he has as its narrator. He has explicitly drawn attention to the fact that knowledge about the journey is characterized by holes in his memory, and that the relation to his companion is really no one's concern during the journey other than the guy's and his own. Throughout,

Semprún uses a considerable amount of space to provide this experience with a form that directly incorporates it into the readers' world. He chooses details from the past, their weight and value on the basis of his present conditions while writing in order to be able to understand the situation that otherwise evades his memory. Knowledge arises not only in relation to the things about which they are knowledge but also in relation to the person who chooses focus, purpose and the form of communication. The readers have the same relation to the text that Semprún has to the past. They, too, have to bring about order in the scattered thoughts and the temporal leaps back and forth and to assess the credibility of the choices that have been made and attempt to see some kind of necessity in the way they are connected in and by the narrative. This situation is also identical with the impenetrability of the journey for the prisoners, the permanent uncertainty of the prisoners and the fragments of shouts, rumours and sensory impressions that crowd in on them during their journey.

However, from inside the train, the sight of the Germans out on a walk outside the train and outside the camp and his own frustrated experience when he is set free outside the camp in spring 1945 acquire a general and simple form that detaches them from his personal experience. In his recreation of the facts, they are reduced, or elevated to two simple general core experiences that are a concrete everyday experiences for all of us. The simplicity is underlined by the uncomplicated and repeated sentences, vacillating between present and past tenses and aspects:

> Seeing them walking down that road, as if it was the most simple thing in the world, I suddenly realise that I'm inside and they are outside. I'm overwhelmed by a profound, physical feeling of sadness. I'm inside, for months I have been inside, and the others are outside. ... They, quite simply, are outside, and I am inside. It's not so much that I can't go where I want, one is never all that free to go where one wants. I have never been really all that free to go where I wanted. I have been free to go where I had to go, and I had to get on this train, since I had to do the things which led me to this train. I was free, completely free, to get on this train, and I put that freedom to good use. I am here, on this train. I am here of my own free will, since I could have not been here. So it's not that at all. It is merely a physical feeling: one is inside. There's the outside and the inside, and I'm inside. It is a feeling of sadness that courses through you, nothing more.

In all its simplicity, the one core experience is the *elementary spatial contrast between inside and outside*. Semprún displaces it in parallel fashion from the concrete relation between him and the Germans outside to a placeless experience of a double relation between coercion and freedom. The first relation is static – they are there, I am here. The second is dynamic – how do I choose to move from the one place to the other, with everything that this implies? He runs the inner film backwards of the forced boarding of the train, ending up seeing it as a result of the free, unforced act that underlies it, namely, his involvement in the resistance movement. He had to take part and not stay outside, but could just as well have chosen not to. In this light, the train journey is now *his* train journey, part of him, because he made a choice. The train journey and his choice come to determine and reflect each other now, while he is writing. Semprún therefore also himself chooses details and situations, sequences and perspectives for the narrative.

In that way, he anticipates the simplicity of the readers' situation. They have chosen to read the book, to cross over the border between inside and outside when they look into the world of the text, and now they have to decide what is right and wrong, truth and lies, reality and imagination. But they too could just as well have left the book unread. Both the author and the readers have a concrete experience of the fundamental cultural situation reflected by the relation between inside and outside which is varied every day all the way around us, linked to choices. The choice may have principal and binding consequences, in Semprún's case of life and death. But we do not always know that in advance. A large part of the book varies and concretizes this elementary core experience, gives it new meanings and lays it like a template over new concrete situations.

The other elementary core experience is *the physical nature of the situation*. It is penetrated by 'a profound, physical feeling of sadness', Semprún says, almost identically at the beginning and the conclusion of the last quotation. Inside and outside are never abstract categories. Acts such as boarding the train and situations such as the contrast between inside and outside can be reinterpreted on personal conditions. But sensed experience is not something we choose. We have them, or rather they have us, it is simply an experience of the shared anonymity of physical presence as such, an anonymity which is marked throughout the book, both, of course, in the overfilled carriage with the dead, hunger, thirst and human excrement and also in the language. The narrator is neither referred to as Jorge nor referred to as Semprún, but 'I', and the guy from Semur, *le gars de Semur*, is never called anything else. They say 'you' and 'old friend', but never mention each other's name. When his companion dies, he is registered as a corpse that sticks close to the narrator's own body. In the brief second half of the book, which takes up only the last eighteen pages, the guy from Semur is dead. The main character leaves the train, outside, but walks into the camp, going to live inside under his first name, Gérard. He leaves 'the world of the living' is the book's last words, but still addresses a living reader.

Why is his first name finally mentioned? The narrative in itself is an implementation of a reverse journey that Semprún dreams of undertaking for many years, but which he did not undertake, or could not undertake, before he wrote about it sixteen years later. In the retelling he not only forms the memories he decides to write about but also opens up the deadlocked situations of the past. They acquire new, shifting meanings. Through the story, they end up having to do with freedom and personal choices more than with the physical camp, and thereby, they can finally be integrated into his life. While watching people who are outside from the train, he does nothing more than look, even though he perhaps sees nothing, as he says to the guy from Semur. He is an empty, anonymous, bodily receptor. In the retelling, on the other hand, he acquires existence while he stands there, watching, while we as readers are outside, being looked at by him. While he looks, he is after all alive, he *is*. He anonymously left the living on entering the camp, but in the narrative he therefore re-emerges for us as Gérard.

Such a depiction of an emerging subjective identity, depicted during its actual emergence, is also happening in Blixen's *Out of Africa*: 'Here I am, where I ought to be.' Semprún uses almost the same words in his retrospective look at boarding the train. No matter how general or personal it is and no matter its content, the knowledge that literature provides is always based on a *concrete focus*. Here, the focus is the immediacy of the physical experience and the choices it forces on us between being on the outside and the inside in all contexts structured by this simple opposition as an experience of bodily presence, a phenomenological experience, as it were. That is the starting point for subjective identity, wherever we are localized, independent of the confusing ungraspableness of the world.

The relation between inside and outside is literature's DNA profile as a model of global thinking. A simple model, but with endless concrete possibilities to assume new forms and content when charged with the readers' supplementary experience. And we cannot avoid activating this experience, because the physicality of our presence and the dilemma between in and out, indicates basic features of our life world.

We have met a similar situation in Blixen when she stood with Farah in the living room, and when she stood in the maize field in the circle of young natives. In both cases, the relation between inside and outside was reversed. The same happened for Campe in Paris when the world outside unfolded itself to him inside the gardens of the Palais Royal, for the Chinese Peruvians on their way into the United States, for me personally, inside and outside at one and the same time during my visit to the school class, and for Frederick Sinnett, who wanted to place the literature of distant Australia inside English literature. Kant fell out of his divinely governed universe and had to incorporate the new unintelligible experience of the world's material processes into new explanations and concepts so as to re-enter it. This he spent the rest of his life doing. It is also the permanent problem of every author: to get the ungraspable world into language, so that it can acquire a concrete, human form to which readers can relate, despite its unwieldy materiality or abstract distance. Readers stand in the same relation to the text. That is also Semprún's project, in literature and life (Semprún 1998).

Knowledge as choice

But knowledge that rests on Semprún's extremely personal choice of material and presentation, is it knowledge at all? It is, at any rate, only a form of knowledge if the fundamental starting point for knowledge in general is choice. And that it is so is not immediately self-evident. For I do not choose if it is true that gravity is universal or that the Earth revolves around the sun. However, the first thorough and systematic considerations about the nature of scientific knowledge have precisely choice as their starting point before empirical data which, from that perspective, are available by being chosen, not immediately given. This is Aristotle's view. He was both deeply interested in organizing knowledge in a new way and in creating new knowledge within the numerous areas that he examined, with an interdisciplinary approach to what we nowadays would call natural science, the humanities, social studies and medicine. His basic ideas had for 2,000 years a profound and almost unchallenged effect on the European conception of knowledge, only fading away about the time of the Lisbon earthquake

Knowledge is a reasoned choice between right and wrong. That is roughly what Aristotle says in his so-called *Nichomachean Ethics* (Book 6), reputedly written for his son, Nichomachos, in the fourth century BCE. He makes two points. The first has to do with the *social dimensions* of knowledge, as in Holberg. The fundamental role of choice relates knowledge and ethics to each other, because both have to do with making reasoned choices between right and wrong, though not within the same fields or on the basis of the same kind of reasoning. This means that reason cannot be separated from its social contexts, no matter how true and irrefutable it is. One can never avoid discussing essentiality, intelligibility, acceptance and use alongside truth. If the producer of knowledge does not engage in this discussion, others will step in, simply because knowledge has a bearing beyond those who produced it. Knowledge comes into being in order to develop the culture of which it is a part, Aristotle says in slightly different words (1941: 1094a, 1–30): the different and specialized forms of knowledge strive to do something good, and taken together they strive to improve life in the *polis* as a whole, that is, organized human life in the city state. He was a cosmopolitan from Athens. This is Aristotle's first point.

The Greek's second point has to do with the *cognitive dimensions* of knowledge. There are two reasons why choice is also fundamental here. The first has to do with the things (*ousia*) we wish to know something about. 'Our discussion will be adequate if it has as much clearness as the subject-matter admits of, for precision is not to be sought for alike in all discussions, any more than in all the products of the crafts,' Aristotle points out, with practical knowledge in mind (1941: 1194b, 15ff). In other words, arguments that are solely based on theoretical stringency, exhaustive knowledge of the material and experimental accuracy, but that ignore the limitations imposed on us by special types of subject-matter, do not guarantee the best or most exhaustive knowledge in all instances. For that reason, various forms of knowledge cannot without further ado serve as a model for each other, but can – and ought to – cooperate and complement each other. Complex subjects require us to combine several types of knowledge, and this means that we have to choose which types of knowledge we are to combine in relation to different things. Knowledge is never in the singular, and no one type of knowledge has a fixed monopoly when it comes to serving as a model for other forms.

This conclusion might just suggest a convenient division of labour. All of us can now become nerds within a separate subject area, each built on a combination of types of knowledge and well-suited subjects – globalization for specialists. But here Aristotle's point that choice is the basis for knowledge gets in the way. Knowledge is not only anchored in things but also in us who make the choices when we convert experience of things into knowledge. We choose the subjects we want to know something about as well as the theories and methods we use in order to obtain knowledge. These choices may be based on something spontaneous: desire, emotions, pain and innate proclivities for certain things as well as other individual or passing contingencies. They do not count. Only choices that depend on our special ability to make reasoned choices, *logos*, count. That is the core of Aristotles' choice system for knowledge. Getting involved with things requires choices, and as rational beings humans we have the possibility of making them and using them to develop knowledge. Within all areas where we can make reasoned choices between right and wrong, we can gain knowledge. We exercise this ability not only within the areas which at various points in history have been called science, a category that changes by virtue of the continued reasoned choices we make. Astrology was hot science at one time – now it is hot air.

The fact that Aristotle is so eager for knowledge to be capable of being justified by reason and not just by observation does not mean that theory and method are to be imposed on everything, only that different kinds of reasoning exist which allows for different types of knowledge with different validity and range. Hence, to acquire knowledge also means to be able to justify boundaries of particular types of knowledge, even in relation to the same object. One can do so, for example, by referring to practical experience, to logical argument, to authoritative texts and opinions, to custom, to law and order. Aristotle also emphasizes yet another aspect. If knowledge can in principle be justified to others, even though not all of them perhaps accept or understand the arguments provided, then knowledge cannot essentially be private knowledge in the same way that opinions and notions can be private. In principle, knowledge can always be communicated to others, even though one does not do so all the time. Therefore, knowledge is nearly always fused with language and is therefore basically a social and cultural entity.

In his book on ethics, Aristotle operates with five basic areas regarding our ability to undertake reasoned choices leading to different types of knowledge: theoretical knowledge (*episteme*), intuitive knowledge (*nous*), practical knowledge (*phronesis*), creative knowledge (*tekhne*) and wisdom (*sophia*). All types of knowledge are followed by the shadow of ethics itself being a matter of choice: right and wrong have to do with practical things, with social behaviour, with intuitions, with truth and cognition, with values – and a whole lot more.

Creative knowledge, for example, supplies knowledge about how we produce things, including literature, art, craft and technology. When we as users realize that an express train, a chair or a film functions as intended, we have chosen or produced true creative knowledge via the things we make. If we are dealing with practical knowledge, Aristotle is mainly concerned with what is right and wrong knowledge about society, human actions and community. If we are convinced that the social community improves, then we have chosen or produced true practical knowledge about society. These two kinds of knowledge are 'logistic', he says. It is applied knowledge and knowledge about application.

The three last types are the cognitive or 'epistemological' types of knowledge. Intuitive knowledge distinguishes between what is true and false concerning fundamental principles for the world order on the basis of spontaneous perceptions. If we drop a stone, it falls to the ground, and if we throw it up into the air 10,000 times, it learns just as little about flying as Holberg's Mother (1941: 1103b: 20–25). Holberg has probably looked over Aristotle's shoulder. 'We cannot justify by logical deductions that the natural place for the stone is on the ground, but how can it possibly be otherwise?', Aristotles intuits. Wisdom unites these intuitive insights with theoretical knowledge, so that they are not only right but necessarily true according to both logic and rational intuition. Theoretical knowledge is special. Today, we would refer to it as science. Here, we gain insight into what is true about reality with logical necessity. It requires scrupulously honest reasoning on top of observations, maybe in an attempt to repair incomplete explanations.

There are complicated links between the various areas of knowledge, scientific justifications and types of distinctions between right and wrong. With or without good reason, some of them are regarded as more important than others; indeed, some are regarded as the only model for true scholarship that the other types ought to try to imitate. Natural science acquired such status as a model of true knowledge in the nineteenth century, and it still often plays that role in the cultural debate as the sole representative of Aristotle's theoretical knowledge. The serious exponents of the various sciences, however, have a more humble view regarding the limited validity of their particular kind of knowledge, always keeping in mind that true knowledge is not valid unless the conditions on which it is grounded are made explicit together with its boundaries. They are well aware that the knowledge a society is in need of must be composed of various types of scientific justification and use. True science is that which provides us with essential knowledge about a composite world, not knowledge that has particular methods, theories and validation criteria.

This brings us back to Aristotle. For him, scholarship is not restricted to particular subjects. All the elements of reality can give rise to theoretical knowledge. That is what he himself practises within astronomy, psychology, physics, poetry, biology, sociology and several other domains. His five basic areas of knowledge do not compete with each other, but they offer complementary models of knowledge in need of collaboration. They are just different, because their concrete scientific justifications for the choice between right and wrong are different. For that reason, they cannot separately provide all the knowledge we are in need of. It is the ability of the sciences to formulate the *relation* between the types of knowledge he is seeking, so that the boundaries between them become dynamic. It is the open complexity of reality that is Aristotle's challenge, not to maintain the system he advances.

Even though we do not endorse his individual results, the actual experiences he has of the radical renewal of knowledge are still topical today. In its report of January 2007, *Atlas of Ideas*, to the British foreign ministry, the think-tank Demos notes in particular the organization of knowledge:

An inflexible, standardised curriculum may be a good answer to the industrial economy's demand for punctual, literate, diligent workers capable of following the rules. An innovation economy requires an education system that is curiosity-led and promotes collaborative problem-solving. (Leadbeater and Wilsdon 2007: 50)

The challenges of globalization have given our reality a new complexity that has removed the fences of the back gardens of traditional subject areas. Our standard conceptions of what knowledge the new facts and problem complexes call for have been shaken. Today, like Aristotle, we also have to *choose* new boundaries between subjects and procedures in order to develop our knowledge.

The knowledge of literature

But what kind of knowledge does literature offer on such conditions? That literature contains knowledge is indisputable, also before the formation of the modern sciences that we know today, including literary studies. That this knowledge is or can be shared by many is just as obvious. Not only because there are many observers, listeners and readers of the works but also because literature by nature is the art of language, and language is the basis of the reasonings that convert observations into knowledge. Everything we can talk about in language – and that is *everything*, even silence – literature is able to talk about. Therefore, literature has always been an active force when the relations between types of knowledge, scientific and otherwise, have shifted (Gratz 1990). No matter what type of knowledge literature provides, it is always a neighbour to other types of knowledge. And it constantly exchanges its knowledge in tandem with the neighbours on the other side of the fence. The knowledge which literature, in its capacity as literature, has to offer can be brought together under five headings. Their focus will always be concrete, based on texts and experiences, as in Semprún's book.

The dynamics of knowledge

Literature mixes the types of knowledge that otherwise are kept separate in our knowledge culture, and confronts them with all kinds of beliefs, convictions and fancy tendencies across cultures and across what is taken for granted in the knowledge society. Knowledge can be acquired and cultivated in isolation, but cannot be used without situating itself in the broader cultural landscape of competing opinions and beliefs. It is here that knowledge is transferred from one area to others, scientific or not. When the schoolchildren learn to click heads onto the bodies of Egyptian gods at Newcomer High School, they gain a knowledge – Aristotle's creative knowledge – that can be subject to a transfer that can be characterized as right or wrong. The transfer points to areas that maybe are new for the those exercising the transfer, or perhaps new in general when we seek to move forward with the knowledge we have, face to face with a problem no one can get an overall picture of. And the transfer meets with resistance from stupidity, prejudices or our tentative approximations to knowledge.

Literature is a laboratory for how knowledge is transferred in complex situations by using all the resources of language and in the broader context of cultural belief systems. Literature does not set out to show what kind of knowledge or belief is the best one. It transfers, often imaginatively and at variance with other forms of cognition, knowledge from one area to another and on to a third area. For example, in the crossings of metaphorical language between areas of meaning, or when the same thing is simultaneously subjected to various angles from different characters, some wise, others completely barmy. It has long been recognized that metaphors, associations and intuitive knowledge play an activating role in sciences when one is attempting to grope forward within areas one does not know anything about (Leatherdale 1974; Schön 1993). Later, the ideas are sorted and made more precise under scientific conditions. First and foremost, literature provides knowledge about this fundamental dynamics of transference. Literature holds the dynamics of knowledge open, whereas others imprison it within monopolies of subject areas and knowledge.

In Semprún, the two companions exchange knowledge about the same things while travelling, but all the time they have to transfer what they know between different horizons of knowledge. The narrator has political, geographical and historical knowledge and an overview to pass on. On the other hand, he gains practical knowledge from the guy from Semur about how to survive on the train. They are like Erasmus and brother Jakob in a muted form. They do not want to have a monopoly, but want to share the knowledge neither of them can create or contain as separate individuals. They transfer knowledge on each other's conditions, so that it re-emerges as new and different knowledge. This keeps them alive.

Boundaries of knowledge

No matter how dynamic knowledge is, in principle it has always limits. It is this fundamental fact literature always holds up in front of us. Everything that literature says is said from a limited position. It may be indicated by a person, an institution, an anonymous community or a linguistic stylistic layer, such as irony. The way in which such a restricted standpoint is formulated in language reveals to the reader that what is being said here is not universally valid. Statements about absolute belief, universal truths or incontestable facts are never more absolute, universal or incontestable than the conditions under which they have come into being and are used.

Albert Einstein shifted the conditions for understanding space and time in the physical world. In doing so, he did not invalidate Isaac Newton's mechanical view of the world and its basis, absolute space and time. But he made more precise the limited conditions under which they were valid. Our uncertainty regarding the basis for knowledge about important global areas today, for example, the environment, political tendencies and cultural conflicts, tempts many people to create dogmatic world views transforming complex facts into simplified statements and political manifestoes. It quietens us down, but we know quite well that they are illusory. The anti-dogmatic knowledge of literature about the limits and uncertainty of knowledge is a sugar rush that keeps us awake.

In *The Long Voyage*, the narrator emphasizes all the time that everything we get to know during the train journey has been chosen and shaped by him at a later point in time, a constant reminder to the reader to be sceptical. His entire linguistic presentation maintains that scepticism, with leaps of thought, leaps of time, the absence of personal names, sentence construction.

The boundary of consciousness

When the outside world, like that of today, is in constant revision, rational and conscious intentions and acts cannot offer an adequate overview. For that reason, spontaneous physical experience – aesthetic experience – becomes a *predominant* way in which we relate to the world around us. To use a keyboard or drive a car are forms of knowledge on the borderline between body and consciousness where we operate using physical experience alone. We are virtually oblivious of the content, unless a new computer or shift from driving on the one side to the other side of the road causes us to wake up. Our everyday lives are full of such semi-conscious motivations and acts, even the routines of scientific practises, but also desires and urges we cannot rationally control, smoking habits, craving for sugar, conscience, insomnia, erection problems and so on. Although it is a certain and important knowledge in our everyday lives, it cannot stand alone.

Literature is full of knowledge about this border area and the way we approach it. Indeed, presenting experiences that balance on the threshold of consciousness and their effects on human reality is a particularity of literary forms of expression. It is an experience of that type which Semprún homes in on at the window of the train while looking out without knowing what he sees. The simple recognition of the fact that he is physically present keeps him going while he falls into the great void of deportation.

Cognitive uncertainty

Literature interweaves people's reflections on their own identity inextricably with knowledge of the outside world and life in society. That a fact is a fact is one thing, but that we are sure that it is a fact is a more comprehensive aspect of knowledge, binding the outside world to our identity as an individual human being living in this world. We may call subjective investment in factual experience for a necessary attempt to gain conviction or certainty. This attempt is the core of the human processing of reality, even if it has not yet been collected into rational patterns of interest and action that can be made accessible to existing sciences. We often have to hold knowledge and subjective self-understanding apart in order to gain special knowledge, as when we say that something is incredible, but true. The temptation to set them apart is often great, for example, when treating patients the body gets its due, while the ill person looks on helplessly. But the more fundamental knowledge offered by literature tells us that they can never be held apart. Our experience of the world and its effect on us are one unity.

Some types of literature present suggestions of such totalities to us, often difficult to live with, as in tragedies where our certainty concerns a disaster we cannot avoid. Other types of literature test our certainty via challenging themes or forms of expression and present us with the demand to find new forms of certainty: Is this really literature? Is this really about the world I live in? Such questions of uncertainty emerge from experimental literature, or when we encounter literature from foreign cultures. Here, we have to try to understand other forms of certainty than those familiar to us, or set about finding a new connection between ourselves and the world around us that we can feel certain about, for the time being at least.

That is the task which preoccupies Semprún. He cannot gain his identity without making a detour via the experience of the outside world he otherwise has left behind him, the journey and the camp. And it will not foster a knowledge which gives him identity, such as Gérard gains in the book, unless he decides to implement the project as a personal project. This totality of knowledge about the world and himself he transforms into a concrete physical and linguistic framework around the self-reflection he passes on to the reader.

Visions

Literature deals with the constant and real influence on human thoughts and actions of imaginary, that is, unreal notions and ideas. Such notions have an unyielding, material and consistent effect, even if they are private and have neither clear causes nor good justifications. They are simply necessary for us to be able to orientate ourselves towards a future that as yet only exists as a vision, whether it be binding or sheer wishful thinking. The various types of knowledge offer one way of relating to the future via arguments as to what is true or false. The knowledge of literature retains the complexity and necessity of visions and their actual consequences.

When Semprún is to tell his story, it is the notion of the solidarity in the train between the two companions that gives it a goal to aim for in the future.

It is that vision which organizes and holds together the half-memories as one whole narrative and one identity, and that makes the journey concrete for us.

These five types of knowledge structure the integration of innumerable texts into the collected knowledge processes of culture. The two former ones mainly deal with the relation between types of knowledge, while the three latter ones deal with the relation between knowledge and personality. These five types of knowledge offer complementary models of knowledge practised in various branches of science and are the indispensable contribution literature makes to the formulation and use of knowledge in any culture. Without them, that knowledge can neither be formulated nor be used.

Fact or fiction?

I've avoided it as long as I could. But the truth will out. If knowledge rests on choice, one can also choose to lie. And the difference cannot always be traced. In his provocative book *On Bullshit*, Harry Frankfurt states that 'it is impossible for someone to lie unless he thinks he knows the truth. ... A person who lies is thereby responding to the truth, and he is to that extent respectful of it' (Frankfurt 2005: 75). Truth systematizes the possibilities for lying, so it must also be possible to lie people into truth. We can confirm at any rate that Semprún has lied about a crucial issue. The physical solidarity between Semprún and the guy from Semur, the story's authentic basis for the unfolding of the action, the many associations, the random selection of details, the core of the narrative, the concrete experience the reader can immediately relate to, that basis is a lie.

In the two subsequent books about his experiences, *Literature or Life* [*L'écriture ou la vie*] (1994) and *Le mort qu'il faut* [The dead man we needed] (2001), Semprún reveals that the guy from Semur has never existed. He has found some notes by his older colleague Jean Paulhan, who supported him and other young writers thirty years ago. Paulhan found *The Long Voyage* honest, but not sensational, and complained that the guy from Semur died and that this made the ending rather sad. This provokes a simple confession in *Literature or Life* and almost an identical though slightly shorter one later in *Le mort qu'il faut*:

I invented the guy from Semur to keep me company, when I took this same journey again in the imagined reality of literature. To spare myself the loneliness I'd felt during the real journey from Compiègne to Buchenwald, no doubt. I invented the guy from Semur, I invented our conversation: reality often needs some make-believe, to become real. In other words, to be made believable. To win the heart and mind of the reader (Semprún 1998: 262)

I would invent the guy from Semur to keep me company when remaking the journey in the dreamed reality of writing. We did the voyage together, in fiction; I have invented the guy from Semur to remove my solitude, in reality. Why write books if one does not invent reality? Or, even better, what seems real? (Semprún 2001: 187, 188)[4]

He has lied, creatively and effectively, one has to admit. But the strange thing is that we do not change our first experience of the reading.

That is not the case with all kinds of knowledge. If a researcher is caught with both hands covered in lies, he is punished and consigned to oblivion, and his results are likewise discarded. This happened in dramatic fashion for the Korean stem-cell researcher Hwang Woo-Suk in 2004. He was part of a campaign for Korean research in the global knowledge competition backed by power and money. Here truth and lies were virtually indistinguishable from each other for a long time in a field of knowledge characterized by the experimental uncertainty of its early developmental phase. But, at the end, his results proved to be a fraud, although he is still to a certain degree in denial himself.[5] This is not the case with literature. The authentic experience the reader has had is not diminished by the fact that the writer has lied to us about his own experience. And that was precisely the object of the exercise: to shift the onus of responsibility for knowledge and the experience of authenticity from the writer and the book to the readers' reality.

It is also this process that Semprún deals with in the two later books about his concentration camp experiences. *Literature and Life* begin with him being picked up by British soldiers outside the camp after the liberation. He notes their horrified look at the sight of him. He has lived for two years 'without a face', he says (Semprún 1998: 3). There were no mirrors, and he has only seen his own body grow thinner and thinner. His emaciation cannot evoke the horror he encounters in some who have seen quite a lot of that; so it must be his face and his gaze that the soldiers react to. He must use others so as to see himself as a whole person with a face. Interwoven into the narrative, we subsequently, directly and indirectly find out the reason why he has to lie about the guy from Semur, so that it resembles truth as much as possible. In his total loneliness, he must himself create a mirror to show others and himself the identity he is in the process of developing during the description of the journey.

In *Le mort qu'il faut* (Semprún 2001: 233, 234), the invention of this counterpart is more concrete, morbid and acute. Kaminsky, a comrade in Buchenwald, somehow finds out that a letter has arrived from Berlin about Semprún, and can surely not be good news. So he has to switch identities with a dead prisoner of the same age. It is François who dies at the end of the book. Semprún gets into contact with the body that is needed before it becomes a corpse, and has a close, short friendship with the person who is going to live on in him. Here, his *alter ego* gains a physical proximity, even though all of it is Kaminsky's invention so as to save Semprún's life.

This is just as concrete as the physical experience of the difference between inside and outside the train. François and Semprún's relation shows that true identity and knowledge of oneself is gained by looking at oneself with other people's eyes, from a different location. The force of literature is that it enables us by way of imagination to construct a fictive counterpart and thereby makes possible a real identity which, as in the train carriage, would otherwise be impossible. Even if there is no 'other' to work as the mirror that shapes our identity and our knowledge about ourselves as well as our awareness of it, that inventiveness is always possible, because we carry this possibility with us in our language, open to literary creativity. The truth Semprún relates to us is not about the train or the guy from Semur, but the truth about the way in which we gain identity in relation to others. But this fundamental truth appears as truth only when it also structures the possibilities of lying and forces us, the readers, to turn it into a truth about human identity.

'An honest lie must surely exist'

It is not always possible, then, to distinguish between truth and lies by delving into the arguments and solid documentation. A lie must be put to the test in a concrete situation. Does it work or doesn't it? – that is the litmus test. It is not a reference in language but an act of language with an addressee. And that act is even more risky if we are dealing with a testimony, not only in court or in a religious community but, as is the case with Semprún or Kertész, with witness literature. Scruples about lying have followed us since ancient times, when the concept of scientific truth came into existence, and later when the basis of the modern legal system was laid in Rome, and later again when the Christian church demanded truth in testimony concerning and before God. On that basis, one acquired a richly graduated system for describing the strength and baseness of lying as well as its ambiguities which is hardly found in other cultures that have not been weighed down by the Christian consciousness of sin and guilt.

Augustine of Hippo, one of the founding Fathers of the Church, perhaps takes the prize for the truest description ever of lying, written c. 400 CE.[6] First, he wrote *De mendacio* [On Lying], then *Contra mendacium* [Against Lying]. He preferred the latter text which is mainly a moral call to arms against the Spanish mystic Priscillianus. The Spaniard believed that one could lie in order to protect the secrecy of the faith against non-believers and thereby protect God's congregation. He did not stand a chance, and was the first person to be excluded from the church as a heretic. One is not a true witness if one diverges from the basic principle about which one is to bear witness: always to speak truly about God. This is a question that the global political situation has made acute: Can one lie in order to begin a war and call it a just war, as Colin Powell, the American Secretary of State, did in the UN Security Council in the run-up to the war in Iraq in 2002? Wikileaks and other evidence made known by whistle-blowers makes the question pertinent in a world of both globalized conflicts and communication technologies.

Augustine's first treatise is more analytical than moralizing and therefore comes to present the possibilities of lying in many variants, no less than eight main points with numerous subpoints and modifications. Read by the devil's advocate and without its religious rhetoric, it is almost a practical manual with great potential for spin doctors in the present-day global and mediatized political landscape. And when Augustine gets to the relation between lying and witnessing before man and God, it is the devil's advocate that is speaking through the hard-pressed writer: 'An honest lie must surely exist' (Augustine

2005a: §§20–21 and 36). Augustine cannot escape from the fix his analytical acuteness has put him in. One can lie in order to praise someone, even Christ, to non-believers, one can lie in order to protect someone, one can lie without realizing it and one can omit to say the truth, because one is not asked. What can we do with a beast that has so many heads? Augustine is unsure, and truth evaporates into thin air.

But we are more painstaking in religious matters, he assures us, all the while uncertainty still continues to spread. One cannot, of course, have truth in one's heart without the mouth also generating truth with the body. Even so, the mouth of the heart is able to speak the truth, while the mouth of the body is silent without lying (Augustine 2005a: §37). And in a good cause one can, in an emergency, lie or forget the truth for a moment as long as it does not offend fundamental Christian principles such as charity, empathy, humility and the purity of the body. He finally tightens things a little, for even though this discussion might rock from side to side (Augustine 2005a: §38), he reminds us that all lying is a sin, even though the passable lie is only a small one. So, one must always accept responsibility for one's own lying.

It is this uncertainty and responsibility which Semprún's book, and all other literature, maintains. Concerning Kaminsky, who controls the exchange of identity with the dead prisoner in *Le mort qu'il faut*, he writes, tongue in cheek: 'Kaminsky is a fictitious name. The character is partially real, however, probably in all essentials' (Semprún 2001: 233). It is safe to say that the revelation of his lie about the guy from Semur has not led to his mending his ways, but is an underlining of the uncertainty that makes the lie effective. Can we now believe any longer that it is true that the guy from Semur actually is a lie? The crucial thing is that the lie is not gambled with in literature for us to try and see if it will be revealed, but in order for the responsibility for the choice between truth and lies to become our own. What the actual decision looks like is actually a matter of indifference. That is why Semprún's entire narrative has a concrete focus which the reader recognizes and understands through the supplementary experiences he cannot help activating: the camaraderie in the train and the immediate experience of being physically present. It is also our reality, no matter the veracity of what Semprún says. With this focus, all of us always have an elementary point of departure in a shared life experience, enough for assuming the responsibility for distinguishing and choosing between right and wrong, irrespective of the means used by literature to get us to that point.

Truth and lies stand side by side without us being able in advance to distinguish between the two. The reader must personally choose between lies and truth that resemble each other. This is a choice that literature constantly holds open, no matter what type of knowledge is the issue – but always with a concrete focus. Literature does not hand out knowledge like a parcel we unwrap, nor does it do so with its five Aristotelian kinds of knowledge mentioned earlier. Literature is the honest lie Augustine pretends to be looking for. Here, we learn concretely while we read, co-present with the book, that the necessity of choice indicates the conditions for knowledge in a complex reality, *our* reality.

On a small scale, literature is a challenging experiment with the conditions for knowledge that belong to globalization's conditions for everyday life. The first time it really came into the spotlight was back in 1992 in Rio de Janeiro during the first global conference on biodiversity, and it resulted in the first attempt to create a knowledge-based international convention. The final report states in its preamble that 'where there is a threat of significant reduction or loss of biological diversity, lack of full scientific certainty should not be used as a reason for postponing measures to avoid or minimize such a threat' (Rio Convention 1992: s.p.).[7] This type of argument is characteristic of the Kyoto Protocol of 1997 and the climate change panel in Paris in January 2007 as well as in the Paris agreement during COP21 in December 2015. The only reaction which constitutes a real lie will be to wait for complete clarity to manifest itself, do nothing and ignore the impact of such ambiguities in the actual everyday life of individuals; that every day is the focus of literature, while still holding open the problem of knowledge and turning it into a process of human interaction.

If we are unable to function under such conditions, we will meet with the same fate as Erasmus, who ends up throwing away his knowledge that the Earth is round onto the dung heap lying there spreading out over the flat earth. Intoxicated by his conviction that knowledge is in the singular and builds on the power of authoritative monopolies, he is unable to distinguish between truth and lies, unable to see it as a permanent process of questioning. At the end of the comedy, he is cheated by a lieutenant and conscripted into the army (Holberg 1990: 186–192). The lieutenant pretends to make a bet with Erasmus. Is Montanus able to prove that children are to hit their parents? Yes, that is exactly what he is able to, with the aid of this formal learning and logic that can always drive practical knowledge from the field. He gets his ducat. But the lieutenant wants to make another wager: he can make Erasmus into a soldier. It is easy since Erasmus has accepted money from him, real money, even though they were part of a false bet. Erasmus suddenly becomes as practical as his brother Jakob and the lieutenant: There are no witnesses! Erasmus shouts in despair.

But he has no mastery of practical knowledge. There *are* witnesses, and they are more than willing to testify so as to get Erasmus down. Based on lies or not and indifferent to Augustine's considerations regarding the sinfulness of lying, their testimony has its effect. So, Erasmus becomes a real soldier who can buy himself free by accepting that the Earth is flat, paying a ransom that is as fictive as the wager itself. Both the practical inhabitants of the village and Erasmus are helpless when they are to administer their monopoly of knowledge in the coexistence of truth and lies on the border between staging and reality. The home team of the village cannot grasp new knowledge that exceeds their powers of comprehension, and the away team from the capital cannot anchor knowledge in the world of experience where it is valid. Literature is a form of communication which, through its forms of presentation, gives us the opportunity to see and do both and is necessary in a globalized world of uncertain knowledge and unknown consequences of established knowledge. The chapters of the second part discuss some of the literary forms of presentation.

Part Two

Literature in a Global Perspective

Memory for the Future

Literary forms of presentation

Literature is not a thing, but a project that works like building a ship while it is sailing. Its tools are developed when they are used, not ready-made beforehand. The writer explores what the text is about during its production and adapts and revises the tools along the productive trajectory, also forcing the reader to approach the texts in the same way, constantly ready to revise methods and concepts while reading. Such focused, productive strategies are what I will refer to as *forms of presentation*. The term is not a technical one to be found in literary manuals, where one usually peers down into literature's large toolbox. There one finds small, specialized tools, such as rhyme and rhythm, slightly larger ones, such as imagery, narratives and points of view, even larger ones, such as style or compositional principles for novels, sonnets and comedies, and the really solid implements in the form of genres and subgenres, such as drama, poetry, autobiography, the historical novel, French tragedy, haiku poetry and folktales. All these 'gear and tackle and trim' (Hopkins 1877) are mainly used by writers and readers to structure the individual texts and to understand their connections as they unfold in the history of literature. This practical work with literature has to do with its tools and techniques which Aristotle referred to as *tekhne*, creative knowledge, the knowledge required to get it right when producing a particular thing.

In Part Two of the book, I do not intend to go through selected tools or techniques to see how texts are constructed. I want to examine how literature, on that basis, helps to interact with the global cultural processes the direction and form of which we are not yet able to see clearly. Forms of presentation have to do with interacting with the world outside and make this interaction visible in the texts. The word 'form' is important. The Greek word *eidos* means both 'vision' and 'knowledge', and one of the regular translations of *eidos* is precisely 'form'. Form is that which enables us to perceive something as a specific thing, so that it can acquire meaning in a broader context. By its forms of presentation, literary texts give the unwieldy cultural phenomena and processes a form that enables us to grasp them in the texts, precisely as vision and knowledge, and, therefore, contextualize the texts in a larger cultural framework.

Consider a chair. Lots of tools and techniques have been used to make it. We can turn and upend it, sit on it and get supplementary information from its maker, just as a writer can read aloud and talk about how she wrote her collection of poetry. We can group chairs into easy chairs or office chairs, just as literary works can be ordered into genres. If the designer is visionary enough, a chair can also be a new kind of chair as designers have made them in the twentieth century. We can also make a history of chairs as far back as we want, just as we can with a history of literatures. And we can catch a host of broader meanings relating to taste, style and function based on the actual form of the individual chair.

However, the chair is also a form of something else than the chair itself. It presents us with our vision and knowledge of the human body. The ergonomic office chairs are not simply the result of craftsmen having become more proficient, or of new materials having appeared on the scene. It's a translation of a new vision of the body in the process of finding forms in different materials and media to present it. Take a trip to a manor house museum and see just how uncomfortable the chairs were that wealthy people possessed in the past. At the time, people were able to make intricate pieces of art craft, sail across the Atlantic Ocean and construct complex astronomical implements. Of course, technically speaking, people could also have made chairs that were 'body-friendly'. But the idea that the body's physical well-being was a problem that could be solved by making furniture with certain forms had not yet been born (Blixen 1979: 46–50; Mauss 1980). Conceptions of the body do not have a particular form of presentation that allows us to pin them down. The chair is only one of them, tables with adjustable height another, invalid-friendly doors for trains a third, fitness equipment a fourth, the computer mouse a fifth, implements of torture a sixth and so on.

The interesting forms of presentation in a culture are those which are to interact with other forms of presentation and the human lifeworld at large in order to give form to a cultural phenomenon that otherwise would not have forms in which to move in way that makes it accessible. Physical well-being did not have general and varied forms of presentation until during the eighteenth century and into the twentieth century. Some of the forms we now know supplement each other, for example, office chair, writing desk and computer mouse. Others are complementary, such as a high bar stool and a writing desk, and give form to the social structuring of work and home life. Such forms reflect not only the content of particular toolboxes that practically and traditionally are linked to particular materials, such as wood, plastic and metal. They represent the relation between the concrete form and its broader cultural–functional context. I explicitly write cultural–functional and not practical–functional context. Chairs have always been part of the latter. But, in a cultural–functional context, they also cover the changing ideas we form regarding the body, that is to sit, stand, work and be taken care of, the various types of knowledge we develop about its nature and its needs, and our possibility of presenting the physical body in itself in other media, a presentation that moves from the astrological chart of the Zodiac man to the anatomical descriptions of the Renaissance.

I have chosen the term 'form of presentation' instead of 'form of representation', which has a resounding echo dating back to Plato's and Aristotle's' different views on *mimesis*. Representation entails that something which is present elsewhere is presented once more for us by the text or, in case of Aristotle, the performance of tragedies in particular. In contrast, 'presentation' points both to the fact that the text makes something present for us in the text and that this operation takes place in the present while we read or watch it. Taking place in the present therefore means that forms of presentation invites an interaction between a text and its readers or, to put in more general terms, its users. In the case of the chair, that is how we check in what way it is a form of presentation of the body every time we actually use it. Is it made for or against the body?

The same goes for the literary texts. Through his artful lying, Semprún makes the readers to interact with his text. Unavoidably, they activate their supplementary experiences in order for the text to get its true meaning, which, on a larger scale, is also what makes a literary tradition an active part of culture in any present moment. It happens through an interactive use of the texts of the past, imitation being one of the most widespread modes of interaction. 'Interaction' has often been used as a term which is particularly relevant for digital media labelled as interactive media. The way interaction unfolds may differ in various media, in some cases being more of a hands-on process, in others more reflexive in nature. However, interaction is a general presupposition for any media to make forms of communication work.

When, in this section, I talk about literature's forms of presentation, it is based on this way of thinking. The forms of presentation reflect the mutual relation between literature and its broader cultural functions and present an unfolding process which is different from literature itself but which it takes part in, precisely by its attempts to give it form. Such phenomena can also be formed differently and in other media than language. With the use of the entire toolbox and all the creative knowledge that can be mobilized, literature gives this relation a concrete and special linguistic form with a broader cultural meaning which unfolds in an interaction shaped by the actual forms of presentation. The forms of presentation I have selected for the following five chapters have that character. They are culturally indispensable and more comprehensive than literature itself, but without literature they would not exist or function.

The broader cultural context that this book has in view is the open cultural processes of globalization. The dynamics of literary forms of presentation is based on *border-crossings* which we can localize in geography, culture, mentality, communication, literary and cultural histories and many other areas, but which as yet do not have clearly demarcated forms. The relevant border being crossed in the context of globalization is between local anchorage and global perspective. This dynamical engagement with the human life world is a fundamental aspect of literature as a model for global thinking, also prior to modern globalization. It is in the nature of literature to cross borders of all kinds. The five forms of presentation I have chosen are attempts to present this border-crossing dynamics in textual forms. At the same time, they have a long, transcultural history and, thereby, underline a basic condition for all cultural understanding. An understanding of the present age that does not build on a historical reflection is not an understanding at all, but just a tip without an iceberg.

The first chapter deals with memory as a literary form of presentation for crossing *temporal* borders by way of language, and in the next chapter on translation, the interest is in how literature crosses *cultural* borders by way of language and other media. If the two first chapters mainly concern media dependent border-crossings, the last three chapters focus in particular on crossing experiential boundaries, the experience of *body*, *place* and *movement*. These five border-crossings are decisive for the experience of globalization, and the literary forms of presentation are essential for our understanding of that experience.

Inner and outer memory

Memory has always been a distinctive feature of literature and other forms of art.[1] The standard opening of a fairy tale is 'Once upon a time ...'. The nine Greek muses protected the arts plus astronomy. Their mother, the supreme muse, Mnemosyne, is memory itself, and she had her nine daughters with the supreme god, Zeus. Both the word 'muse' and 'mnemosyne' contain, like the word 'museum', the meaning 'to remember'. We often think about memory as if it were identical with the content of what we remember. 'I had a farm in Africa,' is how Karen Blixen begins her memories of Africa. Yet, memory is first and foremost, also for her, a way of investing the past in the present with a future-oriented perspective.

From that point of view, memory is primarily a concrete activity, not a freezer conserving the past, and it therefore takes place in the present where it actually deals with the past. This process directs the present towards the future using the past as material. We choose to focus on particular parts of the past and push aside other parts as being less important. We can also go back and change our priorities as when rewriting a national literary history. We can even make sure that something will at some point in the future become a memorable past, as when we take a photo at a family party while it is taking place. Memory is a future-oriented process which, uninterruptedly, takes place in the present; at a banal level when we jot down a note for things to do the next day, or at a serious level when we attempt to process grief so that we can move on, or at an existential level when we are reminded of our death when thinking of the next generation, or at a monumental level when the Neolithic peoples raised their mounds. All of this has to do with that which will be remembered, not what we remember or remembered. No matter how important the memory content is, it can never be detached from our having chosen and sorted in the past with a hard hand with certain particular future-oriented aims in mind.

In literature, the process has two variants that partially overlap each other. One is the process that takes place *in* literature. This is the *inner* process of memory. It unfolds in the texts which in language, action, images and themes work with memories, their purpose and reliability. Not all texts have this perspective and some have it more than others and in different ways: historical novels, autobiography, travelogues or witness literature. This is a process the writer controls. The other process is that which takes place *with* literature. This is the *outer* process of memory. It is active when we write literary histories, promote literary canons, provide support for literature or call a street Dickens Boulevard. This process comprises all texts, no matter whether they themselves deal with memory or not. It is outside the writer's control and mainly depends on all the changing conditions of use that literature, like all other cultural products, is subject to in culture and society in various historical periods, long after it came into existence. Dante was not present at the official opening of Dante Square in Copenhagen, nor was he asked to give his permission when an audio network provider took the name Dante.

Some of the uses depend on the writer's text having had and still having a broad appeal to readers. Other uses are quite coincidental and have to do with changing media and market relations within and outside the literary field, often set in motion by people who have never read a single line by Dante or Shakespeare but only know their name and fame. Such uses do not have any necessary relation to the texts, most often none whatsoever, but they are a cultural reality. And this reality becomes more visible and insistent the broader it is and more so to the extent that it goes global. During the Hans Christian Andersen Year in 2005 with celebrations of the 200th anniversary of his birth, the old Danish fairy tale writer was used with various degrees of success to a little of everything to make sure that Denmark would be remembered worldwide. He is a global brand for Denmark, just as Shakespeare is for England, with all that it entails in the way of T-shirts, beer mugs and TV spots with inscriptions in languages from all over the globe, although also research and new translations of the texts were launched, everything in one huge hotchpotch. Inner and outer memories have their separate purposes in literature and do only accidentally meet in the texts.

Inner memory and identity

The texts we have read by Karen Blixen and Jorge Semprún develop inner memory as identity formation. When Blixen has completed her introduction, it is that kind of memory that is the most important: 'Here I am, where I ought to be,' she says, transforming memories into a new and forward looking identity. We have seen earlier how both she and Semprún themselves organize in masterful fashion the selected details from the past they wish to pass on to the readers. And perhaps they distort the facts or invent them out of thin air as Semprún did with his comrade from Semur in order for him to keep the process of memory going. This leads to his book primarily dealing with the two comrades, not the horrors of the concentration camp. And this redesigning also gives him access to the traumatized parts of the past and to tackle fundamental identity issues. Memory becomes a literary form of presentation for broader cultural themes, for Semprún the multifaceted crossing of the border between inside and outside and the relation between choice and freedom.

A look at Blixen's letters from Africa and other historical sources to do with her farm show other and more difficult sides of her life she simply passes over in *Out of Africa*: marital problems, syphilis, a financial situation that was in tatters during all the years she lived out there, humiliating begging letters to her family for money, a basic naivety in locating a coffee farm where no coffee can grow. For both writers, the actual process of remembrance takes place in the present while they write. Semprún refers directly to the fifteen to sixteen years that have passed before he was able to use memory as a form of presentation to structure his future. In her introduction, Blixen simply shifts discretely from the past tense to the present tense of the verbs, before triumphantly exclaiming that she is where she ought to be against the evidence of a good deal of factual detail.

It is not the actual facts of their memories that are interesting, but that two writers, like everyone else, are obliged to use the basic difference between present and past to be able to turn the present towards the future. But there is no nostalgic longing to neutralize the difference. Nor any fear of looking backwards. What they pass on to the readers is that this process takes place every time memory is working, also for the readers. The texts are constructed in such a way that the readers, in the concrete now when they grasp the book and are grasped by the text, are involved in a continuation of this process of memory opened by the writers. The aim of this process is always to create an identity that one can transport forward, even when the text itself has perhaps been forgotten.

The basis is individual and thus concrete, also for the reader as an individual person. But the perspective is collective, because the writers painstakingly transpose individual memories into a common language, no matter whether it is the identity of fictive characters or their own that is involved. What is common is not, however, only contained in the language itself but also in the way they build it up. Blixen places a filter of common European images and ideas over the alien landscape. Semprún focuses on immediately recognizable basic situations of physical experience and twosomeness in the train. Both thereby they open up for our supplementary experience, so that the formation of identity reaches beyond the individual horizon of the writers and the characters.

Outer memory and tradition

The outer memory of literature is otherwise constructed. Broadly speaking, it covers three things: *literary history, cultural traditions* and more or less random *associative cultural networks*. Let me take an example which in turn covers these three types of outer memory before I return to the inner memory in more detail. The Irishman Jonathan Swift published *Gulliver's Travels* in 1726. It was immediately a great success. It was reissued and expanded a couple of times and was frequently translated, adapted and imitated and later turned into cartoons, children's books and movies. It is a satirical travel account entirely in the Enlightenment tradition. Just as in Holberg's comedy on

Erasmus Montanus, Swift uses the indirect, satirical presentation in order to cast an alternative, critical light on his own age, a method that is chosen so that people are brought to think for themselves and thereby better remember what they have read. It presupposes all the Enlightenment optimism on humanity's behalf: people are capable of independent thinking, of learning, of developing, and are able and eager to improve society.

Literary history

Literary history is one systematic way of remembering. Since his own age, Swift has become incorporated into all literary accounts of the eighteenth century. Like all other historical writing, literary history must also provide us with source-reliable knowledge about its subject with well-checked names, years, quotations and so on. When one examines Swift's texts, both literary and other, he acquires a more finely graduated place in history than the quick reference to satire and optimism. As an Irishman, he balanced between being British and an almost colonized member of society, both in relation to Britain and in relation to many Irishmen. He was a clergyman in the Church of Ireland, a member of the Anglican Church, not a Catholic, as were, and are, most Irish. From this position on the periphery of the mighty empire, his optimism is not untempered in his satires. And with our present age as a platform, Swift's satirical diversity affords him a place, like Holberg, that transcends his own historical time. In the outer memory of literary history, Swift is positioned as a general representative of the period, but with his own special profile.

Cultural traditions

The connection between the facts of the past and the interpretation of the present therefore also establishes a broader cultural tradition that incorporates literature. To that end, ever since early times, people have been interested in finding methods to remember as well as a media in which to retain what is remembered. That we have an ability to remember earlier events is of course no guarantee for our remaining able to do so, or that we remember what is most important, let alone correct. What we remember are mere drops in the ocean of what we forget. A method is called for, and natural memory must be supplemented by artificial memory if it is to be reliable. One possible method is memory training and learning by rote, *ars memoria*, one of the most important educational disciplines in Antiquity before writing finally took over.[2] The use of images, rhyme and rhythm was important techniques for remembering. Plato's conception of education as an imitation of models is also a methodical memory that builds on the literary toolbox. Later on, writing, images and exhibitions at museums and other locations dominated as ways of remembering and made the earlier mnemonics superfluous, and today, the use of databases is probably the most important medium of memory with an almost instant global accessibility, if not blocked by local authorities. The most important thing about methods of remembering is that they can be learned, controlled and repeated, thus providing us with the certainty that we can remember correctly every time we process the past, while stable media ensure that this certainty also holds in the future. In that way, a cultural tradition is established.

Swift belongs to such a tradition by being reprinted, commented on and reinterpreted, and in many places becoming part of the standard school curriculum, with standard interpretations of the basis of standard texts in standard anthologies. But traditions often rest on a semi-conscious blend of belief and knowledge and an unclear relation to the facts of the past. It is enough for traditions to live on if they are sufficiently clear and conscious to be able to be repeated in social acts. Traditions thus more often work because they are powerful than because they are right, and are therefore more often than not situated at the centre of an ideological battlefield. This is in evidence when literary histories and literature take part in this broader institutionalized management of tradition, either to give it a new direction or to preserve it.

Swift thus gained a revered place in the English canon and, with the opposite effect, in the Catholic Church's *index librorum prohibitorum*. He was also remembered by those who have only heard about him or, at any rate, about *Gulliver's Travels*. In this connection, it is irrelevant if he is an optimist or pessimist, lived in London or in Dublin, was a Catholic or not. He contributes to a cultural tradition with isolated parts of *Gulliver's Travels* in particular, that is, only two of Gulliver's four journeys, to the Lilliputs and to the Brobdingnags; the latter with a name very few people indeed can remember. Here, Swift translates the relation between at home and abroad, the strange and the familiar to the relation between the large and the small. This contrast is as effective as Semprún's between inside and outside and it has a long intercultural tradition in mythology and tales. Swift therefore also has an immediate appeal to everybody's experience and imagination via their supplementary experiences. It is those two parts of the book that have been turned into a dozen films and TV versions in the course of the twentieth century, even with Mickey Mouse.

Although Swift's book deals with recollections from Gulliver's four great journeys with very precise references to time and locality, these details are a matter of complete indifference in this context. Only sections of the text with an immediately captivating and elementary basic structure have themselves been remembered under changing historical conditions. The sharp social satire has changed and is remembered as a mixture of folktale for children and a detached example of a general tradition of social criticism.

The role of literature in literary history depends mostly on the texts themselves. But the broader cultural tradition only deals to a more modest extent with the texts and the historical knowledge about them. Here is it the more comprehensive agendas that predominate, especially the relation between the national perspective and the international context. The cultural encounters following globalization on the world stage, in the school class, in family life, and our individual lives are clashes between traditions and the memories on which they build. Here, there are often powerful forces at work which a correct historical presentation cannot compete with. It is not a battle for the past but for the power to repeat it in the future. The national angle on literary history still has most power over the role of literature in a local cultural tradition, but it is being broken at present both by the own movements of the texts across borders and the challenges posed by globalization. Swift belongs to those who rose above their local affiliation.

Associative cultural networks

Literary histories respect the unity of the texts, and traditions seek to create cohesion, even though they often just combine loose fragments from the past. In the open cultural networks, on the other hand, there is no respect of textual details and precise contextualizations, but continuous attention to reset the ramification of the structures of meaning beyond any literary context. Here, too, Swift contributes with street names, statues and websites. Not everything called Swift has to do with Jonathan, just as not everything called Dante has to do with the writer of *The Divine Comedy*. So, when the associations start rolling, one should make sure one does not roll along too.

One of the many shoots on these networks is called *Yahoo!*, the American internet portal with a whole series of internet services, including search machines and e-mails. The founders, the two engineering students Jerry Yang and David Filo, changed the name *Jerry's Guide to the World Wide Web* to *Yahoo!* in 1994, inspired by *Gulliver's Travels*. At least, so they said. But perhaps, they also said, all the name means is *Yet Another Hierarchical Officious Oracle*. Swift does not have any exclamation mark after Yahoo, but Yang and Filo had to insert one because of modern copyright to names, not out of respect for Swift. It turned out that otherwise one could not distinguish the internet portal from a barbecue sauce and a motor boat. The reason why the two young men knew Gulliver and possibly also Swift was probably that they had heard about him at school or seen a film. Or found something or other by browsing on the internet along with the names of the two Japanese Sumo wrestlers they called their computers after. Gulliver is here being remembered on the conditions of globalization, but not his own.[3]

On his fourth and final journey, Gulliver visits a nation of intelligent horses. They govern their country with more balanced reason than the humans Gulliver has left behind him back home. They have some half ape-like creatures to do all the hard work. They are pugnacious, coarse and governed by their immediate urges. They are *the Yahoos* (Swift 1975: 235–318) and resemble human beings so much that the horses consider Gulliver to be a Yahoo. When he explained European civilization to them to convince them of the opposite, they merely became all the more convinced of his primitive nature. The search machine was given this name because this simple, coarse and spontaneous behaviour was ideal for *Yahoo!* A chance isolated fragment, completely devoid of context, now acquires its own life in a new context, the search engine, probably better known today than Gulliver and Swift put together.

While the inner memory of literature is a form of presentation for the formation of individual identity with a common identity as perspective, outer memory shapes the *development of tradition*. The completely open networks do not make much form out of literature, and literary history is a separate discipline that deserves its own discussion. So I will restrict myself here to the middle of the three forms of outer memory: *the development of cultural traditions*. To that end, I read Jonathan's Swift's short satirical essay *A Modest Proposal* from 1729. The mutual relation between the text and its broader cultural context is literature's contribution to the development of tradition and in general to the discussion of what tradition is as outer memory in a globalized context. Afterwards, I will look at Malcolm Lowry's novel *Under the Volcano* from 1947 as an example of the form of presentation of inner memory, with a focus on the border-crossing conditions of the formation of identity.

Travel accounts and local self-criticism

Experiences far from home have always had their special genre: travel accounts. No culture exists without stories about travels. The fictional ones are usually based on the writer's or others' actual travel experience, while the real ones are often spiced with more or less imaginative details and subjective touches. Travel accounts contain the most striking global thinking prior to modern globalization.

The travel account offers a form for a general discussion of the limitations of the local, because one can thereby construct a fictional anchorage from where one can look at domestic local experiences from the outside. It offers a simultaneous inside and outside look. When we use labels like the foreign and the strange, we implicitly take the local as our starting point. And when we present local conditions, in praise or criticism, it is with the outside world as an implicit perspective. This kind of double-talk can be used for satire. The satire and the ironical form are more important than the actual travels and their exotic events. With or without journeys, literature thereby continues the tradition for an outward looking critique from the inside of life at home, also when new types of relation apply between the local and the world outside. It is that tradition which *Gulliver's Travels* repeats and develops.

But the exotic has to be portrayed in its own right before it can become a satirical technique. The French explorer André Thevet wrote in *The New Found*

Worlde, or Antarctike [Les singularitez de la France antarctique, autrement nommée Amérique] (1557)[4] about the indigenous Tupinambas he visited in Brazil: 'And when they see the Christian eate salt meats, they reprove them therefore as a thing impertinent, saying that such meats will shorten their liues' (Thevet 1568: Ch. 30, s.p.). There is an abyss between this wondering meeting with exotic reactions to traditional European eating habits and what Gulliver brags to the rational horse about what is common food culture among his own countrymen, the European Yahoos: 'I assured him that this whole globe of earth must be at least three times gone round, before one of our better female Yahoos could get her breakfast, or a cup to put it in' (Swift 1975: 268). She probably has chocolate in her china.

Something has happened just about 200 years after Europe met up with the rest of the globe. For Thevet, the foreign is strange compared to the alleged European normality. Gulliver, in a 180° turn, looks upon English everyday life as alien. This is now looked at from the outside with a side glance at the dependence of the daily breakfast on setting the entire colonial globe in motion, both in order to obtain South American chocolate and the Chinese porcelain cup. However, Thevet contributes to Swift's satire. By his monarch, he was sent out to several places to draw a map of the world in search for suitable colonies, preferably with cocoa beans for the royal housekeeping. We have gone from a genuinely wondering explorative experience out there to a satirical double look at the domestic duck pond, but against the same backdrop: the rest of the world. The great outside world has become local tradition at the upper-class breakfast table, and thus part of the local self-understanding.

Let us follow that change before returning to Swift. The largest description in Antiquity of the geography and culture of the world is Pliny's *Natural History* [Naturalis historia] from the first century CE. It is a voluminous description of all the known and also partially unknown world, full of all sorts of observations from the peripheries of the Roman Empire and beyond and with a number of imaginative descriptions of creatures great and small right out to the edge of the world. The further away from Rome, the stranger the people. They become less and less human, first in terms of language, then customs and after that colour of skin and appearance, getting closer and closer to animals and finally going beyond both animals and humans in their monster-like figures, such as the one-footed people with feet so large that they can easily be used to shield against the sun, the Scythes with cannibalistic tendencies, the micro-humans or macro-humans – just as in *Gulliver's Travels*. We are normal; the others are weird. That is the basic formula, described with a relatively undogmatic and curious interest in the world's diversity.

Pliny's work created a rock-solid tradition for our relation to the foreign. It was copied and repeated right up until the voyages of exploration in the Renaissance, and illustrations were made based on his descriptions of savage peoples, mermaids and monsters right through the Middle Ages and its bestiaries and encyclopaedias (Hassig 1995). Accounts home from the overseas journeys mixed images and descriptions from Pliny with what was actually seen well into the eighteenth century. What else was one to do? The new world was so radically different that one had to use the already accepted patterns of experience and models of knowledge to create forms of presentation of the new reality. The new was perceived as confirming Pliny, or as exceptional peculiarities. In 1520, the German priest Ioannes Boemus published *The Manners, Laws and Customs of all Nations* [Omnium gentium mores, leges et ritus], based on extracts from these old descriptions.[5] He died in 1535, but the book appeared regardless in his name in new translations in Europe from the end of the sixteenth century, where translators and publishers added more recent extracts of half-documentary reports of new journeys. They still saw the new as exotic peculiarities, *singularités*, as Thevet called his report from Brazil. But the new discoveries also, and together with the tradition from Pliny via the images he inspired in the medieval bestiaries, laid the ground for new cosmographies as, for example, Sebastian Münster's bestselling *Cosmographia* (1544) and thereby fostered a global awareness that now began to move beyond mere curiosity and exotism.

Precisely around 1550, a radical change took place in the conception of the unknown world and of the travel account itself. The clear distinction between domestic and foreign, normal and abnormal became blurred. Bartolomé de Las Casas participated from the very beginning around the year 1500 in the conquest of the West Indies as a soldier and later as a monk (see Todorov 1982). He wrote home in *The Devastation of the Indies. A Brief Account* [Brevísima relación de la destrucción de las Indias] (1552) and accused the Spanish soldiers of unchristian and bestial cruelties towards the indigenous people. They were peaceful, decent individuals, Las Casas found, just like true

Christians, but now lost their souls because they fled from both butchery and baptism: if the Spaniards were examples of Christianity, then no thanks. The status of Las Casas gradually rose, and he became a controversial bishop in the West Indies. He did not build on fanciful rumours but on his own experiences. Who are savage, who are civilized? Could Europe learn any virtues from the savages in the midst of the material greed of colonization? Doubts about the limits of humanity proliferated, and the savages started to become noble. The exotic encounter with the alien, the foreign, gradually turned into a reverse and critical look at the domestic.

It is this line that continues in André Thevet. He writes, for example, about cannibals in *The New Found Worlde, or Antarctike* only a couple of years after Hans Staden, a German mercenary in Portuguese service, were taken prisoner by the same Tupinambas. Thevet visited them more as a modern anthropologist. For centuries, the Tupinambas became a standard reference when one wished to talk about the savages. Staden wrote about them in German under the title *Hans Staden's True History. An Account of Cannibal Captivity in Brazil* [Warhaftig' Historia und beschreibung eyner Landtschafft der Wilden Nacketen, Grimmigen Menschfressen Leuthen in der Newenwelt America gelegen], also in 1557, but somewhat more fancifully than Thevet.

Thevet had more enlightening ambitions and was able to tell the amazed Europeans that the Tupinambas were neither hairy nor savage. Cannibalism was basically horrible, but not a wild orgy. The meal was part of a social war ritual, and the poor prisoner who was going to be eaten was treated with respect and accepted himself his role in the ritual. Even though Thevet insists that he has experienced everything himself the depiction is still in the old style, with references to a host of ancient sources about strange peoples and customs to make it all comprehensible and reliable. He was inspired by Pliny's account of the Scythic cannibals and of other peoples and animals he had encountered. It was, however, probably a secretary, Mathuron Héret, who sprinkled ancient learning over Thevet's scattered notes and made a coherent text out of it, but even so. It was a text that was eagerly devoured throughout Europe. Thevet is a continuation of a long tradition and fits new experiences into familiar moulds.

Later travellers, such as Jean de Léry in *Story of a journey to the land of Brazil otherwise called America* [Histoire d'vn voyage faict en la terre du

Brésil] (1578),[6] had good arguments to question the reliability of Thevet's account. Not so much the cannibalism, for Léry also visited the Tupinambas. But he doubted that Thevet himself actually could have been there in the time slots and locations he listed. Léry announced that he was the one with the true account, but now without Pliny. Léry too became very widely known. The European self-critique gained new fuel with the repeated mention of the humane cannibals, including in Michel de Montaigne. He based himself entirely on Thevet and Léry and noted in several of his essays, including 'Of Cannibals' [Des cannibales] and 'Of Coaches' [Des coches] (1580) that the Europeans themselves were no better. He himself and others had after all heard about anthropophagy during sieges and starvation disasters in France, and even carried out in much more primitive a fashion than what happened among the Tupinambas. Furthermore, the new European weapons of war and use of torture were many times worse than any form of cannibalism. All things considered, we were more savage than the savages.

The bloody religious clashes between Catholics and Protestants in France, with Thevet and Léry on their respective sides, contributed to the struggle for the right global perspective on the home country. The question of the cannibalistic symbolism of the Sacrament which, among other things, divides the Christian persuasions lurked in the background, ready to be criticized by declared atheists, who were now beginning to appear on the scene. The actual expression 'the noble savage', however, probably first appeared in John Dryden's drama *The Conquest of Granada* (1670) (Fairchild 1961: 29). The savages had ceased to be actual beings and became philosophical and moral examples, completely independently of travel reports. In the writing of these authors, a time perspective also began to appear. The noble savages lived in a natural state that the highly developed societies had lost, a thought that developed towards the end of the eighteenth century in Jean-Jacques Rousseau, and was cemented in the Romantic fascination with the lost, golden past, located somewhere between the Garden of Eden and the Crusades.

All the travel accounts were translated into English. The British stood in the wings of the global stage, waiting to take over from the Spanish and Portuguese colonial powers, especially after the Spanish fleet was given a broadside in 1588, and to outmanoeuvre the French attempts at colonization with its great ambitions but small results. So in England, the interest was considerable.

Many of the translations were picked up by William Shakespeare, who had read Montaigne. In 1611, *The Tempest* was performed for the first time, in which Caliban, half fish and half human, is a play on the word 'cannibal'. He is the son of the witch Sycorax and owns the island that Prospero lives on with his daughter Miranda after they have been driven out of Milan. This makes him a slave. The noble Prospero wants to raise him, but as soon as Caliban learns language, he also learns how to swear and all the other questionable things one does as a civilized European. He becomes as crafty and cruel as any Spanish colonial soldier, although he does not eat anyone. His educator, Prospero, is powerless, because the rearing is a result of the built-in conflicts of his own traditions which are stronger than his good intentions.

Shakespeare's text has lasted as the period's most tangible expression of the change that has taken place. It can be performed today with the same appeal as Pliny had for centuries. Montaigne's new form of expression, the subjective essay, also becomes part of the tradition by means of which one subsequently discussed the relation between the known and the unknown. An essay always has a concrete personal point of departure from which it spreads out towards the whole world in a mixture of self-reflection and reflection on the outside world. With the emergence of a modern reading public via periodicals and newspapers in the eighteenth century, the essay became the basic journalistic form of these media to open the relation between local life and global conditions.

The unknown or foreign ceased to be a place out there with strange peoples, described with curiosity by travellers who used an already-existing European model to make them inferior and monster-like. They now became a universal platform of a self-critical consideration of Europe's own culture as a whole. Thereby, the European homebase was itself questioned as a kind of local culture, not a universal culture, let alone an ideal universal model. At this point in history, global thinking started to become modern in its critical questioning of any universalizing idea of local cultures. The tradition of considering the local in relation to the unknown, developed in the travel literature, continued as a double view of the local everyday culture, seen from the inside, but at the same time with the global context as an outside perspective. This double view is a form of presentation for the outer memory, including the use of irony as a linguistic tool.

A double perspective

This is the water in which Swift swims, and not only in *Gulliver*. In a mixture of exotic account, but with a local, self-critical and socially modifying aim, he advances *A Modest Proposal* in 1729 (Swift: 11–18),[7] a classic of English literature less than ten pages long. Shakespeare's fantastic-realistic play and Montaigne's essays renew a tradition with a guaranteed long shelf life on the basis of their innovative forms of presentation, and Swift's satire in ironical style is part of the same movement. Irony is a difficult form of expression which presupposes that the reader knows more than appears on the textual surface. Otherwise, one doesn't get the point. What is this 'more' that Swift wants us to activate? Let us read his modest proposal before we answer.

Like Montaigne, he first describes what he personally believes everyone can experience in Dublin just by going outside their own door. There are swarms of beggars, children and adults. Ireland is both poverty-stricken and hunger-stricken. Mostly because of the Irish upper class, but also because of the British colonial power, he suggests. Children are an insuperable burden: they become thieves and robbers at a very early age as well as non-useful members of society. Perhaps they migrate to the colonies and there they may even join up with the Spaniards. After a simple economic calculation in the reformist style of the age, he comes forth, without batting an eyelid, with his well-reasoned proposal to the benefit of everyone, parents, children and society as a whole:

> I have been assured by a very knowing American of my acquaintance in London, that a young healthy child well nursed is at a year old a most delicious, nourishing, and wholesome food, whether stewed, roasted, baked, or boiled; and I make no doubt that it will equally serve in a fricassee or a ragout.

Stone-faced, he makes this ironic statement with a reference to an American who may come from Latin America where the cannibals are supposed to live. There is nothing to indicate the irony. The listing of economic and other advantages in the preceding two pages are 100 per cent sustainable: the parents can sell their children, the children live well for as long as they remain alive, marriages are improved, because the man no longer beats his pregnant wife, the rest of society gains sufficient food and gets rid of beggars, thieves and an insatiable surplus of population, the church gets rid of many Catholics, who are known to have most children, and Irish cuisine can attract rich visitors by serving the delicious small creatures. The skin can even be used to make fine ladies' gloves. He does, however, reject the idea of using large children instead of animals for hunting. That is too cruel. Furthermore, their meat is too tough, his American informs him. Swift's proposal sets a win–win situation.

As mentioned, the irony works because the reader knows more than is there in the text. A small part of this extra knowledge is provided by the text itself. As when Swift says that the proposal will be excellent for the local squires, who have already eaten their parents and despite this cannot get any more out of them. Aha, we say, cannibalism as an image of the self-destructive internal suppression of society, but there is not very much else to assist the slow-witted.

The larger context he is drawing on is the entire tradition I have just outlined of seeing Europe with an outsider's eye as a savage place. The text only needs to give a couple of details, and then the reader adds the whole picture. Such details are the American with cannibalistic experiences. Swift also refers to the fact that one can become a soldier on Barbados, to a French doctor with dietary advice, to an inhabitant of Formosa on a visit to London, and finally to the Laplanders and Tupinambas, who are noble savages in the many travel accounts from Boemus to Thevet, Staden and Léry and on to Montaigne, Shakespeare and all the minor and now forgotten writers.

Swift's proposal assumes this platform to be able to work. We are led to believe that his proposal follows a widespread solution elsewhere – why not here? But in addition, he has at the same time turned Ireland itself into a savage colony, seen not only from Britain but also as a consequence of the behaviour of those in power in Ireland. For that reason, the poor women and children are spoken of as breeding stock and 'our savages'. Ireland is reduced to Tupinamba status, so why not behave in the same way, only more consistently? After all, we are civilized and can systematize the whole thing, as later in a concentration camp.

But doesn't this make it a text of a satire that can only function in this particular historical situation without taking part in developing a tradition for global thinking? No, for Swift implies yet another context with a far greater range. This context consists of the concrete experience of completely elementary identity-creating experiences and life conditions that we all share: life and death, parents and children, individual and social community. This is stuff to set our supplementary experiences in motion. Such features cannot be turned self-destructively on themselves without any society collapsing. But in Swift's satirical text these positive necessities become destructive tools: life has death as its aim, and the parents exterminate their children and society results in the annihilation of the individual.

We are not given a moral lecture but a concrete exemplification of this logic that all readers can understand; go for a walk and see it with your own eyes, Swift urges us to do. We react with a spontaneous feeling of something being terribly wrong. This belongs to what Aristotle calls intuitive knowledge. By minimizing the presuppositions and making them indirect, Swift maximizes the reader's own involvement. It is not only injustice *per se* that he is attacking but its absurdly self-destructive nature. The double view is on the one hand concrete: this exists; and on the other a matter of principle: this is impossible and self-destructive. Swift draws on what Ulrich Beck later calls a 'universalistic minimum' that is embedded in a 'cosmopolitan common sense':

> This includes substantive norms which must be upheld at all costs: that women and children should not be sold or enslaved, that people should be able to express their views about God or their government freely without being tortured or fearing for their lives – these norms are so self-evident that no violation of them could meet with cosmopolitan tolerance. (Beck 2006: 49)

What is new in Swift is not only that he uses a cultural tradition to contrast the known with the global world in order to understand local, concrete everyday life, but that he now can assume that the ordinary, enlightened reader does so too. Everyone has heard all sorts of things from the colonies. This is before global human rights created a 'cosmopolitan common sense', but it is that sense Swift is activating. And, even more importantly, he assumes that the irony promotes the reader's ability to personally supply the detailed references to the great outside world, so that they form a whole and reach a conclusion: we are ourselves like the colonial societies we have already ruined.

When Swift makes use of this common sense as the most relevant framework for local self-understanding and self-criticism, he carries the old tradition for the contrast between local and foreign into a new era that reaches out towards our own. Hardly surprising that the subjective form of the essay in Montaigne, the Shakespearean type of fantastic realism and the satirical irony of Swift have a long afterlife. They enable literature, on its own conditions, to lift the tradition out of the local understanding and make it future oriented and dynamic. Irony is still a tool that makes memory an active literary form of presentation. And also outside literature, irony is an important driving force in the self-critical management of the tradition of outer memory. Inner memory, on the other hand, functions differently.

The many voices of inner memory

The main character in Malcolm Lowry's novel *Under the Volcano* is the British consul Geoffrey Firmin, living in Mexico (see Ackerland and Clipper 1984). Around him, at all levels of the text, an inner memory process in several dimensions is taking place that includes the individual characters, their relation to each other, their cultural anchorage and the way in which the text involves the reader in the memory process. For all parties, it is a question of finding a firm basis when individual and cultural memories do not offer a stable identity, but they themselves are obliged to create it, quite simply in order to stay alive. That is why the process is so visible and so insistent in its existential inevitability.

Towards the end, the consul sees an older man on the back of an Indian who 'carried the older man and his crutches, trembling in every limb under this weight of the past, he carried both their burdens' (Lowry 1971: 223). He simply continues forward with his burden, also with the unused crutches, and at some point this will force him to the ground. He does not have any other task, and he resolves this one as best as he can. There is not anything he has to remember, know or do, apart from remembering to go on doing what he does now, life-asserting and self-destructive at one and the same time. It is identity on such conditions that the inner memory presents in this novel with its multiple criss-cross connections. It is not suitable for quick reading but for intense reading that makes the reading physical and concrete and activates our own memory while reading if we want to capture the many new and criss-crossing repetitions. What was the connection back there and now, where I read something similar to a few pages back? – That kind of question inevitably arises for the reader, just as for the characters in their search for meaning and identity. In that way, inner memory becomes concrete experience while reading.

The framework, however, is not complicated. The centre of the events is a small Mexican town 2,000 metres above sea level with the Indian name Quauhnauac, and they take place of 1 November 1939, All Saints' Day. The novel begins with two Europeans, the physician Dr. Vigil and the film-man Jacques Laruelle, sitting at one of the small town's numerous bars. They are speaking broken English, and the Indian place name and local language no one can really manage. Spanish is the local European language, also for those who do not completely master it. One remembers one's dead here on All Saints' Day, also called the Day of the Dead. With sorrow, but also with colourful processions and popular entertainment and a large, turning Ferris wheel.

The town is intersected by deep trenches and clefts and situated between two volcanoes, a location that in itself is a constant reminder of boundaries and lines of division that are as real as the language barriers of everyday life. The outer boundary of memory between life and death is marked by the church festival and the competition between the graves and the public houses. Between these outer poles other boundaries make themselves felt. The past of the characters, together with and against each other, has taken place in Europe, an Atlantic Ocean away. Historically, we are on the very edge of the Second World War, just after the ending of the Spanish Civil War, a boundary between civilization and ragnarök lies around the characters. It is these spatially reinforced time boundaries the characters are dealing with in the novel.

Exactly one year earlier the British consul died; his life and fate are known to the two Europeans, but not completely understood. The rest of the novel, Chapters 2–12, takes place on the same day one year earlier. We read about it in flashbacks up to the death of the consul, pitched down into one of the many clefts after having been shot by the local police following a visit to a brothel.

The text itself is thus also part of the total memory process, via a construction that gets us involved as readers, as if we are actually there. Time and place are extremely sharp and easy to grasp.

But that is not the case with the life stories of the same day a year earlier. The consul has called his wife, Yvonne, back to Mexico. Whether he loved her or not, they were each other's firm basis in life. 'Nothing can ever take the place of the unity we once knew and which Christ alone knows must still exist somewhere' (Lowry 1971: 12). It is memory as an open, future-oriented process he wants to keep in operation, from the abyss he is reeling around in. The letter to her is read by Vigil and Laruelle and is cited by the narrator in the first chapter. She arrives. They have an argument, and with Hugh, the consul's brother, a macho who has taken part as a volunteer in the Spanish Civil War, but who is now completely without any chance of carrying out heroic deeds. The smouldering world war, however, offers new potential. He ends up by returning to Europe, while Yvonne is killed by a runaway horse, and by mistake the consul is shot by a local policeman.

We are not unfamiliar with texts that organize memory through flashbacks. But here the literary finesse is used in a more comprehensive demonstration of how the workings of memory which aims at creating identity inevitably causes boundaries to become fluid, outside the individual's control. This is a result of the very way in which memory functions, even though the motives of the individual characters are clear and well considered. Memory entangles them in each other's lives, in local life and the broader cultural tradition that is present as an echo outside their own control. They have an interconnection, but without completely knowing how and how far it extends when memory is at work. It does not place us in the fixed, recognized boxes, dictated by known history and particular events that we can conclude ourselves. So the whole book balances between several consciousnesses at the same time in order to indicate the semi-conscious, identity-giving interconnection all are involved in via the memory, which runs off with us as long as we live.

The consul is constantly under the influence of alcohol and drugs, to a certain extent with style, but also with a hazy consciousness. The effect is not to give us a psychological portrait of an alcoholic, but to reduce the conscious control when the process of memory unfolds. This takes place as associative leaps in the heads of the characters, openly receptive when thoughts about local conditions, other characters and common cultural conceptions merge in the consciousness in their desperate striving for identity. The consul starts by thinking of his passion for Yvonne when he writes his letter, but ends up in a different place in clauses that are just as convoluted as his memory traces:

> His passion for Yvonne (whether or not she'd ever been much good as an actress was beside the point, he'd told her the truth when he said she would have been more than good in any film he made) had brought back to his heart, in a way he could not have explained, the first time that alone, walking over the meadows of the sleepy French village of backwaters and locks and grey disused watermills where he was lodging, he had seen, rising slowly and wonderfully and with boundless beauty above the stubble fields blowing with wild flowers, slowly rising into the sunlight, as centuries before the pilgrims straying over those same fields had watched them rise, the twin spires of Chartres Cathedral. (Lowry 1971: 12)

The concretely reawakened passion, here and now in the first words, is broken off by a parenthesis with an echo from one of their past quarrels that have to do with their ambitions and abilities and that brought their relationship to a halt a couple of years earlier. But the thought of Yvonne leads him further back, to before he met her when he was 'alone', expressed in a past perfect tense '*had* brought back to his heart'. Now, this association reopens a cultural affinity with the French cultural landscape. Here, he shifts into the repeated use of the present participle, '… *rising* slowly and wonderfully and with boundless beauty above the stubble fields *blowing* with wild flowers, slowly *rising* into the sunlight, as centuries before the pilgrims *straying* …'. In that way, he attempts to hold onto the re-experienced state of goal, meaning and interaction, so that it becomes an endlessly extended now, an ongoing process larger than himself and is captured by the non-finite verbal forms of present participles. Here, together with the pilgrims, he is raising his eyes to the final goal. Only in the final clause is the goal, the church, mentioned, which lies at the end of his train of thought, the clauses and the pilgrimage that terminates the winding phrase. But the use, again, of the past perfect: '*had* watched them rise' also marks that this meaningful collective past including both the consul and the pilgrims, is now inaccessibly frozen.

The entire oscillating process of memory between *his* past and *his* present as well as between an ongoing collective process and a collective past takes place while he is writing and feeling his passion for his ex-wife. We move from an existential identity in his passion for Yvonne via his crumbling social identity in the exchange of words about acting on to a highly personal emotional experience in the field – almost one of a higher order, outside time. It unites him with one of culture's old expressions of identity and meaning, one where the individual and the collective fuse – the pilgrimage. This is a dream outside language, which even in the convoluted clauses presents in dreamlike fashion the wish for identity as if it had been realized here and now. In their targeted striving, the characters use memory, for it is the only thing they have. But precisely memory places the target out of focus, because the process of memory follows its own partly random associative paths that cut across conscious control. It is this condition the Indian with his unused crutches accepts when he personifies the workings of memory and drags the old man off without letting himself be distracted.

So there are always more voices involved *en route*. Memory is never completely our own. It always places us on a border between ourselves and everything else and everyone else that influences us. The parenthesis in the above quotation is the consul's memory of having given Yvonne a plain answer. But he is unable to explain the rest of the quotation, he says. So here the words are those of the narrator. Above the head of the consul he tells us about the experience the consul has had. The consul's voice from the past and from the present and that of the narrator are mixed together in the quotation. The consul's two friends sitting remembering in the first chapter cannot understand all that either, but they cannot stop themselves remembering. Yvonne has slightly different interpretations of what the consul has said and not said during all this, and is a counter-voice to the consul. The policeman who finally shoots the consul misunderstands the situation. All of them find themselves on the border between themselves and others. Yvonne sums up this insight just before she dies, and therefore it is once more the narrator who tells us what Yvonne says to herself:

> There is, sometimes in thunder, another person who thinks for you, takes in one's mental porch furniture, shuts and bolts the mind's window against what seems less appalling as a threat than as some distortion of celestial privacy, a shattering insanity in heaven, a form of disgrace forbidden

mortals to observe too closely: but there is always a door left open in the mind – as men have been known in great thunderstorms to leave their real doors open for Jesus to walk in – for the entrance and the reception of the unprecedented … (Lowry 1971: 334)

One cannot exclude experiences, not even when, as here, one reinterprets them into distant threats. Just as the consul's memory of Chartres, the pressure of experiences forces itself onto us with its own unpredictable strength. Memory operates on this interface between the conscious and the unconscious, between one's own consciousness and others' and between individual consciousness and the collective.

The shared cultural memory to which the consul refers with the pilgrims outside Chartres also includes the reader. There are many references to the literary tradition and to cultural history. They are often provided by the narrator. Some also drift like detached ice floes through the characters' heads in various degrees of understanding and misunderstanding, according to who they are, as it of course is when we associatively fetch material out of cultural history. Others lie in the narrator's formulations and images. Most of them have to do with the inevitable, but also vain attempt to find an ultimate identity and find tranquillity, with a rounded past behind and an assured future ahead. Like the consul who attempts in vain to identify himself with the pilgrims. There are recurring literary references to such authors as Dante and religious ones to Christianity and Judaism. With Dante they have in particular to do with the contrast in *Divina Commedia* (1320) between paradise and hell. The characters seek a paradise-like peace, but the way in which they do so turns it into an experience of hell. Their entire project to move upwards leads to a permanent fall. These references are integrated into the characters' lives and do not require special background knowledge on the part of the reader. It mostly lends the characters' individual lives an aura of collective cultural history, as Swift's Tupinambas did for his contemporary readers.

Let me just take one of the common symbols that have to do with memory and identity. The large Ferris wheel turns round and round at the amusement park where the novel takes place, so that one sometimes sees things from above, at other times from below in a constant motion. But it is also a wheel of fortune, an ancient idea implying that it is never completely one's own decision and will that determine the ups and downs of individual fortune. The circular movement is like a whole year in the twelve months that have passed since the consul died, repeated in the novel's twelve chapters, and as the twenty-four hours we hear of in the book's retrospective look. This circular time, linked to the natural course of the day and the year, is an ancient conception of time as repetition. This we attempt to maintain in the repetitions of memory here and now. But repetitions bring something unexpectedly new each time, both when time revolves and when memory works. For that reason, repetition is also the attempts made by the characters to change things, to create a new future together. Time thus also becomes a linear human act, oriented towards the future, into which the characters fling themselves headlong, with a splintered memory as luggage. But the great wheel that turns visibly in the town behind it all also churns as a hellish machine, as some say in the novel. Following its turns, the characters merely repeat the path towards death that no one can help remembering lies at the end of things, also of their linear route.

The whole book focuses on memory as the process that creates identity between the human will to repeat in order to change, renew, live on, move forward, and the process that just as clearly has its limit in our ability to gain an overview and shape what we meet, a limit that in the last resort is the death all meet as the wheel grinds on. The beauty in which the life of the individual and the larger context fuse – as for the consul at Chartres – consists of brief, individual situations where the wheel stands still for a moment. This short pause can then fuel the continued process of memory. For that reason, the novel is neither bleak nor desperate. It is light-hearted in many ways, because the characters find meaning in their very involvement in converting the memory of a broken-down past into an identity that points forward.

When the consul has finally been shot and lies in one of the town's many clefts, the narrative allows life to flow through his head. No one can live without love, he mumbles aloud. 'How could he have thought so evil of the world when succour was at hand all the time?' (Lowry 1971 : 375). What he now remembers is his entire life as a large, unused possibility for a future that he overlooked. It was there the whole time, no matter how much he was entangled in old conflicts and bonds. The world is always full of possible choices, just as for Semprún in the train. It is the consul's summing up of this relation between his own limited, deadlocked ego and this large world that gives him identity as he dies. 'And now he had reached the summit,' he says just before he instead ends up at the bottom of the cleft (Lowry 1971: 375). But the consul is only one voice. Some people throw a dead dog down after the dead body in the cleft. Inner memory is a matter for each individual, all the time, each with his own voice and perspective, but always mixed with the other voices and other conditions than those we determine ourselves in our local setting.

Creative memory

Swift and Lowry belong to their separate ends of the modern world. Both of them have an idea about memory as something that can bring back a form of wholeness, without either of them completely believing in it or being able to find solutions. It is that wholeness which the consul mentions to Yvonne as 'the unity we once knew', while Swift calls for a sense of social decency that has been lost. The younger with an individual perspective, the older with a social angle. The German-American philosopher Hannah Arendt started just after the Second World War to discuss the consequences of the memory for individual and collective identity. What does memory mean for the relation of humans, cultures and societies to each other in the open, fluid world of the post-war era? One of her answers, from 1957, sounds like this:

> Nobody can be a citizen of the world as he is the citizen of his country . . . . It is true that for the first time in history all peoples on earth have a common present. . . . the present realities, insofar as they have brought us a global present without a common past, threaten to render irrelevant all traditions and all particular past histories. (Arendt 1957: 539–541)

Arendt was able to think globally before it became really modern. Among other things, she is thinking of the large groups of homeless and stateless migrants who at the point in time are crossing Europe and the rest of the world as refugees and displaced persons. They have no past that can be anchored or reused via the memory, and that which is found where they, perhaps temporarily, settle down is not theirs. If globalization means that each culture is rid of relevant memories about the past, then personal and collective memories are also made obsolete. However, Arendt is only right if memory solely has to do with unearthing something from the past that can be confirmed in the present.

But Swift and Lowry also emphasize another aspect of memory. Outer and inner memories can create a new context on the basis of the shards and fragments of the past. For Arendt, migrating individuals also have memories, even if only of persecution, placelessness and expulsion. Both Semprún and Kertész have precisely transformed such memories into future-oriented identity. It is this active, creative process of memory, with the emphasis on the administering by the present of the fragments of the past which literature undertakes. It is that creation of new possibilities on top of shattered contexts which Swift tries out through irony, and which Lowry attempts to embrace with the many voices and memories that intersect each other. Swift presupposes the active participation by the reader for the irony to be dissolved, and Lowry signals with the fluid processes of memory that all characters, despite their individual impossibility, have something in common with each other and with the larger cultural context that echoes in them. Memory does not unpack an old content, and literature enables us to configure new ones.

It is this creative experience that the Nobel Prize-winner Derek Walcott refers to as 'the bitter taste on the tongue'. He is from the West Indies and has lived as a migrant in his own country, as everyone else has done there since colonization. So, the aim for Walcott is to forget that dream of the great collective history that Arendt, despite everything, dreamt of. One has to accept, he says in the essay 'The Muse of History' (1974) the sweetness and bitterness of fragmented memory and the complex reality of the simultaneous presence of several times and places that it reminds us of. He finds that precisely literature can portray this complexity as a universe of possibilities, soberly but not naively: a literature in which 'there is a bitter memory and it is the bitterness that dries last on the tongue. It is the acidulous that supplies its energy ... For us in the archipelago, the tribal memory is salted with the bitter memory of migration' (Walcott 1996: 357). Everywhere, migration is a common local condition in a globalized era, also at the centres of the world, but obviously most clearly seen from the peripheries. We are on our way from one place to another; we belong to more than one place at any given time. Our memory is a trace of the processes of migration, also there where we settle down but do not necessarily put down roots.

Walcott's contemporary fellow author from the French-speaking Caribbean, Édouard Glissant, is less preoccupied by the inner processes of memory in the text and more with national literary history as outer memory:

> Once peoples have been colonized by the West, their histories have *subsequently* never been unambiguous. From the moment the Western world interferes, the apparent simplicity of these histories erase the complex contexts, where that which comes from the outside and that which comes from the inside become foreign and opaque to each other, a tendency that is intensified when it comes to 'composite' peoples like those in the Antilles …. A national literature poses all these questions …. The national literature must also express the connection from one people to another and the totality this connection contributes to. If the national literature does not do this (and only if it does not do this), it is merely a regional phenomenon, i.e. folkloristic and old-fashioned. (Glissant 1996: 180, 189)

One can say that Swift, with his ironic practising of global thinking, anticipates Glissant's standpoint, while Lowry operates on Walcott's conditions. His characters are individualized European migrants. Swift's Tupinambas and Lowry's characters lived very close to Walcott's and Glissant's West Indies, the former to the south, the latter to the north. They form a cultural continuity that is important for the relation between the local and the global today.

The consul's concluding, blinkingly short awareness that he had had the freedom to turn memory in other directions and to create a future come right up to the surface in Amitav Ghosh's *The Glass Palace* (2000). We first meet Rajkumar Raha as a boy who was the victim of a boat accident during a storm in which his family has perished. He ends up in what was then Burma, just before the British expelled the king and incorporated the country into British-controlled India at the end of the nineteenth century. He also had to leave Burma. When the royal family was sent into exile in India, he as an eleven-year-old boy saw one of the girls, Dolly, who took care of the princesses. These girls were removed when young from distant villages, brought to the court and given English names. Both are migrants deprived of their past. She burns herself into his memory, and he seeks her out twenty years later. In the meantime, he has become wealthy in the timber business; she still only knows the enclosed court, now reduced to a collapsed court in exile, and is afraid of anything new. Rajkumar says to her:

> Miss Dolly, I have no family, no brothers, no sisters, no fabric of small memories from which to cut a large cloth. People think this is sad and so it is. But it means also that I have no option but to choose my own attachments. This is not easy, as you can see. But it is freedom of a kind, and thus not without value. (Ghosh 2000: 147, 148)

The consul glimpses that freedom when it is too late, and literature uses it as an open resource when it makes memory a form of presentation that creates a future-oriented identity and reorientates common local traditions with a global perspective. A literary form of presentation taking on that task on is translation, the subject of the next chapter.

The Creative Dynamics of Translation

Translation and cultural function

'World literature is work that gains in translation.' This is one of the provocative definitions proposed by the American literary researcher David Damrosch – '*What?!?*' many people would exclaim and add: 'Don't texts lose by being translated: meanings disappear, the language loses its suppleness, misunderstandings are rife and the cultural contexts either are reduced or get lost completely? Shakespeare is and remains original only in English'. From that point of view, translations are erroneous, whether the text gains from them or loses. This staunch conviction defines the ideal norm of translation as transparent and neutral, although at the same time recognizing that as a concrete practice this goal is never attainable. *Traduttore, traditore,* one says in Italian.

Damrosch's cheeky one-liner is therefore the expression of a different conception, both of translation as such and of its actual functions than the standard one, which would only apply to what I will call a technical translation: a version of a text in another language which unambiguously repeats the meaning of its source text. However, the knowledge, ideas and presentation of reality that literature passes on to us are not information of the kind dealt with by a technical translation. The reaction then could be that literature simply cannot be translated. Yet, no matter which culture we delve into, global cultural history testifies to the fact that translations of many kinds of texts and forms of expression have always taken place, not least of literature in its many manifestations across cultures and epochs. Translation is an indispensable and inevitable precondition for the life of cultures. This applies both when cultures are changed or stabilized, no matter if this occurs in relation to their own inner life or in relation to other cultures; just think of how the Christian church has used Latin and various national languages to establish itself as an institution in a particular local area and at the same time build up or reinforce its global ambition.

To claim that translations of complex literary or religious texts are in principle impossible that is thus untenable. In a globalized culture, they are essential and unavoidable, also across language boundaries we as yet are hardly able to handle. Here, even technical translation calls for much more than grammar and a dictionary and can therefore not justify a neutral ideal norm either. The preparations for the Beijing Olympics in 2008 and the Shanghai World's Fair in 2010 thus ran into the problem of translations from Chinese into *Globish* and avoid *Chinglish*. A technically correct translation from Chinese is, 'Do not disturb tiny grass is sleeping', but all it means is an order: 'Keep off the grass!' However, one does not recur to such an explicit bluntness in Chinese culture. When the standard symbol for an invalid toilet is provided with a Chinese text that literally would be translated into English as 'Deformed Man Toilet', it is correct in a highly incorrect way, culturally speaking.[1] Being a speaker of *Danglish* myself, I sympathize with the Chinese translators and wonder how instructions in Chinese to Chinese visitors look outside China. If the reader thinks that this kind of linguistic skipping around does not have anything to do with literature, then read the Chinese-British author Xiaolu Guo's moving and funny tragic-comic novel which is all about cultural and linguistic confusion and its personal consequences during a year in the United Kingdom and Europe in a passionate love affair, *A Concise Chinese-English Dictionary For Lovers* (2007).

Shakespeare went global through multiple types of translations of which none are neutral, some are deficient, a good deal efficient and all are an inseparable part of the undeniable reality of cultural processes. He was actually only an acknowledged local writer in England until he gained greater European success in the latter half of the eighteenth century. After that, translations and performances accelerated, and so it has been ever since. Today, he is the very epitome of literature that is universally valid, at any rate if we look at the case with the eyes of a European-influenced Western culture. But the Shakespeare of the court and general public in London around the year 1600 was hardly the same as the bard who now all over the world grips generation after generation via new translations, performances, film versions, TV series, operas and musicals. Even though we feel that some of this is rubbish, some of it sublime, Shakespeare would have loved it all. He was also a practical theatrical tailor who cut his cloth to make money.

His new global role did not come all by itself just because his texts were there. It was shaped by translations, education systems, the media and public cultural life as they developed in the British Empire in the course of the nineteenth century to promote the global value of the culture of the motherland. Certain translations or interpretations of Shakespeare are therefore nothing less than indoctrinating, while others expand our knowledge, ideas and conceptions of reality beyond our everyday experience and imagination. But all the effects are gained through translations. This is the idea contained in Damrosch's assertion. What he is saying is not so much that translations are positive but that they create a change, both where the text translated belongs and the place where the translation is active. Translations make a cultural difference. That is the gain of translation for all parties, the translated text, the source text, the receiving cultures, the text's home culture, the media landscape and all the rest.

This has to do with the fact that languages do not just consist of dictionary meanings and grammar, but express conceptions of reality. In 'English and the African Writer' (1965), the Nigerian writer Chinua Achebe points to his double relation to African languages and English:

> Those of us who have inherited the English language may not be in a position to appreciate the value of the inheritance. Or we may go on resenting it because it came as part of a package deal that included many other items of doubtful value and the positive atrocity of racial arrogance and prejudice which may yet set the world on fire. . . . I feel that the English language will be able to carry the weight of my African experience. But it will have to be a new English, still in full communion with its ancestral home but altered to suit its new African surroundings. (Achebe 1965: 28, 30)

Language exchange is an innovative cultural dynamics across cultural boundaries with mutual innovative effects on the languages involved. For that reason, translation is a literary form of presentation, not a technical capacity.

In other words, translations have an independent but not isolated cultural role within and outside a language area, and are not simply a passive and unreliable appendage to an original text. They bring inspiration in from the outside, and they direct the cultural antennas of the inside towards a larger world and are never just a one-way activity. The languages involved in translation challenge each other's possibilities of expression. Whether this is a sign of weakness or strength cannot be decided in advance, for the linguistic and cultural interaction can of course fail. The most important thing is to see translation as an open and creative cultural process where cultures can make a difference to each other with the aid of languages and texts.

The technical translation of information is of course still important and indispensable. How could I otherwise read my washing machine manual? But it does not define the ideal and neutral model for translation against which every translation must be measured. It is just a variant. The same applies to literary translation. Although it is more complex and operates at many levels, from grammar via imagery to implicitly understood cultural assumptions, it too is only one version of translation as a broader linguistically based but not linguistically isolated activity. Damrosch's English slogan can therefore be rephrased: World literature is literature that in translation can make a difference to the relation between a local culture and a globalized context. This is the focus of my approach to Gustav Mahler's *The Song of the Earth* [Das Lied von der Erde] from 1908, a literary and musical translation at many levels that has made a cultural difference from a global perspective.

Originality, responsibility and reliability

First, though, we must get rid of a couple of basic misunderstandings regarding the traditional conception of translation, also literary translation.[2] Both have to do with originals – the writer and the text. Not because the writer is a one-off original, although that is often the way it looks, but because he or she has been accepted, rightly or wrongly, as the responsible originator of the text. The standard neutral mode can only be maintained as an ideal when we are dealing with a reliable origin and an original text. The originator can be a person, an association, a public authority or a company that is responsible for the text that is established as original. Texts to be translated from EU, NATO, UN or a company exist in a form that these organizations are responsible for. Originality with reference to the originator is about responsibility for the source text, not about originality. If there is any disagreement regarding the translation, and it is not the translator's fault, one can of course go back to the text and its responsible origin and inquire and maybe get a new and improved original text. This happens occasionally with legal texts or user's manuals proven to be ambiguous. As for the text it is then clear that original basically means reliable on the conditions set by the responsible originator, who need not necessarily be the writer but can just as well be an editor.

Under these and only these conditions, translation is a neutral, passive piece of work that at most can weaken the intention of the original author and the meaning of the original text, but never strengthen it. The main task of this translation is *not* to cause a difference in meaning and effect, but to ensure identity and repetition. If we translate literature, it is also part of the task, but only a part. This is due to the fact that in literature, the author or original texts, sometimes both, often have an unclear status, and responsibility and reliability are hard to establish. That has been the case ever since Moses came down from Mount Sinai with a copy of the tablets of the law after having smashed the originals. Even when we can unhesitatingly point to a single original text and identify a single author, this confirmation has seldom or never had any further influence on whether a translation has made a difference or not.

Many texts from Antiquity and from other cultures we only know in fragments, mixed transcriptions and unauthorized reissues, produced under unclear historical circumstances and without author's rights or individual and institutional responsibility that can be upheld in court. Despite this, they have been translated in great numbers and had such an impact that world culture would not be the same without them. Two examples: the Bible with … well, with whom as the author? and Shakespeare's texts … well, what original texts?

The Bible is the world's most translated book and perhaps the world's most influential book. On the front page of the Danish Bible translation, it says 'den hellige skrifts kanoniske bøger' [the canonical books of Holy Scripture]. That they are holy means that they are God's own words; that they are canonical means that the text is recognized by the church as being the original text. The church, not God, is responsible for the texts' reliability as text. Unlike the Qur'an and other holy writings of other religious communities, the Bible is not conceived as being revealed in one piece in a language that cannot be translated. And for good reasons, all Christian communities from the earliest times had to recognize that it came into being with a lot of different writers, numerous translations and the interference of the Fathers of the Church as to what belonged to the Bible and what should be omitted. The omitted parts are referred to as the Apocrypha, or 'hidden' writings and are considered by some to be forbidden and by others merely to be edifying writings that are not sufficiently holy and thus not reliable.

The first Bible is the Old Testament from the third century BCE, translated into Greek from Hebrew and only then established as one total text. According to myth, six from each of the twelve tribes, seventy-two men, translated it and – amazingly! – ended up with identical texts. So, it must of course be God who was the author, and their result, translated or not, must be the original text. But that was only the Old Testament, though including the apocryphal texts. It had the status of an original text, but is nevertheless called *septuaginta*, after the approximately seventy translators. Yet, when turned into the Jews' Hebrew Bible the apocryphal writings are excluded. In principle, Protestants do not include these writings, although they often print them even so. They are, however, included in the Roman Catholic and Orthodox Bible. Confused? – There's more to come.

In the course of the first centuries CE, the various writings of the New Testament came into being. In the fourth century CE, and over roughly a 100-year period, people in the early church discussed unremittingly at a number of church meetings which writings were God's work and which were the work of man in the Old and New Testaments, and also in which order the books should be placed. This process marks the formation of the biblical canon. The canonization had two functions. An outer defence: excluding writings one could lose without major damage during persecutions and book burnings; and an inner institutionalization: including writings believers could count on as being reliable as God's word across all persuasions and disagreements, for which the church took the responsibility.

For that reason, they were to be translated into Latin, the common language of the church. Hieronymus took care of this around the year 400 when Latin was still a spoken language. Hence, it is called the *vulgata*, and with updates to *nova vulgata* in 1979, it is the Catholic Church's authorized basic text. So, yet another translation functions as an original, partially on the basis of *septuaginta*, which of course is already a translation. Latin was still spoken at the time, and *vulgata* means that it is translated into this spoken Latin, not into classical Latin from Roman Antiquity. So Latin is not simply Latin. Even so, the Bible is original, the church stated. *Vulgata* superseded *septuaginta* to a certain extent, which continued in the Orthodox Church to be the recognized version of the Old Testament, while this branch of Christianity ordered the content of the New Testament differently than in Rome.

For many years, calm descended on the translations, but there was strife between church factions with differing originals. Later, between the thirteenth and sixteenth centuries, came the division into chapters and verses as we know them today, also in the Jewish Bible. Cross references were also included in the Gospels as part of the main text itself, although God himself can hardly have used footnotes. So the original was reorganized a little, not in order to improve on God's word, but to make it easier to remember and refer to the words within the Christian Church and to confirm the Christian interpretation of the Old Testament as the anticipation of the arrival and the life of Christ which, of course, was never intended by whoever composed it before the birth of Christ.

However, around the time of Luther's Reformation, translations got going again throughout Europe. Despite the resistance of the Catholic Church, it was the same operation that Hieronymus had undertaken about 1,000 years earlier. The Holy Scripture was translated into the vernacular languages so that people could understand God's word without the mediation of the church. This was a linguistic and cultural challenge as well as a development of inconceivable impact. The European languages quite simply became modern during this operation. Their ability to express universal relations had to be cultivated and gain authority in their vocabulary, syntax and written form – at that time with no authorized spelling. So the translations came to mean just as much for secular society and its enlightenment as for church and belief. They gave the vernacular a new opportunity to talk about a larger world. As a form of presentation, the Bible translations made a difference to the relation between local culture and a globalized context. One may have doubts about originality, but not that this wave of translation was a gain for text and culture alike.

But how does one ensure that the Bible, through all its versions and translations, is the original text? One can only do so by deciding it, not taking it for granted. This applies to all original texts. One does not find them, one defines them. Their authority as original texts is identical with the reliability that a deciding authority gives them. Therefore, each church community can have slightly differing original texts all of which are God's word. But how does one ensure that God is the original author? Now, that is a much thornier issue. It can only be decided dogmatically. The inter-denominational American website *GotQuestions?org*[3] thus states at many points that it is ultimately God who has determined what should be included and what not by inspiring the writers, translators and editors responsible. But anyone's faith can falter, so the writers of the website 'play it absolutely safe' with lengthy pseudological arguments that this is the case whenever they are asked 'Is the Bible really God's word?' So even in this instance the originality of the writer rests on an argumentation and is never given just like that.

The original copy

Shakespeare is globally a translation giant, almost on a par with the Bible. While the Bible shows the general ability of the translators to make a cultural difference on a global scale, Shakespeare's texts and role as a writer show the historical conditions for originality. When originality rest on decision and argumentation, its validity is also of a limited historical scope and cannot be used as a basis for a general conception of translation. Shakespeare pushes things to their ultimate conclusion. No single manuscript written in his own hand exists and practically nothing is known about his personal history. So originality is a difficult construction. The collection that contains the greatest number of texts in the fullest versions is that of the large folio-format publication of 1623, *First Folio*, published seven years after his death. Less comprehensive editions in the smaller quarto format are known from the preceding years. The publishers of *First Folio* were various colleagues of Shakespeare and people in the book business; at least eight people were involved, one of them blind. So to claim that the result comprises original texts by an original author calls for convincing arguments.

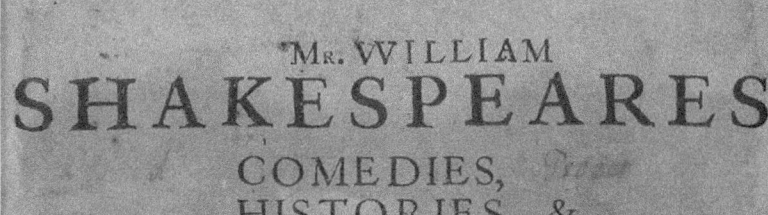

Figure 6.1 Title page of First Folio (1623).

The publisher does his best. On the title page, he writes 'Published according to the True Originall Copies'. Here a modern reader opts out: true original copies – what does that mean? Shakespeare wrote at a time before authors had intellectual rights, author's rights and copyrights. Such things only developed during the seventeenth and eighteenth centuries, and precisely in England, with Queen Anne's law of 1709. Not that there was complete lawlessness prior to that, but copyright did not by law automatically belong to an individual writer or publisher, such as a printer, a theatre company or a book seller.

The working method was for one or more writers to scribble a manuscript for a play, the so-called 'foul papers', drafts or sketches. On the basis of these, a 'prompt copy' or 'prompt book' was made, roughly the equivalent of a fair copy. It was made by some professional writer or other, perhaps a member of the group, who was 'prompter', or a kind of 'permanent secretary'. This copy had to be approved by the censors. The result was an original copy including text and some stage instructions. It thereby became the property of the theatre company and could be performed, copied or sold, possibly to a printer who thereby automatically gained the copyright. They were now to be set by typographers, and anything could happen in that process. The rough versions were probably thrown out, while the author started out on some new dramas. The printed copies or further transcriptions of them were used for memorizing and rehearsing and could also be altered in the process. Shakespeare-research has done its best to compile the printed versions into a text that today is authorized by researchers and not censors as an original text (Halliday 1964; Rose 1993).

If copyright was difficult to control for the author, it was an even worse matter regarding the author's rights. This did not worry Shakespeare at all. He grabbed hold of anything that came his way as best he could, from all sorts of possible sources, historical texts, travel accounts about cannibals and noble savages, other plays, popular tales, translations from the outside world, classical texts, anything that could conceivably be used to retell, reuse and recreate a story (anything with re-). There was nothing original in the basic material for his work. He was like the medieval folk singer or storyteller; all of them took part in the inexhaustible reuse of classical and popular tales about gods and heroes.

The original behind a translation is better called its 'textual basis;' it is determined in reverse order, so to speak, by the aim and function of the translation for the recipients. The text by Shakespeare we select as a the textual basis for a translation can be selected in view of a theatrical performance, but it can also be intended for research purposes and be an academically correct reproduction of all the textual variants we know of with footnotes and all the rest, definitely not fit for a performance. Also, the EU translators have to choose the authorized version of a document for it to be able to function with the necessary authority in the parliaments of the member countries and elsewhere. With more than twenty languages involved, this is a tricky business. The textual basis of the Bible translation is that which has been canonized within a certain religious persuasion in order to support its particular version of Christianity.

In practice, André Lefevere and Susan Bassnett argue in 'Where are we in Translation Studies?' from 1999, this means that a text is translated with the emphasis on one or more but not necessarily all of the following aspects: (1) informational content, (2) entertainment value, (3) logical or emotional convincingness and, finally, (4) basic cultural understanding, that which they call its 'cultural capital'. The four aspects both indicate useful guidelines for translation beyond the technical level and expose the challenges that translators have to face when larger contexts become an integral part of translation.

Cyril Birch's translation of *The Peony Pavilion* (1598) by Tang Xianzu, a Chinese sort of parallel to *Romeo and Juliet,* shows these challenges. In some places, sexual innuendos blend with lyrical innocence in an ambiguous informational context, and together with the rich use of embedded quotations from Chinese classics, these *double-entendres* both define part of the 'entertainment value' and render the emotional complexity of the play. But most modern readers, Chinese and non-Chinese alike, will have a hard time to grasp the quotations in the cultural context, although the non-verbal dimensions of performance itself may help. Birch's solution is immediately understandable with regard to the three first aspects, well known also from Western literature's use of metaphors. To trace the quotations, however, are as difficult as in erudite European texts from the Renaissance with no explicit references. Activating the cultural capital is always a problem.

Just a brief example, Sister Stone has a problem that made her a nun: no man, even well hung, can penetrate her, which she then describes in a long misquotation of a medieval text of formal perfection, *The Thousand Character Text*, which uses one thousand and only one thousand different characters, a *tour de force* like a crown of sonnets. However, the text was used to teach children the characters and elementary grammar, but Sister Stone's voluptuous teaching over quite a few pages is of a less innocent nature, for example:

> Of course, I could just run away and
> live far from men and worldly strife
> but wasn't there some way to bring him where
> joy reigns supreme, while hands and feet ....
> Aha, got it! For want of better he's after the "flower in the rear court"
> (Tang 2002: 83)

This contrast between innocence and sensuality also echoes the relation between the two young lovers, Bridal Du and Liu Mengmei. The translation grasps the information, emotion and entertainment, but not the larger cultural context. Birch has to insert a note to inform the reader about the existence of the classical text behind Sister Stone's bawdy soliloquy and the strategy of misquotation. In an earlier note, he also explains that a host of quotations are included in the text, which he, as in the quotation above, marks with double quotation marks, but without reference to the sources. He tells the reader to go to scholarly editions for full information. Recent and successful performances inside and outside China mainly focus on the emotional content with the contrast between the world of sensual experiences and the sublime love of the young lovers and the social constraints that surrounds it. This contrast is far from unknown in literature around the world and can be grasped without footnotes by an audience and by readers of Birch's captivating translation. He activates a 'transcultural capital', as it were, but also a contested one: as Catherine Swatek points out in her introduction, the strategy to include the sensual aspects on stage and not only as textual innuendos has called for official Chinese protests as a vulgar distortion of the sublime classical play (Tang 2002: XV–XXX).

Here as elsewhere a translation is an independent and risky creative effort like a work of art, not a passive appendix to a given original text. It may be unsuccessful, but it continues literature's own process of coming into existence as a selective, function-determined and contextualized adaptation of the texts and meanings of a tradition. Around 1800, at a time when the sovereign self-expression of the individual artist was given pride of place, the German Romantic Friedrich von Hardenberg, aka Novalis, nevertheless stated: 'Translation is just as much a creative act of composition as accomplishing one's own works – but harder, rarer' (Novalis 1960: 237). He distinguishes between various function-determined translations (Novalis 1975: 439). There are the *grammatical* translations, which I have called technical. They require a rock-solid, formal linguistic competence. In addition, he mentioned the *changing* translations. These are the cocreating translations of literature which both capture their cultural background and grip the actual reader. This occurs when we read a work that makes us wiser about other times and places and yet at the same time speaks to use directly in the here and now. It is such translations Damrosch has in mind and that I will deal with shortly.

Finally, though, Novalis additionally mentions the *mythical* translations. These not only reproduce the language and the cultural dialogue; they create, so to speak, a new work of art in another language and in another context, one with its own new independent life. Those are the ones Damrosch hopes for. Keats' poem 'On First Looking into Chapman's Homer' (1816) elevates Chapman's translation to this status (Keats 1973: 72). And this is how most believing Bible readers think about their Bible. It is not a German, English or Danish translation, but quite simply the Bible.

Novalis adds that 'not only books but everything can be translated in those three ways' (Novalis 1975: 440). Although he is referring directly to different media such as music or pictures, what he has in mind is more generally the changing repetition of the words and meanings of a tradition on a par with literary creation as the key to the cultural life of tradition and cultural dialogue. This broader conception turns translation into a form of presentation for the inner infinity of culture with language and literature as an important but not isolated driving force. One must recall that the actual foundational ideal for literature was for many years an active imitation of models, not an original form of self-expression, in the way as Mozart reused a classical formal musical language and also transcended it. Both Mozart and Shakespeare, in their own separate ways, show that precisely the reusing of the medium they happen to work with, musical scores or language, plus the addition of a personal imprint causes tradition and cultural boundaries to shift and open up towards the future.

The technical linguistic translations are the one extremity of a number of cultural repetitive mechanisms. The other extremity is the comprehensive cultural renewal of tradition via revised translation, text processing and reuse of words, concepts and meanings in language and other media, in other words: a host of varieties of rewriting. Even the most original creation rests on a traditional basis that is repeated in new forms.

The music of the world

Gustav Mahler's *The Song of the Earth* is a symphonic work with six movements each of which is built around a song. It involves several dimensions of translation. None of them is identical with technical translation, but the literary translation is, in an unorthodox way, integrated in a three-part translation process. The first part is Mahler's musical translation of traditional forms of music and cultural meanings into new forms of musical and literary expression. The second is the translation of words to music. The texts come from Hans Bethge's *The Chinese Flute* [Die chinesische Flöte] from 1907, an adaptation of Chinese poetry via English, German and French translations. The third link in the total translation process is Bethge's transfer of Chinese poetry to German and Mahler's own further adaptation of Bethge's texts. Today, the work is performed all over the world as a milestone of European classical music, a branch of music which, combined with American jazz, Euro-American rock and contemporary forms of rhythmic music constitutes the broadest cross-national forms of music with a global outreach.

The symphonic song cycle is rerecorded at regular intervals and is always available in several versions at such music giants as HMV, Virgin Megastore, Amazon, Fnac and other global media chains. The global perspective also lies in the textual basis of the work and the structure of the music. The text is a translation, the music is an active reuse of tradition, and the theme embraces the whole world beyond cultural boundaries. It is the linguistic aspect I intend to deal with mainly in order to underline the fact that literary translation is always part of a broader culture translation process of media and meanings. This process characterizes the linguistic translation, which in turn is utterly crucial for the overall structure and broader impact of the symphony. The translation is a form of presentation that helps to give the work its worldwide appeal as a cultural border-crossing.

Mahler demonstratively makes full use of musical tradition in all his works. If we do not cause our cultural inheritance to shift by the way we use it, it loses its function and becomes a dead monument of an otherwise forgotten past. For that reason, Mahler almost always operates with the same basic form, the symphonic, which is renewed again and again. He, if anyone, was able to take simple popular melodies, dance tunes and folk songs – especially those known from German Romanticism – turn their sentimentality inside out and at the same time reveal their unknown potential for being included in comprehensive forms of musical expression. That is why he lets traditional and new elements collide at high decibel levels, often in fragmented forms. Mahler is true to tradition precisely by going beyond its limits. That is what makes him modern.[4]

Precisely because Mahler's production always has the reworking of tradition on its agenda, his music is highly reflective. Frequently, words are added, often texts by the well-read composer himself or adaptations. He made generous use of the German literary tradition in such works as the early *Songs of a Wandering Youth* [Lieder eines fahrenden Gesellen] (1885) or *The Youth's Magic Horn* [Des Knaben Wunderhorn] (1887–1896) and adapted these works to his own ends. Or, as in *The Song of the Earth* (1908), he made use of the literary and musical tradition of another continent, filtered through various layers of translation and the European tradition for *chinoiserie* and other forms of oriental expression.

The Earth is the symbolic focus of *The Song of the Earth*. With its composite semantic content of history and eternity, life and death, nature and culture, mysticism of origins and sensory presence, cosmos and everyday reality, Earth as a highly complex symbol acquires various concrete meaning in different locations across the globe. At the same time, it is open enough for the individual artist to be able to take it over and add new lines of connection.

It is a transcultural symbol that has always travelled between periods and culture and changed meanings and nuances while moving across the Earth to which it refers. The translation and reuse of tradition is, so to speak, the outside of this movement. But it is also reflected on the inside in two themes of particular importance in the texts that Mahler has found and adapted to his own ends. One is the *journey*, movement across borders, on a large or small scale. The other is *art* and its ability to renew itself by reaching out beyond cultural boundaries and change itself, something that Mahler himself exemplifies.

Mahler was familiar with the entire modern internationalization of the view of culture and art from Immanuel Kant and Johann Wolfgang von Goethe. This view is an extension of the cosmopolitan view of culture in the Enlightenment as well and central to the idealism and classicism of late eighteenth century and early nineteenth century that was Mahler's philosophical and cultural home ground. Already here and earlier, there is evidence of a strong European interest in the Orient. Mahler knew this from such poets as Goethe and Friedrich Rückert. This platform is an important precondition for his almost immediate use of Bethge's reworkings of Chinese poetry for both textual comprehension and musical expression with a Chinese influenced musical idiom as a new dimension in his music. The book appeared in 1907, and *The Song of the Earth*, is from 1908. It is only possible to work that quickly if one is not starting from scratch.

From sense to mood

The Song of the Earth comprises six songs, or six symphonic movements with a solo voice. Each song is an adaptation of a text from *The Chinese Flute*, although the sixth and last song 'Der Abschied' [The Farewell] is made up of two connected poems from the collection. The final song is at the same time the longest text and, especially, the longest movement – almost half of the hour-long opus. A farewell to the world and a farewell to the work, one could say, containing both the theme of travel and that of art. The alternate songs, nos. 1, 3 and 5, are sung by a high male voice, a tenor, and the remaining songs are sung by a low female voice, normally a contralto or a mezzo-soprano, although occasionally by a baritone, which Mahler had suggested as an alternative possibility. He himself, however, never got to hear the work performed. At first glance, the musical whole is thus constructed of a number of elementary divisions into pairs: the final song is divided into two, also musically speaking – this entire song makes up half of the work, while the other five together make up the other half, the relation between the high male voice and the deep female voice, each performing one half of the songs. In addition, there are the two themes of travel and art.

This binary structure is not, at any rate, a reflection of Bethge's chronologically ordered textual selection of Chinese poetry. So even before we look more closely at the texts, it is clear that Mahler chooses in such a way that he can make a cohesive whole out of text and music, turning the musical and verbal translations into his form of presentation of a view of the world. The anthology comprises eighty-three texts of anything between ten lines and two pages from 3,000 years of Chinese poetry, from c. 1000 BCE up to the year of publication, 1907. Just under a third of the texts are by the two major poets from the Tang period, c. 600–900 CE, Li-Tai-Po and his slightly younger contemporary and friend Thu-Fu (with Bethge's spelling). And if we include other Tang poets and those of the following great era, the Song period up to c. 1200 CE, we have almost half the anthology. It is poetry from these two periods, especially the Tang period that makes Chinese poetry continue to be regarded as something out of the ordinary. The rest of the anthology is made up of ten or so poems from the preceding 500 years and almost thirty poems that cover the subsequent c. 1,000 years, with most emphasis on the nineteenth century.

Bethge did neither know Chinese nor the other Middle Eastern or Far Asian languages from which he rendered poetry into German during the following years up to his death in 1946. He did, however, possess a comprehensive cultural and literary-historical knowledge of the 'cultural capital'. For *The Chinese Flute,* he used existing translations in German, English and French. The basis of the older poems in particular is a French translation, which has once again being rewritten in French, from which it was translated into German, from which Bethge composed his own version. And from there, Mahler continues with his own alterations. It is not linguistic reliability that has pride of place in such a working method, but the effect produced. The more recent poems Bethge reinterpreted on the basis of an English translation.

Despite, or maybe because of, the many layers of text, Bethge's translation was used by other composers than Mahler and it saw several reprints before the Second World War. By means of this and other anthologies, Bethge brought a foreign lyrical mode of expression to Germany that could be understood by his own time and even be a source of inspiration for innovative creative efforts. Perhaps he has distorted the translated Chinese texts so much that they have become too contemporary and European which his own comments do not conceal. The use of translations and adaptations is a way of developing art and culture in a transcultural perspective that Mahler continues in his own adaptation of Bethge's choices in order to attain the poetical-musical precision he needs.

There are of course certain linguistic features Mahler can neither select nor deselect. He was ignorant of them, and so was Bethge. It is of independent value to read a textual analysis of the basic Chinese texts by Teng-Leong Chew, a bilingual American-Chinese connoisseur of Mahler. But it has nothing to do with Mahler's work. Chew goes behind the first French translations of the Tang poetry, points out comprehensive errors and omissions during the entire course of development up to Mahler. Chew's work points out that translations are both necessary in cultural meetings and risk being extremely erratic.

The fundamental difference between Chinese and Indo-European languages, Chew points out, lies in the syntax. Using some striking examples from the same poems that Mahler works with, he shows how the relation between words and word classes is organized according to the linguistic context in which they appear, not on the basis of fixed grammatical forms as we know them from the morphology of Indo-European languages. The words stand next to each other in ambiguous semantic and ambiguous word-class relations, and a syntactic connection is established on the basis of the linguistic context. The subjects of sentences are not defined, whereas we in English simply write 'I' or 'he'. This means that one and the same word, for example, 'music', in one context can be the verb 'to play music', in another can be the adjective 'musical', and in a third context is a picture of the rhythm of nature, in all cases the context also determines what the Indo-

European languages incapsulates in the various of forms of declinations or conjugations.

If this sounds strange and difficult to native speakers of Indo-European languages, think of a homonym like the English word 'bow'. It can mean 'to incline the body forwards', 'the front part of a boat' and (with a different pronunciation) also 'a knot with two curved parts and two loose ends', 'a weapon for shooting arrows', 'a long thin piece of wood with hair from the tail of a horse stretched along it, used for playing string instruments'. We seldom find it difficult to choose the right meaning when we have the word in a definite context. The same applies to a word like 'could'. 'He could do it' may refer to the past, that is, 'he was able to', but also to a possible future: 'Maybe I could do it tomorrow', or to indicate politeness 'Could I have a fork, please?' Heard in context, however, we can distinguish without difficulty different grammatical forms and meanings of the same cluster of sounds or letters.

What Chew refers to as a minimal syntax can therefore be used as an auxiliary translation to test various possibilities regarding context. The translator may construct some small standard sentences in the language into which something is to be translated to test out such possibilities. Chew himself is most interested in correcting the translations before those of Bethge. But it is also this open syntactical structure which he regards as a feature of Mahler's use of coordinated contrasting musical elements and which causes him to ask whether knowledge of these syntactical features would have been an inspiration, over and above the thematic one. All of this, however, lies outside the possible choices for Mahler to have made.[5]

But he can choose to omit. In the anthology one finds a number of poems which – whether in accordance or not with their Chinese basis I do not know – have mutual love as their theme, where the lovers meet and are united, or where friends meet in an enclosed circle. Such situations are not present in Mahler's work, where love is an incurable longing for a lost or unattainable person, and friends occur particularly at a distance before and mainly after their meetings. Lovers and friends are left behind on their own. Bethge also has poems about war, revenge and killing where people set out into the world to do battle. Such a resolute, extrovert act with a potential for physical conflict is not a theme in Mahler either; he only retains the purposeless, melancholic cross between flight and distraction, of which there is plenty in the anthology.

Instead, the positive and negative social dimensions of war, friendship or love are omitted in favour of human isolation in a suspended moment, before or after they collide with a collective reality. Such introvert features are also strong in the more recent poems of the anthology, but Mahler, as in the rest of his work, sticks to adapting that which belongs to tradition as do the Tang poems.

The relation between art and nature is also different in Bethge. Song, poetry and playing feature in most of Bethge's texts. Most of them deal to a great extent with giving longing and experience an artistic expression, slightly melancholy and resigned, but also with a cheerful recognition: everything is after all as swiftly changing as the clouds, also intoxication and love, but joy is no less for being short lived, for example, in 'Auf dem Flusse' [On the River] (Bethge 2001: 47):

> Ich fühle mich den Wolken nah verwandt
> Und plötzlich weiss ich: Wie der Himmel sich
> In diesem Wasser spiegelt, also blüht
> Das Bild meiner Geliebten mir im Herzen
>
> [I feel myself with clouds closely akin,
> and suddenly I know: Just as the sky
> is mirrored in this water, so too blooms
> the image of my loved one in my heart]

This is what art can: in glimpses make a natural impression and an emotion concrete, fix them for an instant in the senses, so that we for a brief now see that we are part of the great world and nature. Art is not just the expression of feelings or longings. First of all, it gives reality a form, so that we experience this simultaneousness of concrete presence and transience. Clouds, water, grass and birds are often images with this function, yet not in Mahler. In the very last lines of the sixth song, he changes 'Und ewig, ewig sind die weissen Wolken' [And eternal, eternal are the white clouds] (Mahler 1998: 19), namely, in their changeability, to '... ewig/ Blauen licht die Fernen!/ Ewig ... ewig [Everywhere and eternally the far distance lightly turns blue!]. Here, the concrete natural element, clouds, as a symbol of changeability, is turned into the abstract, Romantic distant blue, which then is made static and eternal, a forever unbridgeable distance.

In Bethge's texts, art does not air feelings or longing but gives concrete presence in the world the form of a series of images of the moment. They must be repeated, as is the case in poem after poem, because the world is transient. It is not a linear prolongation out into the distance or into eternity beyond concrete experience which, however, is the direction that Mahler's alterations take with regard to the artistic theme. Bethge here is in accordance with the basic mood of classical Chinese poetry. Although he knew no Chinese, he was a man of wide reading. Mahler shifts the choice of texts and their adaptation in the direction of introvert European poetry of longing from the turn of the last century.

Mahler goes further

In *The Song of the Earth*, Mahler chooses seven texts and perhaps has his eye on a few more. He reshuffles Bethge's chronological order and thus changes it into his own aesthetic structure. The first song, for tenor voice, Li-Tai-Po's 'Das Trinklied vom Jammer der Erde' [The Drinking-Song of the Earth's Sorrow], is no. 15 in the anthology, with the same title. The second song, for contralto, '*Der* Einsame im Herbst' [The Lonely Man in Autumn], is no. 45 about a woman, with the title '*Die* Einsame im Herbst'. The third song, the tenor's 'Von der Jugend' [Of Youth], is no. 16 with the title 'Der Pavillon aus Porzellan' [The Porcelain Pavilion]. The fourth song, for contralto, 'Von der Schönheit' [Of Beauty], is no. 18 with the title 'Am Ufer' [On the River Bank]. The fifth song, for tenor, 'Der Trunkene im Frühling' [The Drunkard in Spring], is no. 19 with the title 'Der Trinker im Frühling' [The Fellow-Drinker in Spring]. Finally, there is the sixth song for contralto, made up of two connected poems, no. 12 'In Erwartung des Freundes' [Waiting for the Friend] and no. 13 'Der Abschied des Freundes' [The Farewell to the Friend], now with one title 'Der Abschied'.

Already here one can see that Mahler changes gender from female to male, and that concrete things, places and active persons, such as a pavilion, river bank, fellow drinker, become more abstract, passive or global terms that are open to more vague associations: youth, beauty and intoxication as a passive state of drunkenness rather than the active fellow drinker. In the final song,

Mahler removes the narrative element in Bethge's two poems, from waiting to departure. He only mentions the open farewell, with its associations of homelessness. Although these titles are not part of the musical performance, at most mentioned in the programme, Mahler is meticulous in adapting them to the introvert mood poetry. He could have made do with giving them numbers.

With the alteration of personal pronouns and grammatical gender, Mahler ensures that the opposition between the two voices is not to be perceived as being determined by gender. It is the contralto who sings about '*Der* Einsame im Herbst', not the female '*Die*', as in Bethge. Where it says 'I' or 'my' in this and other songs for female voice, we are dealing with feelings and emotions of longing that are not gender related. In the final song for contralto, '*Ich* stieg vom Pferd' is changed to '*Er*' [I/He dismounted]. The relation between the sexes, as in 'Von der Schönheit', is a partial aspect of the songs, not the main theme. It is the contralto's songs that raise the great issues of eternity, supernatural longings and the indeterminate nature of life. The male songs are all by Li-Tai-Po, and much cheerful drinking and poetry writing takes place, with a slightly jaunty acceptance of the finite nature of the world and the inevitability of the grave. The 'Wüst liegen die Gemächer meiner Seele [Desolate lie the chambers of my soul] of the first song (Mahler 1998: 21), in which the abstract soul is concretely placed inside a space and a person, is changed to the general and less concrete 'liegen wüst die Gärten der Seele' [Desolate lie the gardens of the soul]. In other words: the two voices represent two attitudes to life that are common to humanity beyond a gendered perspective.

The tenor voice is that of the poet who forms life through the body and intoxication, the aesthetic grasp of the world so to speak. He does not change life, simply freezes its beauty for a brief moment. And that is enough. 'Schon winkt der Wein im goldnen Pokale/ Doch trinkt noch nicht, erst sing' ich euch ein Lied' [The wine is already sparkling in the golden goblet,/ but don't drink yet. First I'll sing you all a song!]. In Mahler's 'Das Lied vom Kummer/ soll auflachend in die Seele euch klingen' [The song of sorrow/ will echo through your souls, laughing out loud] the change shifts the focus slightly, once more with a discrete emphasis of the less concrete: from 'you all' to 'the soul' and from the individual singer to the sound of the song. The words 'Seele' and 'klingen' are strongly underlined by the music. The most important elements in the theme of art lie in the tenor's songs.

The contralto voice, on the other hand, uses the theme of travelling to characterize the introvert movement, the educative journey so to speak, that turns away from the perceived world, a permanent journey towards rest as a release from the loneliness of the rejecting physical world. 'Ja, gieb' mir Ruh', ich hab' Erquickung not'[Yes, grant me rest, I am in need of relief] Mahler writes, changing 'Schlaf' [sleep] to 'Ruh', so that the longing for death becomes clearer.

This tendency culminates in the final song 'Der Abschied', Mahler's most drastic adaptation. Bethge writes 'Der Bach sing voller Wohllaut durch das Dunkel/ Von Ruh und Schlaf' [The stream sings full of melodiousness through the dark/ of rest and sleep] (Mahler 1998: 18), but Mahler changes the second line to 'Die Erde atmet voll von Ruh und Schlaf' [The Earth breathes full of rest and sleep]. A little later Bethge has: 'Ich stehe hier und harre/Des Freundes, der zu kommen mir versprach [I stand here waiting/for the friend who promised to come to me], while Mahler writes 'Ich stehe hier und harre meines Freundes;/ich harre sein zum letzten Lebewohl'. [I stand here waiting for my friend,/waiting for him to take the final farewell]. With the repetition of the waiting [harre] of the absolute, death-sounding final farewell it is the actual time of waiting and the death to come that are brought to the fore, not the concrete waiting or the farewell.

Travel and melancholy

It is not only in the linguistic details that Mahler pulls the texts forward towards his own time and across towards his own European cultural scene. This is also the case with the two themes, art and travel, which are presented by the two separate voices. They have certain transcultural basic forms, with changing nuances in various cultures and historical periods, and are shaped by Mahler in his particular time-determined combination of musical and poetical repetition of tradition.

The theme of travel is known in European literature in two main forms since Antiquity, each with a positive and a negative aspect. There is the great journey out into the world. We meet it in myths and folktales, in Homer, in the sagas, in stories of the crusades, in voyages of discovery, South Pole expeditions and modern extreme sports. Here, the celebrated heroes express themselves with courage, muscle and a thirsting for knowledge and insight, while we admiringly look on. But there is also a reverse side. The journey can be demonized as a monumental restlessness and pursuit, as in the story of The Flying Dutchman. Not strength to travel, but the inability to take root is at the centre. Opposite this, we also have the small journey as an excursion, hike or keep-fit exercise. Here one finds oneself in a balance between body, nature and the outside world at the everyday level, while one pauses for thought and becomes wiser.[6]

While the great journey is mostly a European phenomenon, the small one is also deeply anchored in the East, with the many wandering poets and barefoot philosophers such as Li-Tai-Po. In the course of the eighteenth and nineteenth centuries, a bourgeois urban culture develops in Europe with leisurely walks for everyone in the public spaces of the town, expanded with the nature worship of Romanticism to comprise walks outdoors, preferably on one's own, in the national landscape. And later this became organized leisure activities, in Mahler's age as *Die Wandervogel Bewegung* or the boyscout movement, conceived as a socially emancipatory experience on a small scale. This micro-journey also has its negative aspect. It can stiffen into rituals and right-brand running equipment, or quite simply into a melancholy flight from the society from which one even so cannot escape. This melancholy version is a European twist of the theme of the small journey and is the basis for *The Song of the Earth*.

Tang poetry looks at the matter differently. The small journey has nothing to do with release, and nature is not viewed as a leisurely alternative to social reality. The repeated and perhaps pointless walk, in nature or in social surroundings, is an expression of life's changeability and transience. The loneliness is real because of the changeability everywhere, just like death, but not full of the frustrated expectation that things ought to have been otherwise. There is no reason to seek death or say farewell to sorrow. Both will come even so, as the singer states in the first song 'Das Trinklied von Jammer der Erde:' 'everyone only lives and dies once' and 'sorrow comes, sorrow comes' as it soberly states in Chew's close translation, while both

Bethge and Mahler give a little sob: 'Dunkel is das Leben, ist der Tod' [Dark is life, is death].

The artistic and philosophical project for Mahler and other European artists of his age is to give the individual malaise and unrest a collective interpretation. Mahler uses the Earth-symbol to make the individual's longing universal and to view its development as a journey towards the eternity of a collective, universal nature. Thus, Mahler's emphasis on the various meanings of nature is the theme of the three songs for a female voice, nos. 2, 4 and 6. In the final song, it is this aspect of the travel theme that is to be the mainstay of the entire conclusion of the work, while the woman's first song, 'Der Einsame im Herbst' [The Lonely Man in Autumn], depicts loneliness as a state where a social and natural balance has collapsed, and where longing for release is the goal. This is the basic departure situation of the small journey. Music and text work with and against each other. A thin orchestral opening, with notes like single drops, merges with the situation, while the ecstatic music to the sun at the end of the song covers the dream of release that the text rejects. The whole thing flattens out into nothing.

The other song, 'Von der Schönheit', makes the theme of travelling clearer. A group of young girls is picking flowers by the river in their own world of beauty. A group of male riders thunders past and breaks the circle. And here Mahler alters Bethge by allowing one of the girls to fall in love with a rider in passing, and dream she is part of the journey, an illusion that only pains the heart. The music both floats in the thin upper air of dreaming and longing, allowing the riders, with almost coarsened spoken singing, to break into the circle of beauty. The final song, which I will return to, has precisely the farewell as its title, not the arrival and the completed journey.

Art between magic and sense perception

The theme of art also appears in a European version typical of the age (Chai 1990; Bell-Villade 1996). The aesthetic self-awareness had, broadly speaking, two variants at that time. On the one hand, the work of art itself was emphasized as something that was unique and – continuing the Romantic worship of the original genius – was seen as an example of the fact that art could create new and unique experiences. Language and sound became more important in themselves as material structure than the meaning contained in the works. On the other hand, an attempt was made to restore a magical or religious function to art. From its isolated position outside the collective material and social reality, art is able to create or open people's eyes to meanings beyond everyday reality. While the first version makes art a provocatively sensual fragment of reality, the other shifts art out of this reality and into a spiritual and universal dimension of existence to which only art can open the door. In his texts and his philosophy, Mahler belongs to the latter movement, while his music points towards the former. That is the built-in tension in his entire production.

In oriental poetry, also in the texts that Mahler uses, this material and spiritual dilemma is not present. Eternity and cosmic nature are present in the individual things, and it is that which the artists write about in repeated and varied descriptions. The eternity involved here does not lie beyond the world as a stable cosmic eternity, but is identical with the very eternal multiplicity of the small things in the world, manifesting itself there in a steady stream of new moments. The poems describe these moments in the outside world and they become themselves such concrete experiences for the reader.

The three songs for tenor voice, nos. 1, 3 and 5, show art in a European perspective as aestheticism without any obligation, which is judged negatively, while the contralto voice both represents – and in the final song also goes beyond – the alternative, religiously tinged conception of art. The first tenor song is a trouble-free drinking song about death and transience. Wine 'ist mehr wert' [is worth more] than all the world's riches. Mahler chooses to repeat this 'ist mehr wert' three times, in a musical invocation, so that the eulogy is almost turned inside out. Shortly afterwards, the generally rising melody drops disharmoniously twice to deeper levels, both at the negative 'wildgespenstische Gestalt' [wild, ghostlike figure] and then just after the positive 'in den süssen Duft des Lebens' [into life's sweet scent]. So, despite everything, the occasional song is not merely froth.

The next tenor song, 'Von der Jugend' [Of Youth], has its title changed from 'The Porcelain Pavilion' in Bethge's anthology. The scene is a depiction of a festive gathering of young people in an elaborate porcelain pavilion on an island with a bridge, isolated from the world and surrounded by mirror-glass water. Here one writes poems and amuses oneself. Through the reflected image, it becomes impossible to distinguish between image and reality and everything is frozen into a miniature painting. Bethge therefore writes 'the surface of the pond' and not the 'surface of the water of the pond:' the surface eventually becomes both the shiny surface of the porcelain and that of the gleaming water, a unity retained in the title. Mahler changes this to 'the surface of the water' and, as in the change made to the title, keeps the distance between reality and image open – one is water, another is the pavilion and something else again is a mirror. Central to Mahler, therefore, is the youth that poetry cannot recreate or retain, not the sensory unity of water, building and persons that the poem creates here and now, according to Bethge. For Mahler, art can be artful, but to no avail.

The last of the tenor's songs about the intoxicated poet, 'Der Trunkene im Frühling' [The Drunkard in Spring], returns to the cheerful–sorrowful situation of the first song, but now without any company. The artist can only write occasional songs and create small conjuring tricks outside reality. And he is then, lonely and abandoned, more a drunk than a fellow drinker, and with no one to sing for except himself. As long as I sing and am drunk, what do I care about spring, is roughly the gist of the song. Here, this form of aestheticism is only a poor consolation, while the spring lies out there like a dream the drunk cannot reach, neither as poet nor as a drunk. He is like a homeless today looking for a bridge to sleep under or a hot-air grill above the metro.

Art cannot grasp the drunk's dream of a spring, while at the same time languishing music is put to the words 'der Lenz ist da' [spring has arrived], music that confirms the dream. The Earth that is sung about in the first song is only material reality, and the death and rest that are also found in the fifth song have more to do with resignation than fulfilment – 'was geht mich denn der Frühling an!' [what do I care about the spring!]. Although the longing of the travel theme is a mockery, the music retains the dream by clinging around the text, both in the gentle praise of spring and the ironically triumphant fanfare of the last line. Beauty and sensory perception do not enclose themselves in the music in an aesthetic way, but awaken a human longing that cannot be fulfilled. Music is art itself as magic.

The tenor becomes lonely from his jingling poetry and skating around over the cheerful–sorrowful surface of reality, while the contralto in the first two of her songs already is lonely and full of longing and can do nothing about it. In these songs, the art which the tenor represents thus appears in a negative light. In 'Der Einsame im Herbst' [The Lonely Man in Autumn] the withered, misty landscape is described: 'man meint, ein Künstler habe Staub von Jade/ über die feinen Blüten ausgestreut' [as if an artist has scattered jade dust/ over the fine profusion of flowers]. Here, Mahler has changed Bethge's 'Halme' [stems of straw] with 'Blüten'. The withered autumn landscape not only gets a thin layer of beauty from art, but its profusion of flowers is destroyed by the artist. The powerful art of the tenor is destructive in the universe of the contralto.

The farewell

The changes to the three songs for female voice are more comprehensive than those for male voice. This is evident in the final song 'Der Abschied' [The Farewell]. The tenor ends in loneliness, the contralto begins in it. Now, the two movements are to meet. The Earth here becomes unambiguously a cosmic universal symbol. In the previous songs the Earth has been the material reality for art and travel, for love, social intercourse, landscape, the changing of the seasons. 'Der Abschied' starts with a concrete scene from nature, with the moon rising above the trees. Mahler broadens the perspective by adding 'am blauen Himmelssee' [by the blue sky-lake] to Bethge's text. After this, he once more expands Bethge's concrete picture of nature with his additions 'Die Erde atmet voll von Ruh und Schlaf,/ Alle Sehnsucht will nun träumen' [The Earth breathes full of rest and sleep,/ all longing now wishes to dream]. Human subjects are gone, the Earth and the emotions operate by themselves. This is not the infinite universe that is so to speak injected into things of the actual world, as in the mirror-images of Tang poetry. It is, conversely, the things of the actual world that expand with a cosmic perspective of infinity. Here, we are looking at Mahler out on his own, with neither Li-Tai-Po nor Bethge at his side.

After the first of the two poems Mahler takes from Bethge, he sums up, once more with his own addition: 'O Schönheit! O ewigen Liebens-Lebenstrunkne Welt' [Oh beauty! Oh world intoxicated with love and life]. These are important lines. Here, he integrates both the beauty and intoxication from the tenor songs and the love from the contralto songs, now within the framework of the world as cosmic entities – eternal and never-ending.

In the adaptation of the second poem, he goes further on this basis. Now, there is drinking once again. Not as with the drunkard poet but as part of the journey, an acceptance of the difficult parting: 'Er stieg vom Pferd und reichte ihm den Trunk/ Des Abschieds dar' [He dismounted and handed to him the parting drink]. From here on, only the theme of travel features in the rest of the work, both as the great journey out into the unknown world and the small journey out into the mountains to find rest and be released from demonic restlessness. The unreleased positions of the poet and the contralto are integrated and reinterpreted under different conditions.

The very last lines are often referred to as Mahler's own. In fact, however, the changes from Bethge are not greater here than elsewhere. But the reason for claiming this is perhaps that Mahler here is supposed to convey his own message. It would be more justifiable to claim that the final lines make it possible for him to conclude his work and thereby *perform* his message, so that we can *hear* it here at the end of the journey, audibly, aesthetically. The text is brief and concise in Bethge: 'Die Erde ist die gleiche überall,/ Und ewig, ewig sind de weissen Wolken' [The Earth is the same everywhere/ and eternal, eternal are the white clouds]. Clearly, this lies completely within the aesthetics of Tang poetry, and the slightly narrower version of it in the songs sung by the tenor. Mahler changes this perspective:

Die liebe Erde allüberall
Blüht auf im Lenz und grünt aufs neu!
Allüberall und ewig
Blauen licht die Fernen!
Ewig ... ewig.

[Everywhere the beloved Earth
now blossoms in spring and grows green once more!
Everywhere and eternally
the far distance lightly turns blue!
Eternally ... eternally.]

It is not the word 'eternally' that produces cosmic visions. This word can most certainly be used to convey the eternal, concrete changeability of the material world, as in the Tang poems. Yet here, the infinity comes from the generalizing and pleonastically absolute nature of 'allüberall' and 'die Fernen'. There are no human beings. The farewell applies to everyone and everything human. The distance is in itself the eternity. The emptiness does not indicate a frustrated homelessness, but comprises the Earth and the universe taken together, beyond hopeless longing or melancholy.

The music dies away into absolute silence without any definite final chord or a clear tonal structure. The concluding silence is a stillness that *is*, just as the clouds and the surface of the water in the poems, because it is created through the music, here and now, and afterwards hangs there as a lost sound-image. It creates a silence that continues in us, and it is repeated when the work is listened to again. In the repetition we take part in a world to which we, as aesthetically sensing beings, belong. There are no others. It is all-encompassing. The song of the Earth is of the Earth where we live, create traditions of meaning that we have to adapt, translate and pass on as new form in unforeseen contexts. In Mahler, translation – between languages, layers of tradition and medium of expression – has not only become a form of presentation for going beyond cultural boundaries but for a utopian, global lack of boundaries that language, being local, can never express on its own without an integration and translation in another medium: music. Being itself void of specific meaning and at the end bordering on silence, it nevertheless hits the body here and now in its sensual appeal. The role of the body for the literary forms of presentation belongs to the next chapter.

Embodied Worlds

Meaning without guidelines

The novel *Tsotsi* (1980) by the South African dramatist, writer and film-maker Athol Fugard deals with the world seen with the body.[1] As literature and culture, it sounds trivial and not particularly global. The former is correct, and the latter is not. It *is* trivial, but not in the sense of being boring. The body is with us wherever we are, yet even so we do not know it, not even our own. We cannot stop ourselves from exploring it, fearing it slightly, becoming ecstatic and animated by bodily sensations and noticing pain. Like music, feelings enter the body directly; we know this, although we cannot determine how – involuntary blushing, urination and erection. We are not alone in this. Behind all cultural differences, our bodies are organized in the same way. Otherwise, we would not be able to go to a doctor anywhere in the world, or have children across ethnicities. We also react immediately and uniformly to starvation, child mortality and abuse the world over with spontaneous understanding, before reservations, explanations and cultural differences make themselves felt. As humans, such reactions are built into our supplementary experiences we invest in events also outside our realm of immediate experiences. TV images of physical joy and suffering travel swiftly round the world. The body is trivial and global in an insistent way all of us share.

Our body is the most individual and private part of our being, in fact so close to our own individual identity that we cannot distinguish between having a body and being our body. With it, we notice the strongest violation of our identity and the most spontaneous experience of strength or frailty, before reflection takes over and places things in perspective. Hunger, sleep, sex, language, all these and more are found everywhere where there are bodies, without exception. But the way in which we eat and become satiated, in which we sleep and even define what is a comfortable position for resting, in which we enjoy our sexuality or in which we feel we are called to speak or stay silent, such sensations differ from culture to culture. Nothing surprises us more when we meet other cultures than their habits within these areas.

That throughout the world we all share being bodily creatures does not mean, then, that we are identical. It does mean, however, that no culture and no individual can avoid forming the common bodily functions in special ways. The body is a globally shared basic condition for different meanings of local identity. Without these meanings, there will be no identity for either culture or individual. But our bodies do not tell us what this meaning is supposed to look like, nor does it place a certain number of possibilities at our disposal, like inflections in a language. For that reason, its meaning has to be constantly confirmed, modified or renewed on particular cultural conditions. Our individual bodily experiences are included in certain shared culturally determined meanings.

So, the body is global, long before anyone thought of saying globalization. Today, though, the body is in a special way an expression of the tension between a local culture and its global conditions. In the present-day Western world, and also in other places where its body culture has made an influence, the body is not just a part of my individuality. Within our highly individualistic culture, it is also my individual responsibility and my individual project – in relation to health, illness, diet, fashion, well-being, urges and so on. But this individualization project is increasingly being carried out on globalized conditions. The pharmaceutical industry, sports industry, hospital system and health tourism are international, just as fashionwear, make-up and tattoos. Porno tourism and internet-based child porno are international, although illegal, and plastic surgery in some areas is referred to as scalpel tourism. There are abortion ships in international waters, surrogate mothers in developing countries, international adoptions and the import of donor organs. The individual body under individual responsibility is today a globalized product and thereby so are the fundamental cultural values and identities that support it. To understand what a body is today is to investigate new literary forms of presentation that give meaning to a connection between the individual body and global cultural conditions, forms which comprise both the way the body appears in the texts and the interaction with readers through the aesthetic and thus physical appeal of the texts.

The last two chapters in the second part of this book have to do with two other relations of a similar kind: place and movement. Like the body, place and movement are global common conditions for various kinds of cultural and individual identity. All three factors structure space, time and action, with human existence as their point of departure. Certain basic changes have for a long time been prominent in the debate. With today's global means of transport and communication, basic cultural elements, such as place and movement, have also changed. Not only does our body tell us about many places at one and the same time and the many cross-border movements that has shaped its physical appearance and symbolic meaning. Time and space, and thereby place and movement, have also entered new physical and symbolic manifestations (Kern 2003). Time and space have not of course ceased to exist as delineated phenomena, as the most ecstatic globalists preach, but they are not as simple as they have been earlier either.

As we have seen in Chapter 3, place is not only the place we are. It is a meeting place where many movements meet, and where we enter into direct contact with persons at various places around the globe and with various media across time zones. To understand what *place* is today is to explore new literary forms of presentation of the connection between place and the multiplicity of possible contexts.

The centre for the conception of movement was for centuries a movement of our body from place to place. The thousands of years of travel literature have given form to this mode of thinking and still do. Places were demarcated localities, and movement was so to speak forgotten as soon as the destination was reached and the distance covered. Differences in customs and values were a simple result of spatial distance. And if the strangers entered the local confinement, physical distance to them was often established once more in special precincts or regions of the city or the country like ghettos of various types. But when cultures are entangled in each other as a result of electronic movement just as much as by bodily journeys, movement takes place on the spot, without our having to travel and spend time moving ourselves.

The distances must to a far greater extent be overcome by movements through and across media or across value systems rather than as movements in space. We still get jet lag, though, and continue to be surprised by the behaviour of other places. But this experience is only part of the meaning of movement today. To understand what *movement* is today is to explore new literary forms of presentation of the connection between distance and movement through many media and cultural platforms, bodily movements being just one of them.

Today, no formation of identity takes place individually and collectively unless we are able to mould body, place and movement in new forms of presentation that produce new meanings with major cultural import. The means to do so are never constant and never self-evident, even if body, place and movement are the framework of our most spontaneous life expressions. To feel one's way forward to generate new meanings is an ongoing cultural assignment, with literature in the front rank. In Chapter 2, I have described patterns of experience, models of knowledge and forms of communication as a *basic structure* that are indispensable for the cohesion of any culture. Body, place and movement are the *basic components* of the structures, filling them with a special content: individual and common identity through the forms of presentation we are able to construct. The structures give cohesion to our lives and those of others, and via such forms, the components charge them with identity. In *Tsotsi*, this process takes place with the body as its point of departure.

Controlling the body

Four young men are sitting in a bar in a black ghetto, a township, close to a South African city around 1980, at a time when the apartheid regime still has a firm grip on things. We are not on the scene of the great national and international world, but it is there nevertheless. The distant city entices somewhere on the horizon. The white man who is asked the way to it only answers that it takes a couple of hours. By car, of course, which they don't have, and drives on. The bulldozers, on the other hand, get closer and closer to the ghetto. To clear up and build new dwellings. For only the whites. Lorries take the blacks to unspecified dwellings or to prison. And things move fast, for 'the white township had grown impatient' (Fugard 1989: 166). The local continuation of colonial power and the commodities, work requirements and the planning of an international industrial society follow the events like a shadow that is never clearly thematized, only indirectly present in the third-rate versions in which the ghetto materializes them. There is no cultural or black self-awareness here, only a hardened mirror on a miniature scale of the norms and actions of the competitive outside world. The township youngsters are violent big-city trouble-makers and might have been from any global big-city culture whatsoever, but marked locally.

The four young blacks know very well that there is a big world outside. But they do not know anything about it, nor that they actually have been formed by it. Most of them are also illiterate. They only know that it is distant, random and opaque, and that it invades their local ghetto reality with a faceless power and cruelty at any time and any place, and have always done so. Tsotsi has lived with small gangs ever since his home was destroyed in a police raid, his mother removed, while his father worked in some distant place or other. The boys are to retaliate using the same means on a smaller scale. The more their overview disintegrates, the more the world is concentrated on their own body. That they can control, and with it they can control their reactions to the world. They react quickly, strike and kill before asking. Knife and fist are not the extension of thought. They *are* all the consideration that exists. Their communal bond is a gang with a leader that can control the others by beating them. And he does precisely that, Tsotsi. The name means hooligan or thug. Their names are merely epithets – Butcher and Die Aap (the ape) – that reflect their bodies. Boston is a former teacher who has slightly gone to the dogs. Violence, cynical attacks and every-man-for-himself, this is the logic of their everyday lives.

Under such conditions, the body forms the connecting link between the local ghetto and the rest of the world. Nothing else is possible. The world is that which the body can reach with senses and the chop of the hand, and the body is also a shield against it. So, the body bears the traces of the world it does not know, but shaped by the form in which they know it: threats, power and injustice. But since the world is always larger than what the body can attain, the body contains an often unrecognized vulnerability and exposedness. That the world is seen through the body, even when the world is reduced to swift reflexes, does not therefore mean that the world is quite simply identical with the body, or that one can raise the drawbridge to the world by enclosing oneself in one's own body. That is not possible, for it *is* a larger world. So, for the young guys as for the rest of us, the body always indicates the moving border between ourselves and the world around us we are connected to, with or against our will. The body always has that role, even when the world on which we depend lies beyond our senses and concrete knowledge. It is that role which is the thread running through the cultural and literary history of the body and also in the novel.

The four young scoundrels don't give a damn about that history. But they are part of it even so. When we meet them in the bar, they are sitting in their body-holsters, on their guard:

> they sat silent a long time until the youngest of the four, the one they called Tsotsi, until suddenly his hands were together and the other three looking at him and waiting.
>
> Boston smiled, Butcher twisted in another spasm of impatience and hate for the silent man, Die Aap waited impassively.
>
> Tsotsi saw it all. The smile that hid fear, the eyes that hid hate, the face that hid nothing. You I can trust, he said to himself, looking at Die Aap. You I must never turn my back on, and it was Butcher he looked at. And you, Boston. You smile at me and your smile hides fear. (Fugard 1989: 7)

The body is an individual casing in which they hide, and which protects their thoughts, feelings and urges. It is a sign of maximum individual self-control. But the body can take power away from them. A smile or a quiver in the body, as here, is enough. Enough for the others to be able to read the body, see its weakness and take over control. So control of the body is not an individual project but an identity project that is enacted between the characters and defines their mutual ranking. Tsotsi is the leader, and no one is able to read him, whereas he can read the others.

Despite the fact that they all share this bodily experience, it is a lonely world with power and no solidarity up front. They are alone together. But the narrator gets past the lines of defence and describes Tsotsi's thoughts. In that way, his individual bodily existence nevertheless becomes accessible to a common understanding. The narrator makes sure that we realize all the time that the world is formed on the conditions of the individual human body, but is also a cultural expression, not an individual separate world.

But when identity in relation to others is linked to an individual and social body control, there is also a permanent risk of losing it in an unheeded or weak moment. They kill a man, Gumboot, shortly afterwards and take the few valuables he has on him. And the reason? His body stood out from the others – a smile, a tie and a visible pay packet. Lack of control! He doesn't deserve anything better. But Boston throws up. Wimp! Although even Tsotsi feels some uncertainty when he is alone after the murder.

> Tsotsi feared nothingness. He feared it because he believed in it. ... The problem of his life was to maintain himself, to affirm his existence in the face of his nullity. He achieved this through pain and fear, and through death. He knew no other way. When Gumboot died, and in those last few seconds before death had looked hard with hate and then fear at the young man who had chosen him, that moment Tsotsi had known he was alive. It was as simple as that. (Fugard 1989: 32, 33)

The random violence and drinking, the pumping of adrenalin by experiencing the fear can scarcely be overcome, all this is no longer just characteristics of a chance black guy in a ghetto. The possibility of cutting oneself would also be a tempting choice. The way in which he experiences tiredness suggests this: 'The ache in his legs was no worse than a ten-day-old knife wound' (Fugard 1989: 29). All this has long since been documented as a characteristic of a strongly individualistic culture, not only in the Western world but everywhere where its ideas, forms of social organization and urban life forms have influenced local life forms. The less conscious, the more strongly and lethally they enter into the life of the individual across cultural borders. It is this cultural clash the novel depicts via the characters' bodily experiences and the unobtrusive side remarks of the narrator also using the body experience to shape the address to the readers.

Loss of control

Tsotsi's life is a life in the now where he feels his body. He learnt this as a child when he became homeless, first as a weakness that calls for vigilance when he seeks shelter at a refuse dump. Here, he meets other boys like himself:

> It might have been the same day, or the next one. He didn't know. There was no sense of time or of anything past, just the present and being somewhere he had never been before, being cold and hungry. Then he saw them trotting towards him in the darkness, keeping together like a ragged pack of mongrel beings .... On the way he noticed among other things that the oldest was a head higher than himself, while the youngest was so small he had to be carried because he was tired. (Fugard 1989: 121)
>
> You learnt to watch for the weakness of sympathy or compassion for others weaker than yourself, like discovering how never to feel the pain you inflicted. He had no use for memories. And did not have any either. (Fugard 1989: 126)

One day, however, Tsotsi stumbles over the border between the local world and a larger world. He loses control, and does so precisely by following his own precautions. A small, quick routine assault sends him out over the edge. He attacks a black woman with a shoebox, but happens to let go of her for a short instant. She hands him the box and manages to get away. But the box contains neither money nor valuables. A sound comes from it. It is a baby. And as he later says to himself: 'It had broken into his life with a shattering improbability' (Fugard 1989: 45). Rather like when he ran away from home, but without the same possibility of surviving via sober observation and raw physical strength. Gradually his individual body control disintegrates and opens up for the cultural context that the body always carries around inside – memories, compassion, uncertainty and some other intuition of 'shattering improbability'.

The French writer Paul Valéry, in some simple ideas about the body, as he puts it, has provided us with a model for Tsotsi's life until now – 'Réflexions simples sur le corps' (1943). Valéry describes four aspects of the body. We all know very well that the body is not just a simple whole. We look at it in one way when we go to the doctor's, when we enjoy the warmth of the first spring sun, when we have sex, when we look in the mirror before going into town, or when rocking a baby in our arms. Valéry's four categories not only cover four different types of body that Tsotsi exemplifies. The four aspects cohere because they are all forms of the relation between the individual and the outside world through the body. The four forms taken together shape the literary form of presentation that serves to understand Tsotsi's story in a way that reaches beyond himself and his ghetto.

The first body, using Valéry's expression, is the body as *my* body and not just some body or other. It is this body that confirms at every moment of our life that we exist and are present as one independent living being in a concrete world. When I can say 'I', I know that it is a unique physical being that is talking and that it is *me*, no matter my name or others' conception or presence. We repeat and confirm it when we wake up, unless we are delirious with fever, senile or suffer from schizophrenia. Tsotsi has to resort to violence to attain the repetition of this experience time and again.

The second body is the body as a kind of showcase. With it, we look at other people, and they look at us and recognize our identity and presence. The guys at the rubbish dump and the four young guys in the bar establish their gangs around this mutual observation of their bodily expressions. Not in a sense of communality, but out of fear and strive for power. It is here we are given or assume a name, for example Tsotsi. To be made anonymous by becoming a number, to be overlooked or treated as an animal, removes both dignity and social identity. Torture and humiliation of the body, physically or mentally, in detention camps and prisons also break down these two first fundamental cultural bodily functions. This strategy defines Tsotsi's control over the others.

These two aspects of the body both turn outwards towards the world, despite their dogged individualistic bodily control. Although each of us knows we have a body, we cannot circumvent it, hardly even scratch our own back, and experience with our own senses that it is a whole and forms the basis for existence and identity. Only others can do that, but we can, on the other hand, transfer the experience of other people's bodies to our own in order to confirm that it is a whole and thereby that I myself exist as unified subject. However, we cannot confront ourselves with others and make the impact we wish without experiencing our own wholeness as a bodily being, Valéry's first body. Otherwise, the body cracks into uneasy smiles and gestures that betray our dependency. Valéry's first two bodies are entangled in each other.

In both cases, we have added something to the actual naked bodily presence which it does not have in itself. We have added various individual and cultural meanings, so that it is no longer a lump of flesh. In the first instance, we make the body the basis of a holistic conception of ourselves as an independent being in the world, a subject. In the second case, we add a social status to the body that can only be maintained in a permanently repeated confrontation with others, body to body. In that way, we use the body to position ourselves in a social and cultural space. But this means that we are all the time exposed to the unpredictability of other bodies. This is what Tsotsi experiences with the baby that he hides at home in his small den.

Between violence and care

Tsotsi finds out that the baby, in all its defencelessness, makes demands he cannot get round. He has to extend his bodily presence in a different way from previously. Not via power and violence, but by the compassion and empathy that he up till then has feared as signs of weakness. The baby thus makes him feel frightened despite its helplessness. He has to discover other's bodies as physical objects in a new way, first as a biological organism. He lifts the lid of the shoebox 'to examine the contents':

> For a moment he was again awed by what he saw. This was man …. The head was misshapen. It looked more like an egg. The body was covered with patches of fuzzy hair. When his first surprize was passed, Tsotsi noticed the smell …. the smell was coming from the baby. He examined it. The smell was coming from its clothes, the rags in which it was wrapped …. He hadn't done it before. What is more he didn't know what to do, and was forced to pause and formulate each new phase of action. The next phase had to do with the bad smell and dirty rags …. He stopped what he was doing and looked down in amazement. The baby was a boy! The tiny penis rested like a thin finger on the testicles and these together were the size of a small walnut. The navel stood out prominently as a convoluted button of flesh. Tsotsi lifted up the baby and the origin of the smell was obvious. (Fugard 1989: 40, 41)

He now passes through the phases he has forgotten about his own body. It is a human being, and it is a boy. Humanity and gender, these are the most elementary basic features before one through the body becomes conscious of oneself as an independent being with a social identity. He gets no further here than just to wonder, absorbed as he is with the body's basic and ill-smelling functions.

This awareness of the body as a purely biological phenomenon Valéry refers to as the third body. The baby is a body in loose parts, almost like tenderloin or a lamb chop on the cold counter. It is the side of the body that biology, medicine and physiotherapy take care of, positively in health, negatively in war, torture and violence when one knows just where to insert the knife. And we also inevitably add to this purely material side something to give it personal and cultural meaning. We actually see it as one single object, not a store of spare parts. In that way, it becomes either a physical object that is controlled, as Tsotsi has attempted to do up to now, or it becomes one coherent organism that makes us part of a nature that is larger than our own individual one. That is the case with the baby.

If the first three aspects could be labelled body as existence, culture and nature, some thing more is added with the arrival of the baby. This 'more' Valéry tries to encapsulate in his fourth body. Tsotsi's meeting with the orphaned boy, uncontrolled and uncontrollable throughout, changes Tsotsi's view of the world. The individualistic body he has survived with is no longer sufficient. A new type of body with a new meaning has made its appearance, its dignity as a human being which demands company and is an organism in its own right. A new insight of the body vaguely and disquietingly dawns on him: maybe this meaning also includes his own body and the people with whom he normally associates, but who he has either beaten or killed.

Much of our bodily knowledge is rarely fully conscious: manipulating with a steering wheel or gear, riding a bike and writing on a computer – we simply do it. The change is only registered by Tsotsi as something unavoidable that he cannot be more precise about but that causes him to examine himself and the world with new eyes. This turn is determined by the body, but not only by the first three aspects of it. It is up to the narrator to formulate Tsotsi's only half-recognized experience of a meaning of the body beyond existence, culture and nature, thus including the reader address in the form of presentation as it is determined by the body, which now also includes the structure of enunciation. The narrator takes over when Tsotsi meets a cripple, Morris Tshabalala, who he is now not simply able to strike to the ground as he used to:

> What is sympathy? If you had asked Tsotsi this, telling him that it was his new experience, he would have answered: like light, meaning that it revealed. He might have thought of darkness and lighting a candle and holding it up to find [the cripple] within the halo of its radiance. He was *seeing* him for the first time, in a way that he hadn't seen him before, or with a second sort of sight, or maybe just more clearly. The subtleties did not matter .... The same light fell on the baby .... And beyond that still, what? A sense of space, of an infinity stretching away so vast that the whole world, the crooked trees, the township streets, the crowded, wheezing rooms, might have been waiting there for a brighter, intense revelation. (Fugard 1989: 81)

Tsotsi here makes use of his senses to see the world become larger. It is not abstract sympathy but concrete sense perception like light: a conception of the world as a unity, not just as a body, ghetto or that which he already knows. He practises, unknowingly, what Ulrich Beck in Chapter 3 pointed out as 'the universalistic minimum' implied by a global 'cosmopolitan common sense'.

This bodily based vision of the world as a whole belongs to what Valéry points to as a fourth body.[2] We add to the total experience of existence, culture and nature an idea of the world as a unity, also in relation to that which lies outside our concrete experience. Because we are bodily individuals, it is an idea of the world as *my* world, even though we have never seen it, not even on TV, or been present there in flesh and blood. Because we have a body, we are able to imagine being present elsewhere on universally human terms. It is that form of concrete imaginative capacity that globalization calls for.

Those who claim that involvement in the great outside world, in fear or understanding, is of necessity abstract sentimentality have not understood much of what it means to be a bodily being. This imaginative capacity is just as incorporated into our way of using the body as reactions to hunger, cold or pain. Without it, we could not add the necessary supplementary experience we invest in our local and partial experiences in order to imagine them as part of a translocal human lifeworld. Without it, a term like the 'experience of globalization' would be meaningless, composed as it is of an equal amount of experience, mediated information and imagination. Nevertheless, we practise it everyday. It is via this body-based conception that we extend the connection between the three first bodily experiences, back in time in our understanding of life in other ages and other experiences and possibilities, as well as in the bodily based imagination of entire life worlds that we gaze forward towards as new future possibilities and limitations. By means of such conceptions we, like Tsotsi, enlarge our lifespace far beyond what we can perceive with the senses.

For the first time, Tsotsi sees the whole world as a possible human life world. He gradually opens up to the childhood memories he has so persistently excluded. Otherwise, he would have lost concentration in the situations he controls with his fists. His name, David, comes back to him as an alternative social physicality. Finally, Tsotsi – now David – runs home to his concealed baby, but full of anticipated fear that the bulldozer is about to flatten his slum dwelling and take the baby with it – and that he nevertheless *must* run. He can do nothing, and is crushed under a collapsing wall: 'Then it was too late for anything; and the wall came down on top of him, flattening him into the dust …. He is dug out, and to the amazement of the spectators, his smashed skull has a smile on its face.' (Fugard 1989: 167)

The novel speaks of our ability to reach out to the entire world in all its diversity as a personal lifespace, culture and nature. This does not happen despite the fact we live locally, each with own our independent body, but because we do so. Bodily existence makes it possible for us to give a concrete meaning to the idea of a whole life and a world outside local reality. But the story also tells us that this totality cannot be contained within one mind, only in common approaches and shared attempts. Tsotsi is unable to manage this. In order to exist he has to use both violence and care, but he is unable to accommodate both. That is why the narrator discretely follows us as Tsotsi's complementary consciousness, while he is imprisoned within his isolated body. He shows both the sympathy that Tsotsi's does not have fully grasped, and the knowledge Tsotsi is unable to muster. He reproduces the smiling face on the crushed head, recurring from his narrator's word to the view of Tsotsi's body.

Tsotsi has a body-based conception of the world he is unable to maintain, the individualistic world. He is ignorant of its background in a world that with bulldozers, industrial societies, colonial powers and big cities forces its way into his territory, and he hardly knows why he has such a conception. All he wants to do is survive without worrying about memory or tradition. Nor does he understand the alternative vision that hits him like a bolt from the blue with the baby. It is spontaneously felt to be dangerous, but it contains a collective solidarity he lacks sufficient ideas to accommodate and transmute into the body he is familiar with. He is squeezed between these two conceptions, both of which transcend his little universe and yet have taken root in his body. Eventually, he is only present as a smile and a crushed skull. It is such expanding conceptions and their opposites that Valéry comes out with on the basis of our body. It is these that create the individual and cultural differences to which literature gives meaning and significance using the body as a form of presentation.

Body and cultural clash

The characters in the small miracle of a novel, *Earth and Ashes* (1999), also relate to the world through the body. In a different way, but with just as insistent a topicality. It has been translated from the Persian, *dari*, and is written by the Afghan-French writer and film director Atiq Rahimi. Tsotsi does not realize how his body is sucked up by the forms of presentation of a culture alien to his. He hardly even understands the alternative the child offers him, simply by its bare existence. He is whirled round just as defencelessly as the baby in the excruciating world he unknowingly expresses with his body both alive and dead. That is one form of cultural clash that requires meaning in a globalized culture. In Rahimi's novel, things are different.

The horror of the story is initially only revealed gradually. The old grandfather, Dastaguir, is sitting with his grandchild, Yassin, waiting for a lift to reach his son, Murad, who is doing shift work. He works in the coal mine in Kalkar, a long way from the family's village. It is Dastaguir who is the narrator, and the inadmissible event he has to get past his lips and tell to Murad determines the construction of the narrative. We only gradually start to realize what this terrible piece of news is about. And in his hesitation, Dastaguir concentrates instead on the small things and movements immediately linked to his own and the boy's body. 'I'm hungry', are the first words of the novel. And the grandfather painstakingly peels an apple and talks about this small everyday business. Dastaguir tells his story by talking to himself, saying 'you' to himself.

> 'I'm hungry.' You take an apple from the red scarf with a *gol-e-seb* pattern [red & white apple blossoms] and wipe it on your dusty clothes. The apple just gets dirtier. You put it back in the bundle and pull out another, cleaner one, which you give to your grandson, Yassin, who is sitting next to you, his head resting on your tired arm. (Rahimi 2002: 1)

The entire novel is in you-form, except from the direct speech. To concentrate and talk about small things and immediate sensations and body movements is also to push the inevitable meeting with the son a little further away. They wait and wait, eat a little, quarrel a little, sleep a little, hold each other by the hand a little. By means of this, Dastaguir's body expresses his evasive actions, but also the challenge he is facing. Sooner or later, he *must* stand face to face with his son and say what is so terrible. Finally, the grandfather and his grandchild get into a truck and try to gain access to the mine to talk with Murad. Here, the body becomes an immediate expression of mutual obligation and sense of community: the old man is politely treated by the leader of the mine, simply because he is old, even though he is dirty and in the way. A similar sense of community is something the old man himself practises: he has dragged Yassin along with him to the mine and expends his energy on remaining faithful to his son and grandson. The body is in the centre, also in the events we as yet still do not know, and which involve a global world.

The full story gradually emerges. It is during the Russian war in Afghanistan in the 1980s. Their village has been bombed, their home annihilated, and the grandmother as well as Murad's wife and daughter died in the hellish conflagration. Yassin is now deaf, and Dastaguir utterly exhausted. The Russians' war in Afghanistan, followed by the Taliban regime is the one international backdrop. The mine with its international-style shift work and fixed working hours and piecework of big corporations that cannot at all be adapted to family obligations or disasters is the other. Murad is neither allowed to come home to his family nor hold a break to see his father, who must return when at some point someone can offer him a lift back to the no longer existing village. There was also no real need for the father to come, they felt at the mine. Murad has already been told everything, though admittedly not in the version involving the Russians. Instead, the story is that rebels and traitors have destroyed the village, not the Russians. For the mine is run by the government, one understands, which has been appointed by the Russians. And they have plans for Murad, who is clever, is learning to read and is to be promoted. Such a man is not going to be sent anywhere, no matter family traumas or traditional family obligations.

This is before the Taliban take over power, before the Russians are thrown out and before the attack on Twin Towers. But it is this global knot of conflict that is being tightened around the village and is determining local life. Not that the general international conflicts are discussed more closely. We only hear about them in the simple form Dastaguir uses to talk to himself, or in the brief exchanges at the mine that tell him what he has to comply with, politely but without any discussion possible. The grandfather only registers everything as a natural event. Everything merges into what is basically irrelevant to him, the real power of which he can neither comprehend nor is interested in. He translates everything into his own register as regards actions in the world. The great conflicts are experienced with the body. And this perspective is also far more important about what he would like to tell his son than war and mine operation, more important than the destruction of the village and the son's work which is getting close to forced labour. The suppressed story Dastaguir has to tell has to do with the body and with the globally widespread norms for honour and shame.

The body and dignity

Until the bombing and the mine-work, Dastaguir and most of the other characters belonged to a world of physical hard work, bodily contact and practical solidarity. They still live in that world. But it just no longer exists, or is rapidly disintegrating. They knew that world precisely. It doesn't take Dastaguir any longer time to remember an honour killing attempt than to give Yassin an apple. The first thing has the clarity of self-evidence, the other is part of the difficult detour of getting the loss of honour and the shame brought out into the light. The neighbour's Yaqub has behaved in a challenging way to Murad's wife, Zaynab, four years earlier:

> Four years ago your neighbour Yaqub Shah's unworthy son made advances towards Murad's wife, and your daughter-in-law told Murad. Grabbing a spade, Murad ran to Yaqub Shah's house, demanded his son come out and, without asking questions or waiting for answers, brought the spade hard down on the crown of his head. Yaqub Shah took his wounded son to the village council, and Murad was sentenced to six months in prison. (Rahimi 2002: 10)

That's the way it must be, the old man thinks, also when it comes to the punishment. Nor do we get any other explanations than this short, value-laden description.

It is this clear logic regarding the connection between individual body and community that now gets lost. So much so that Dastaguir forgets to observe his religion. What are the flames of hell compared to what he has seen? Not so much as a result of the Russians' behaviour. That could be avenged. But because of the shame, that cannot be overcome. 'What wrong had I committed', he asks a guard at the mine, 'to be condemned to witness …', he stops and continues after a long pause. He has seen his daughter-in-law naked, running at top speed, burned, grimacing like a madwoman from shock and pain.

> I saw Yassin's mother. She was running, completely naked … She wasn't shouting, she was laughing. She was running around like a madwoman. She had been in the bathhouse. A bomb had hit and destroyed it. Women were buried alive and died. But my daughter-in-law … If only I'd been blind and hadn't seen her dishonoured. (Rahimi 2002: 20)

The guard is shocked not only at the cruelty and extent of the destruction, but his comments strike to the very heart of Dastaguir's crisis: 'Men have lost all dignity. Power is their faith, instead of faith being their power' (Rahimi 2002: 22). Dignity has been lost, that is the worst thing. Not only for the Russians or for the naked woman who has brought shame on herself by being naked in public, although the event was beyond her will and control. Now, also Dastaguir's dignity is damaged. He has seen what he must not see; yet it did occur and placed him a level with the neighbour's lustful son. By seeing her body, he has violated the honour of the family, his own as well, and has offended against his religion. It all has to do with the body, both the seeing and the reaction. He wishes he had lost his sight.

This is what he must confess to his son. But how can honour be recovered? Murad cannot strike his father down – only a brother or cousin at most. Here comes the next shock. The polite foreman at the mine is just as devoid of honour, even though they wish to promote Murad, and has lied so that the matter can rest there. For Murad has actually survived a collapse in the mine. Since it turned out all right, there was no need to mention anything about it back home. The foreman and his superiors have also decided that the skilled and valuable Murad cannot come home and bury his dead as tradition requires. And Allah be praised, the foreman says hypocritically to Dastaguir, he can now tell Murad that his father and his child are still alive, so Dastaguir will not need to see him before he leaves. Shamefully Dastaguir had even been deprived of the opportunity to carry out his family obligation and take care of his son. He is totally defenceless against the shame being heaped on him by being kept in ignorance.

> Why praise Allah? If only Yassin and Dastaguir had died as well! That way a father wouldn't have had to witness the frailty of his son, and a son the helplessness of his father. (Rahimi 2002: 47)

The helplessness increases the shame for everyone. The destruction of the village retained at least the size it had always had. We also hear Murad react like his father. Rather die than live with the shame. He refuses to eat and drink, hides himself in the dormitory, but one night explodes round the bonfire, dances around naked and beats his chest and plunges into the flames. 'His companions came to his aid and pulled him out ...' (Rahimi 2002: 88). The three dots imply that nobody really knows if they were real friends. For the mine is investing in him. Shame, and with it the whole world, resides in the body.

Once again we meet the four types of bodily physicality described by Valéry, but not with the same content or emphasis as for Tsotsi. For he constantly has to confirm his existence here and now through violence and pain in a desperate individualism. In contrast, the social bodily contact, Valéry's second body aspect, is under complete control in ice-cold vigilance. The individual bodily existence is centre stage; the social comes of its own accord. Not so for Dastaguir. He notices the closeness of his grandchild, the heavy turban, the urge to chew *narwar*, the proximity of Allah in his physical

misery and finally the dust he feels on his tongue. All this is enough for him
to know that he is alive here and now with his faith, his family, his land and
his own body. Valéry's first body aspect is established completely by itself,
even though he wishes to die.

The social side of the body, on the other hand, is the constant challenge
for both individual physical existence and identity in relation to others. It is
the hub of Dastaguir's existence. The body is a common concern before it is
an individual one. When he wishes he was dead, and when Murad plunges
into the flames, it is not because they wish to confirm their existence by
means of violence and pain and thereby gain power over others. It is, on the
contrary, in order to escape from their hopeless powerlessness. They have not
respected the bodies that hold up the total individual and collective identity.
And therefore they themselves have no identity and cannot gain one with the
body that usually guarantees their place in the world. It is that place which the
bombing and the son's work have put at risk.

Tsotsi's examination in detail of the baby's body – Valéry's third body
aspect – gives him a new way of looking at his own body and his entire world.
The situation is completely different here. To investigate the intimate physical
details of someone else's body – even just to see it naked – is shameful for
both parties and destroys their social relationship. And if it is a question of
relations between the generations that is involved, the identities of all are
destroyed. That is why Dastaguir is so panic-stricken at the thought of having
to tell his son that he has seen his daughter-in-law naked. While he dozes, we
even realize that perhaps subconsciously he has not been able to suppress an
erotic and aesthetic satisfaction in the midst of the shame, and thereby made
it yet greater. Dozing off he dreams that Murad's wife is at the mine in front of
the lorry they have arrived in, before he returns to talking about the bombing:

> Within a black billow of dust, you see Murad's wife running naked in
> front of the truck. Her damp hair streams behind her, parting the dust
> – as if she were sweeping away the dust with her hair. Her white breasts
> dance on her chest. Drops of water fall from her skin like dewdrops ....
> She was burned alive. She was burned naked. She left this world naked.
> She burned to death before your very eyes ... How will you tell all this to
> Murad? Do you have to? No .... She died like all the others – in the house,
> beneath the bombs. She is bound for Paradise. We are the ones burning

in the fires of Hell. The dead are more fortunate than the living. (Rahimi 2002: 70–73)

The observation of the individual limbs of the particular body that are formed into an organism, with a gender, does not enlarge the world as it does for Tsotsi. It causes it to stop. Rather lie than feel shame. Lying is not shameful when it serves that purpose. Violence and care happily coexist in Dastaguir's body-world, as when Murad gives his neighbour's son a bash with a spade for looking at his wife and thus protecting her honour. For Tsotsi, violence and care pull in opposite directions.

Dastaguir is completely present in his social body universe, controlled by honour and shame, and also – as an individual – expelled from it. He cannot start all over again, as can Tsotsi after the police have smashed his childhood home. That is why the old man talks to himself. He sees himself from the inside and the outside at one and the same time. From the inside, he looks out into a world of industrialized mining, big-time politics and international conflicts with global perspectives, and sees his own powerlessness. When he looks in from the outside at himself, he sees his moral strength is anchored in his body now completely useless. He does not need a narrator to add what he ought to know. On the other hand, the story is told on his conditions and at his tempo. This embodies the meaning of honour and shame as concrete, fundamental and universal at one and the same time.

Honour and shame

The world that builds on honour and shame – and thereby on an immediate connection between the body of the individual and the world as a whole – looks very different from the world Tsotsi in vain imagines after he has stumbled over the infant. They are various versions of Valéry's fourth body aspect – the body-based but all-embracing cultural universes. Honour and shame, like extreme individualism, are part of the cultural meetings and clashes that belong to the cultural processes of globalization. The individual body we know from Western culture, but we tend to forget that honour and shame are fundamental regulatory mechanisms throughout the world, until honour killing appeared in the West. We naturally do not accept that form of cruelty, but nor do we understand the strength that honour and shame have as an integrated individual and collective organization of body and culture. The reason is that we have forgotten that honour and shame, with or without honour killing, is a fundamental part of our own cultural history, and we are blind to the fact that they still are, even if in other forms.[3]

The Icelandic sagas, folk songs, stories and authors from Homer and well into the eighteenth-century literature in almost all genres had honour to life and death as a crucial part of their system of norms. A system, it should be noted, that they actively tried to maintain, not to contest. It provides individual and collective identity and holds together the common values of society. Honour is identical with the ability to uphold one's own and one's family's position in a large-scale social community such as a country, a church, a region or a city state, and with the obligation to make that position prevail among others of the same social standing. Honour is therefore not a private but a public matter. Dastaguir is glad that Murad is sentenced, so everyone can see that he has done his duty with the shovel. Shame arises when it becomes publicly known that one does not have the strength to preserve one's honour. That is what Dastaguir is struggling with: the naked daughter-in-law running along the road, the mine authorities that see both Murad's and Dastaguir's helplessness.

Honour is the capacity of the individual, on behalf of the group to which he belongs to give the group the social position it is striving for so that it is visible to everyone. A loss of honour that no one sees is less important. For that reason, Dastaguir can consider lying, not in order to save his own skin, but for the sake of the family. It is, however, not any kind of public opinion that counts. It is a public opinion of peers. For the former aristocracy, honour was only a matter between aristocrats and upwards in the system. Servants did not count. One could behave towards them exactly as one was inclined and, indeed, one ought to do so in order to underline the difference. One was in principle not naked as regards servants, even without clothes on. Subjects could possibly have problems to do with honour in relation to their families, but not in relation to their master. In public, they were part of the master's honour, not their own. The classic right of the lord of the manor to the wedding night with the newly married women underlines that side of things, also underlining that honour and shame are anchored in the body.

That line of thought still applies in those areas where honour and shame are social mainstays.

Honour and shame, firstly, belong to static and hierarchical societies, because they have to do with the stable control of power relations. Change is a bad thing, for some people will always lose when there is change, also honour, and this means that hard conflict is an in-built potential in the make-up of societies with honour and shame as the core of their value systems. Secondly, reactions to honour and shame in the vast majority of cases are taking the law into one's own hands and thus a challenge to any form of central power. For its representatives also have an honour to defend. The balancing act is often in ensuring changes in which nobody loses face, and of balancing the punishment so that it does not unleash new conflicts, often in vain as the sagas tell us. That is what the classical stories deal with when it comes to social norms. Thirdly, honour and shame maintain that the community is stronger than its members, who are precisely that: members, not individuals. When Dastaguir loses the community whose honour he is defending, and which holds him up, he collapses or is reduced to random destruction, maybe self-destruction like Murad who wants to throw himself onto the fire. Violence is hard and cruel when honour is at stake, but never random. It serves a purpose.

But what does it have to do with the body, apart from the carnal pleasures of the squire? Two things: one concrete and one symbolic (Koselleck 1984). The former has to do with things that preserve the family: marriage, sexuality and legitimate offspring. There honour is particularly at stake. The latter links up to the conception of communities as organisms made up of parts that are coordinated into a whole. The community is like one large body. This is an image that recurs from ancient times and across cultures the world over. Kings and princes were particularly important in this context. Their individual body was a symbol of the cohesion of society, manifested in marriage, fertility, strength in war and other collective doings. A strong king meant a strong society. In his magnificent court life, Louis XIV cultivated the body of the king in this dual function as a symbol and a concrete reality and other monarchs followed suit as best they could.

But the body of the single individual, including that of the king, was part of an even greater whole, the cosmos, no matter whether it was created by the

Christian God or by his colleagues. With his individual body, each human being was in immediate contact with the universe, mirrored it. We saw in Chapter 3 how the individual parts of the body correspond to the ideal forms of the universe, as in Leonardo da Vinci's Vitruvian Man. Honour and shame are the forms in which this universal connection is transposed into social relations in which the king is the head of society. And early medicine is the form in which it is then transposed into an understanding of the individual human body.

The vital parts and fluids of the body are directly connected to the signs of the Zodiac, which are the twelve animal signs we know today only from horoscopes in magazines. By regulating these organs and fluids, one brings the body into harmony with the universe and makes a sick body healthy again, to the extent that human skills make possible. Beyond our will, we are bound to the constitution of the body and this means that the life and actions of the individual are also anticipated by the constellations of the stars at that individual's birth. Astrology and medicine are inextricably intertwined, as can be seen from the many medieval depictions of the body's connection with the positions of the stars and planets, the so-called Zodiac Man.

This idea is known everywhere in the world (Kurdziałek 1971; Kiddel and Rowe-Leete 1989). In Europe, the world was considered to be made up of four elements: fire, water, air and earth. These corresponded to certain bodily fluids, *humores*: blood, phlegm, yellow bile and black bile, which in turn corresponded to different temperaments, our humours, and to the skin-colour and temperature of the body. All of this corresponded to signs of the Zodiac and made horoscopes possible (Klibansky et al. 1964; Walther 1999). Generally speaking, it all had to do with not losing the balance between fluids and their effects and of redressing the balance if one fell ill. Letting blood removed the hot blood from a feverish patient to cool that person down and restore the right balance. The entire universe was ultimately at stake, often with a divine perspective, even though honour and shame are not in themselves religious entities. That is what Dastaguir is speculating about. He has a problem with Allah if he cannot do something about his shame. What Valéry painstakingly develops as the fourth body for a readership of an individualized culture, was self-evident in earlier stages of the same culture.

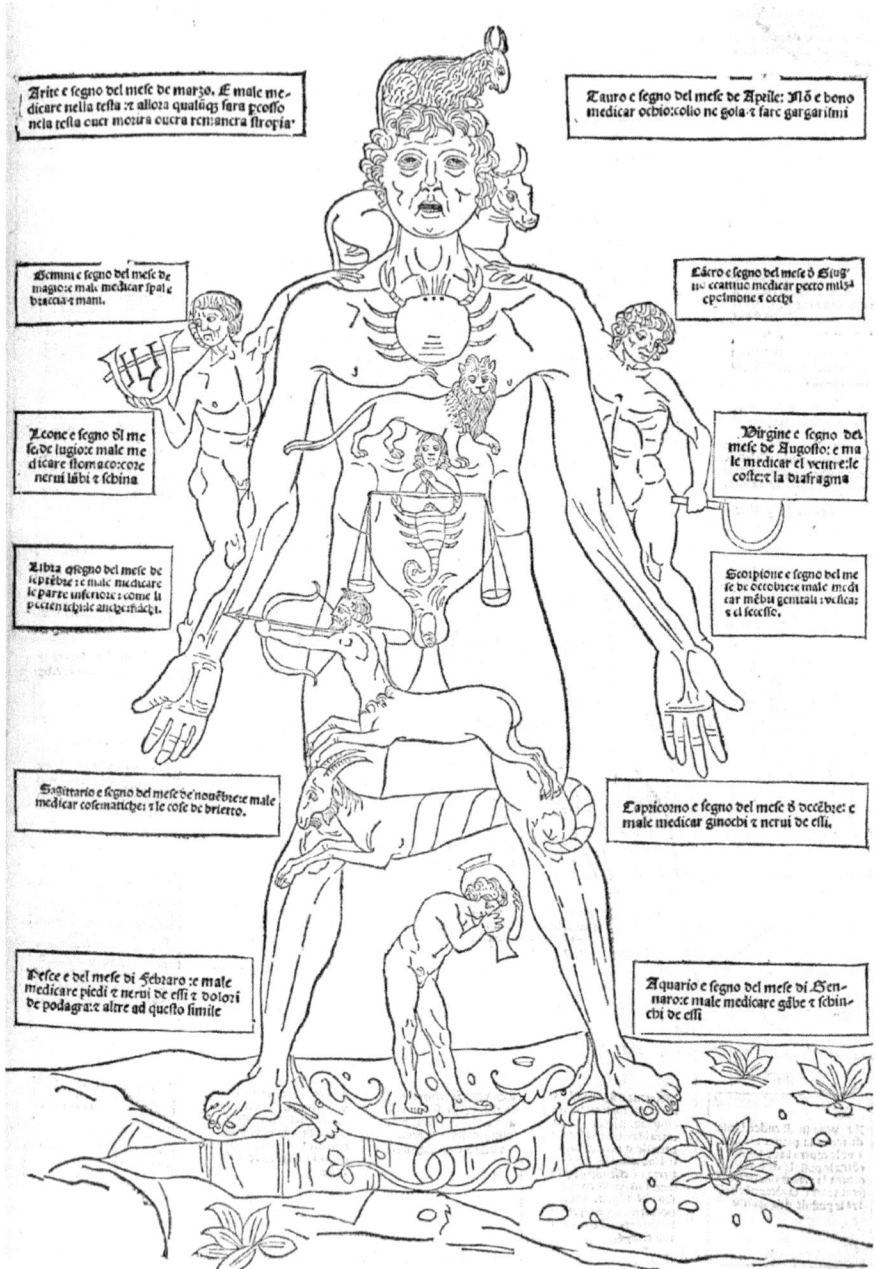

Figure 7.1 The Zodiac Man (Ketham 1493).

This entire system came apart at the seams when the new medicine in the sixteenth and seventeenth centuries started to examine the anatomy of the human body in detail, just as Tsotsi examines the baby. At the same time, the destiny of the individual begins to become more important than his collective life, and organic society is subjected to violent changes, with the voyages of discovery and the wars of religion. We saw this in Chapter 3. Honour and shame gradually become purely social mechanisms without any broader anchorings, and the body that is their focal point is thought of on individual terms. The cosmopolitan of the eighteenth century is one of the expressions of this change. The whole world is no longer a cohesive, static cosmos but an open space that can be conquered by the individual. This idea Tsotsi catches a glimpse of in the light of the baby, but of which Dastaguir has no inkling at all. He puts a little dust on his tongue so as, nevertheless, to feel the Earth to which he belongs.

Pain and suffering also change character.[4] In modern times, it is either an individual test of virility or humiliation, as with Tsotsi, or just the doctors' lack of competence. Pain ought not to be there, unless we ourselves are responsible for it, as it became the conviction in consequence of human rights of the late eighteenth century. In the old, organic type of society pain and suffering are just as unpleasant as they are today, but, supported by religion, they had a collective meaning. Pain was a scourge from God and thus indirectly a sign of God's presence, although in the form of punishment. That was one of the interpretations of the earthquake in Lisbon which we referred to in Chapter 3 and it permeates Dastaguir's way of thinking. Suffering can therefore also be a way to God through martyrdom, which casts honour over the community to which one belongs. The cruel public executions that continued during the eighteenth century in Europe were not an expression of collective sadism. The criminal had, with his or her body, displaced the balance of the great common universe of which his or her body was to be an image. Such a body had to be destroyed in public.

In our part of the world, the old forms aiming at maintaining honour and shame only survive as a closet culture for honour and shame in closed societies and environments with an emphasis on discipline and unwavering solidarity. These comprise, for example, religious groupings, special social groups, boarding schools, biker clubs, the army, gangs and immigrant milieus that share a background with Dastaguir, village environments or peripheral areas such as Corsica. From time to time, mobbing, humiliating initiation rites, punitive gangs and honour killings tumble out of the closet and remind us that collective honour and shame are still a reality.

In contrast to the collective conception of honour and shame an individual conception gradually developed in Europe and ends with Tsotsi. It starts with all the many texts from around 1600 about the conflict between common duty and individual passion. It continues with the individual duel well into the nineteenth century. At the same time, those aspects of the body we cannot completely control, like sex and toilet visits, and to a lesser extent to sleeping and eating, are privatized and referred to special secluded areas of the home. Honour and shame are then often linked to the exposure of the body's intimate privacy, but only as an individual problem. If we, as it is said, are taken with our trousers down, we feel embarrassed. The individual body has put honour and shame on a strict diet and can make do with bodily images of inept clumsiness, not violations that shake sun, moon and stars.

The first undisguised attack on the old code of honour comes from the seedy nobleman Sir John Falstaff in Shakespeare's *Henry IV* (1592, Act V, vv. 130–133). Honour is rubbish, he states on the battlefield among the fallen. It cannot repair arms or legs, or call the dead back to life. Anyone still today embarrassed at being called a wimp and honoured at being called a real man, and who for that reason reacts with aggression or with visible pride, still has honour and shame inscribed on his body. Teasing and mobbing are works by playing with that feeling. But the reaction now is rarely large-scale revenge, for there is no community that derives any pleasure from that. It is guilt or spontaneous violence. Guilt and responsibility as an individual and psychological problem is what Western literature deals with from Shakespeare onwards, while spontaneous violence is Tsotsi's department. One of the guys, Boston, asks him about something he either cannot or will not answer: his age. This reminds Tsotsi of the childhood he wishes to forget, because it makes him weak as a wimp and not a real man. Whether the violation is deliberate or not is of no matter – Boston is badly beaten up on the spot.

The individual dignity of the body

In international law, the expression *habeas corpus* is used.[5] This Latin expression literally means 'you have the body', meaning you are able to produce it in court. It is the beginning of Latin judicial precepts from the Middle Ages and is addressed to those who are to bring the culprit to a judge. The term indicates that everyone has the right to be physically presented in in front of a judge to have the legality of the accusation tested before the question of guilt is examined. One may not be held arbitrarily in prison, simply to be softened up or put out of the way. At one time, this only applied to free men, not to humbler members of society. It was the nobility's protection against the king's power. And therefore, at that time, a protection of their honour is more than their lives. They were not to be allowed to be degraded. But with universal human rights, from the French Revolution to the United Nation and international tribunals, *habeas corpus* now in principle applies to everyone, although not ratified or practised everywhere. One may not be accused with retroactive effect, for then one could not be confronted with the accusation when one possibly broke the law. Nor may one be thrown into prison for an undetermined period without personally knowing what one is accused of, what time limits exist for trying the case, and what a possible verdict might be. Today, the principle has the individual body as the point of departure and thereby human dignity as a fact that results from our very existence, not our social position. Tsotsi's desperate point of departure is this naked bodily existence, but Dastaguir's is primarily his social position.

With a body you have a human right and a human worth, no matter where you are. This could be the motto for some of the most gripping literary portrayals of this global principle and the conflicts it triggers for the relation between body and human dignity which, on might say, is a modern global equivalent of the concept of honour. I am thinking of those who writes about persons returning from conditions of annihilation where identity is removed by physical violation with varying degrees of cruelty, but with systematic humiliation as its tool: concentration camps, Gulag, Guantanamo, Abu Ghraib, Rwanda, South Africa, Argentina, Chile, Bosnia, ISIL – and a frighteningly long list of other places. Here, human rights that have global validity as embodied dignity are violated. Literature is intensely preoccupied with this theme right now.

Imre Kertész's *Fateless* (1975) is one such text from the Nazi concentration camps. The main character and narrator of the novel, György Köves, gradually returns to life in a concentrated sequence of events that are more body than consciousness. He has basically been hauled out of the pile of bodies and taken to the infirmary after the liberation of the camp. In Chapter 10, he talks about this, but has no idea where he is, why and how he got there. Since he himself is narrating, the chapter is one long guessing game as to what it is he registers with his weak senses – he works with the fine brush, the small jerks of body and consciousness. Slowly his body regenerates. He is now able to ask more pertinent questions of himself and others, see a few more connections, although without finding any unifying answers, perceive other people, relate to them with names, language and functions, answer and recall more and more. Finally, he realizes that he is no longer a prisoner, no longer alone and that he has been liberated. But he starts the chapter without any clues whatsoever:

> I have to admit that there is a lot I could never explain, not in any exact way, not if I tried to base my explanations on reason, not if I viewed events from the point of view of life in general and the usual order of things, at least in the way I had known it …. That jam-packed room, which at first glance looked convincingly like a shower and onto whose slippery wooden floor they placed me along with a mass of sticky heels, feet, and abscessed calves, matched my expectations by and large. (Kertész 1992: 139)

He has camp life as his normal and neutral starting point and is on the point of concluding that he has now come to the extermination section. But does not say this, only registers details. He knows though that he is still alive, and that he is being carried like some dangling sack over someone's shoulder. The next step is that his body acquires a social importance. He feels shame. He has first said that he does not have diarrhoea:

> Then my attention and even more so all my powers were totally occupied with the suddenly aroused signs of life from my intestines, which began to make disobedient noises. I mustered all my strength to prevent my insides from giving the lie to my earlier words. (Kertész 1992: 140)

After that, he starts to be able to localize the buildings outside, the rooms inside and other people, while time becomes a blur because of the constant light. But there are language problems, so there is only body language that provides communication, and therefore there is no overall coherence to be found anywhere. He comes to the conclusion that he is in the special section that has been rumoured about. Here, the prisoners are fattened up by the Germans before their organs are removed as spare parts for medical use. Gradually, however, the small hospital becomes a mini-society of which he is a part. He can see its routines, but not its context and his place in it. But in a way he is at home in the camp.

Then comes the shock. Some people cry out in excitement that everyone is free, in every kind of language György doesn't understand but also in German. He hasn't the faintest idea what freedom is. He cannot sense it or understand it with his body. He feels nothing. He can only understand what he sees, hears and notices and make his conclusions on the basis of what to him is the normal world, the concentration camp. And, by the way, they are about to have soup, which he is now able to keep down. So what interest does freedom have for him? Then, however, the loudspeakers blare out that everyone is to stay awake for now they are going to make a good, strong goulash soup: 'Only then did I fall back, relieved, onto my pillow. Only then did something relax within me, and only then did I myself begin to think seriously about freedom' (Kertész 1992: 172).

Once again, the body is the focal point for a discrete reference to the memory of Hungary and the real soup of soups, to another normality than the camp, a place where one has a full stomach and the strength to move around by oneself. Now, he is able to think completely on his own of something and not only react with a reflex to his immediate surroundings and the turning of his body by other people. He is a body, he is himself and he is actually free in a possible new life-perspective without borders. Gradually, the body becomes the centre of the contexts that can be created of patterns of experience embracing the surroundings, models of knowledge concerning freedom and forms of communication for intelligible messages. The body is a path to a world beyond the local borders.

One could be tempted to call Dastaguir old-fashioned, Tsotsi extreme and György Köves special. But they are not isolated cases that can be pinned on a board by history, anthropology, sociology or psychology. Literature does not divide up into concepts and does not say which are right or extreme, special or old-fashioned. All of them show a topical reality in the cross-cultural world in which we live. It is this reality that literature shows. With the different narrators of the three texts, that reality acquires a significance that goes beyond the three life-stories, but is anchored in the concrete events that have to do with their bodies. That is how the texts shape our involvement as readers. We allow them into our own world, but see a reality that is more complex. Not in order to accept it, but to understand it. We also understand that György's newly minted spontaneous freedom does not automatically have a place to take root. The last chapter of the novel in Budapest shows that he no longer belongs to Budapest. His camp experience alienates his view of the home city, and his bodily appearance when he returns makes the local people look at him with a degree of enmity. Places are not fixed geographical localities but dynamic life worlds. In the next chapter, we look at the importance of place as a literary form of presentation.

Travelling Places

The Danish allotment garden

When asked about prototype places of globalization, the cosmopolitans of the eighteenth century would not hesitate to point to the big cities – Paris and London. From 1798 to 1815, some of them published the first journal, *London und Paris*, with reports from the most important cities of the time. During the nineteenth century, the range of cities with a cosmopolitan urban life grew in Europe as well as in the European colonies and the United States, though still measured against the idea of a cosmopolitan hotpotch of mainly European origin: New York, Shanghai, Cairo, Casablanca, Cape Town and many more. However, these cities also maintained their own strong non-European features in architecture, layout and urban life. All of them became examples of the blended meeting places of modern globalization in the making.

With waves of migration crossing the globe, particularly after the Second World War, Europe weakened as the centre for shaping urban locations, and global influences moved simultaneously in all directions – between colonies and former colonies, between former colonies and motherland and vice versa and between some colonies and the empirical centres of other colonies and vice versa. This entanglement of migrating flows created variations of Little Italy, China Town, Londonistan and other ethnic and national enclaves across the globe. Along with this truly globalizing development, the importance of non-urban local traditions from faraway places also entered the big urban centres in a diversity of ethnic neighbourhoods, and at the same time, the effects of urbanized globalization made its influence felt in the local homes of the remaining families of the migrants on the other side of the globe, where people, without ever having seen the urban centres, found it became part of their life through their family networks, with money earned and changing values being brought back. At that stage, the place experience of globalization becomes a fact everywhere. Now, all places challenge the capacity of literature to find new forms of presentation that can provide this experience with meaning.

Therefore, to explore what this development means for the globalization of place experience, this chapter does not travel to the usual centres of globalization. Instead, it spans the globe by going to places on completely opposite sides of it: Scandinavia and Australia. One is small and densely populated, with a long history involving most of the globe; the other is large, with vast tracts of uninhabited land and with a long history outside the goings-on taking place elsewhere in the world. More often than not, both are taken to be closer to the margins of the long process of globalization than to its centres. Nevertheless, these places are an integral part of the process by being involved not only in modern globalization but also in early European history and global pre-history, even the earliest pre-history of humanity.[1]

I will begin with a Scandinavian locality, Denmark. In the *longue durée* of thousands of years, its cultural particularity within changing geographical and political boundaries has evolved in a permanent interaction with regions beyond the Scandinavian territory. However, the closer we come to the modern nation state, the more the continuous and even expanding exchange with the world at large is met with a national localism. This tension is reflected in the changing meaning of place in general as well as in its literary forms of presentation, not least since the disappearance of Denmark as a prominent North European empire around 1800.[2]

Since the Middle Ages, the Danish empire had been an important player on the European stage, but the empire gradually dwindled away during the following centuries. After having taken Norway, part of England and Sweden, Greenland, Iceland, the Orkney, Shetland and Faroe Islands and Northern Germany up to the Baltic countries under its colonial wings, it lost some of its territories step by step until the seventeenth century. At that point, Denmark took instead a small part in the global discoveries already prominent in the days of the Vikings. It expanded to India, Africa and the West Indies during the seventeenth and eighteenth centuries occupying small colonial locations that involved Denmark in the lucrative trade in the Far East and in the cross-Atlantic slave trade. Everything went to pieces after the Napoleonic Wars with a sell-out of colonies ending with the sale of the Virgin Islands to the United States in 1916 and only leaving the North Atlantic domains under the small but still the United Kingdom of Denmark. It now saw itself simply as a small but modern nation state in the mode of nineteenth century nation building. Today, it is a member of the European Union, part of the global economy and, like many other countries, receiving migrants from all over the world, adding a new dimension to the age-old exchange between the local and the global.

This rather turbulent turn-around of what the experience of place means in Denmark and for Danes, or rather those actually living in Denmark, is also a micro-history of what the transformation in general of the meaning of place has undergone globally. Here as elsewhere, the tension between the local and the global is the crucial driving force, the local being the attempts to shape an individual and collective sense of national identity in relation to Denmark as the place of a modern small nation which it was not before, and the century-long understanding of Denmark as the centre of a once-middle-sized empire with some degree of global outreach. This tension is most clearly articulated in the period of Romanticism, when national awareness is growing and imperial self-understanding fading away, accelerated by a political as well as economic collapse during the Napoleonic Wars and after the Congress of Vienna in 1815, when the country was reduced to about its present size. This required a reconfiguration of the forms of presentation of place.

In 1819, the Danish writer Poul Martin Møller travelled as chaplain on one of the ships of the Danish East Asiatic Company bound for China. Møller reached the Dutch colonies in Indonesia and saw Sumatra and Batavia. However, through his travels, he nostalgically deepened more the understanding of his native land than foreign parts. His 'Notes from the Journey to China' [Optegnelser fra Reisen til China] tells of events during the journey, but stops in 1820 in Indonesia. Before returning home in June 1821, he also wrote 'Delight in Denmark' [Glæde over Denmark] (1820). This is how it begins:

> Now the rose in Dana's garden blazes,
> Surely black starlings' trillings outwards spread,
> Bees turn nectar into honeyed glazes,
> On ancestral graves the proud horse grazes,
> And the boy plucks berries crimson red. (Møller 1855a: 63)[3]

Real or not, here we have a vision of a completely balanced idyll in which history and nature, man and animals, and growth and death are frictionlessly united in a simple, clear language. In later stanzas, we also meet the farmer with 'a powerful arm, a wise brow,/crops in the field, milk in his pail'. This ideal place provides labour for the farmer and food to the rest of the Danes in self-sustained harmony.

Møller was far from being the only one to sing the praises of the national landscape, as the new prism for national identity formation. In the first half of the nineteenth century, there was across Europe a profusion of such descriptions in poetry and prose using the same idyllic formula as Møller or celebrating the sublime landscapes in more mountainous regions. Much of the verse was set to music by contemporary composers and was included from the end of the nineteenth century in popular songbooks in many countries. In Denmark, *The Danish Book of Melodies* [Danmarks Melodibog] was worn threadbare in Danish piano-playing homes in the period up to the Second World War. Pictures were also added by painters from the so-called Danish Golden Age to hang above the piano. Most important of all, a major selection of such poems was included in the *Folk High School Song Book* [Højskolesangbogen] of 1894, the eighteenth edition of which was published in 2006. In that way, an 'old guard' of poems became part of the Danish treasury of song, even though the value of the treasure in 2006 had to be adapted to meet international trends – 'keeping pace with globalisation', as it says in the latest edition with songs in foreign languages and in translation being added. No matter the circumstances, the Danish landscape became an ideal place for all Danes, concomitant with what occurred elsewhere in Europe where text, music, painting and school curricula went hand in hand in the evocation of their national landscapes.

Hans Christian Ørsted was one of the a top-ten European physicists of the time with as his main achievement the discovery of electromagnetism, indispensable for industrial development right up until modern globalization. He was an ardent nationalist and took part in the cultural debate about the reshaping of the Danish sense of place and identity, adding language as key factor. In his lecture 'Danishness' [Danskhed] (1836), his idealism almost brings tears to one's eyes:

The land of Denmark has a friendly nature, greatness is seldom expressed right there, but in sea and sky, and there is an almost complete absence of anything fearful; ... Surrounded by this nature, the people have now lived and developed down through the many centuries: Should not then an accord between them both be perceptible? I think it would be hard to deny that the Dane is good-natured, cheerful, modest, disinclined to violence and scheming. ... How can one come to write genuinely Danish? ... Follow your nature with good sense: when a Dane who has been born and bred among Danes and has lived among them follows this precept, he will without further ado become genuinely Danish. (Ørsted 1852: 50, 51, 53)

This idealistic national propaganda has two aspects. First, it was not completely in accordance with the hard facts of Danish territory and its history, and second, this landscape was a poetical and ideological project that was more interested in forming a mentality and a new meaning of place than describing an actual place.

The poems of the time do not draw on many direct references to the outside world, except in the historical songs about the heroic deeds of the past, long sea voyages and later the wars against Prussia in 1848–50 and 1864. Nevertheless, in a great many poems, there is the outline of a reality that is larger than the Danish and follows it like a shadow. In 1820, the educational reformer N.F.S. Grundtvig wrote a still popular song 'Far higher are mountains in other lands found' [Langt højere Bierge saa vide paa Jord], not in spontaneous praise of the Danish landscape but on the occasion of the departure of his friend Christian Pram to the Danish colonies in the West Indies on 10 April 1820 (Højskolesangbogen 2006). Pram was to have something he could sing out there, while the sugar cane was being harvested by the slaves, the tropic heat shimmered among the palm trees and malaria threatened all of them. To Grundtvig, the great outside world was a part of the conditions not only for the appearance of the Danish landscape but also for its meaning and importance.

In contrast to the idyllic poems, there was, however, an inescapable awareness that Denmark was not an ideal place, also before things went entirely wrong in 1864. Then, the country was reduced to the smallest territory in 1,000 years after a war with Prussia, the new emerging superpower. When Møller left for China, Copenhagen resembled Sarajevo after the Balkan wars, with visible signs of the British civil bombardment in 1807. Møller gained his master's degree in 1816 from a university that had no buildings. During the Napoleonic Wars, the country went bankrupt in 1813, and after the Congress of Vienna in 1815, the dual monarchy of Denmark–Norway was separated like Siamese twins in a life-threatening operation. What was left of the multilingual empire were herring and seals around the Faroes, Iceland and Greenland and a few recalcitrant German-speaking citizens in Schleswig, Holstein and Lauenburg. The Germans were only slightly better liked than the Copenhagen Jews, who were the victims of a pogrom in 1819, just before Møller set out on his journey. There were plenty of reasons for singing a great many songs to transform the misery into an ideal landscape, to forget the outside world here and now and allow the international greatness of former times to stand out all the more strongly. But that did not make the songs or the ideal place any more real.

The fact is that the geography that provided material for this construction of a static, age-old idyllic landscape hardly existed. After the enclosure movement of the latter half of the eighteenth century and up to the 1820s, the landscape radically changed with a rapidity never before seen, almost at the speed of the changes during the 1950s and 1960s with modern agriculture's change of the landscape and its products from stooks of crops to the wall-to-wall vacuuming of huge fields by combine harvesters. At the time of Møller, a profound change to an old medieval landscape took place in just fifty years: the removal of the farmsteads from clustered villages out into the fields as scattered buildings in the open land, the redistribution of land from collectively cultivated fields around a village to individually owned farmland around the newly moved, privately owned farms, and a drastic reduction of the extent of woodland.

The cool beechwoods that are sung of so frequently in the contemporary Danish national poetry had practically ceased to exist, though not in the present national anthem, written in that period. Here, the landscape stands with 'spreading beeches'. When the Forestry Act came into force in 1803, 3–4 per cent of the land was woodland – a record-low figure compared with approx. 12–15 per cent today, with continued planting still taking place. 'Teach me, oh wood, to wither happy' [Lær mig, o Skov, at visne glad] the national bard, Adam Oehlenschläger, sang with involuntary irony in 1824

(Højskolesangbogen 2006). He is excused, for, living in Copenhagen, he did not know any better. Most woodland in fact lay close to the capital. And it was here that the painters and poets of the Danish Golden Age were at work. In Jutland, a far more desolate part of the country, Steen Steensen Blicher, a fabulous short story writer, saw a different landscape, even though he also learnt the standard style and wrote about beechwoods and quiet woodland lakes. He was in need of readers from Copenhagen. Actually, he knew more about deserted, wind-blown expanses of heather, which he compared with a desert, and about lonely, hard-working folk rather than the allotment-garden Danes of the Golden Age landscape. The early existentialist philosopher Søren Kierkegaard came from such an area of isolation and hardship. In other words, the Danish landscape was not just one place but several places, and this diversity is a partly suppressed effect of the international conditions of local life in Denmark under the pressure to see national homogeneity everywhere.

In addition, Denmark was not at all one common place everywhere when it came to how urban life was experienced. As early as 1803, Oehlenschläger began one of the poems from his 'Midsummer Eve Play' [Sanct Hansaften-Spil] with the words 'From nauseous brick walls to fields so benign' [Fra kvalmfulde Mure til Marken saa huld] (Højskolesangbogen 2006). So within the city ramparts, one did not live in an ideal place. Møller's idyllic 'Dana's garden' was actually not within the view of all Danes, as Ørsted would have us believe. They had to get out there first away from home. The day-trip into the countryside became a standard figure, and increasingly so after more and more Danes moved to urban areas during the nineteenth century. The international dwelling and work machine of the city was not a truly human and certainly not a national locality according the new national sense of place. 'Look out on a summer's day, when farmers are out rolling' [Se dig ud en Sommerdag] Jeppe Aakjær wrote 100 years later in 1903, but within the same paradigm for place related forms of presentation. The word 'out' is the most important. This tendency continues directly down to the modern worship of nature as a contrast to the everyday hassle of urbanized life and is key component in global advertisement for holiday resorts around the world.

That we have lived for thousands of years surrounded by a land 'flowing with milk and honey', as Ørsted claims, is far removed from the historical facts. He was well aware of this. But it was a bold and encouraging vision in an embattled age. So this type of poetry was more of a utopian project than a description that scanned and rhymed. That's how it was already when they were written, and the fractured picture has only been heightened since. It was an exceptionally efficient project that comprised virtually all the poets of the age. Their literature created certain normative ideas with that particular mendacity that is literature's strength, because it engages its readers. It was a new, useful and necessary project, on top of the real ruins of Copenhagen, the dissolution of the country and an incalculable but surely threatening future: with the blessing of nature and the history of literature, the arts set out to construct an alternative utopian picture of Denmark and offer a unified focus to Danes in a time of deep crisis. The amalgamation of nationalism, language and landscape defined this focus with literature as one its most efficient instruments. It created the distance that was necessary to see new points of orientation towards an uncertain future in a known world that had lost its familiarity.

Landscape as place became a vital literary form of presentation. Words and meanings were given to the Danes' place on new conditions: the international economic necessity and a position as a small colonial kingdom just before closing time, those were the conditions. Yet, in the predominant art and literature, one was to turn one's back on those conditions. They had nothing to do with the genuine Danish landscape and genuine Danishness, but were an expression of the alienating unreality of the cities and of industrialization. Though an illusion, that was a way to gain the strength needed to move on. The great world outside was like a voice in the choir that can neither keep time nor sing in tune, while the Danish songs were sung. The pure of heart and voice just sang a bit louder to drown them out. But if we are to understand the poems as utopian projects back then and use them today, we must also listen to this out-of-tune voice that is a part of the internal meaning of all places, particularly in a time when a new and aggressive nationalism is gaining ground across the globe. It is this relation to a large and alien world Møller's poem deals with.

The reversed global mirror

When one reads the first stanza of 'Delight in Denmark', which I have quoted above, one does not expect that this landscape requires a perspective from outside to be produced. It is in perfect equilibrium, although the little word 'surely' in the second line reveals that the writer is not physically present; he uses his imagination. But that is just his problem, after all. The paradoxical thing, however, is that the distinctive and positive Danishness only appears against the backdrop of the foreign, which simply depicts those features that are a clear counterpart to the Danish idyll. Even if the landscape is closed in on itself, it actually becomes self-contradictory in an involuntarily comic way:

> Yes, our Danish earth is rich and ruddy;
> There is strength indeed in Danish bread.
> That is why the Dane's so bold and ready;
> That is why the Norman's knife was bloody;
> That is why the Danish cheek's so red.

How can rich and ruddy earth the same time be a bloody battlefield? And the knife red from blood, and the cheek red as a sign of good health, how do they combine? Since the list offers no explanatory connections, we can only mockingly guess that it is the native Dane nicking himself during his morning shave that colours both cheek and knife, and then everything hangs together. But there still remain the old urge to conquest and belligerence there like a jarring voice.

It is that voice which Møller unambiguously places outside the landscape. What is foreign acquires an unmistakably xenophobic content that gives Møller a free run towards an unchallenged positive humanity and harmony of the domestic. This takes place in the next stanza:

> Let in harems Eastern monarchs languish
> On purple velvet drowsily now laze,
> Listen to black eunuch's wailing anguish,
> Midst pillars soaring skywards till they vanish,
> Cold as marble god, with sallow gaze.

The contrast between the harmonious Danish landscape, populated by plain, cheerful and active Danes with their passions suitably tempered, and the opulent, lazy, lascivious, lewd Orientals with a weakness for luxury is unmistakable. And it continues for several more stanzas in the same fashion. The violent contempt for the alien is not a description but a rhetorical springboard for formulating a dream about Denmark: 'Out in the East or the West, where'er I wander,/You are in my dreams on Denmark's shore'. A look in Møller's diaries (Møller 1855b: 241 ff) reveals that he actually found people out there to be poor and gracious. The last stanza quoted above and the two others of like ilk are omitted from the *Folk High School Song Book*. The mutually negative dependence between the foreign and the domestic is removed, and the song then functions more as a self-assertive description of a real landscape than in Møller's complete version.

The song was written when he was farthest away from Denmark, just before his return. Møller's most important occupation during the outward voyage through Danish waters, apart from being seasick, is to study life on board ship and read Tibullus' Latin elegies, not Danish writers. Nor do we hear much about his job as chaplain. And he even draws attention to the cleanliness of the Norwegian farmers compared with the disgusting habits of the Danish farmers (Møller 1855b: 230). He has to get really far away from home before he can idealize the Danish farmer: 'Poor the man that Danish soil does plough,/Shakes down apples from his tree,/Strong armed and shrewd of brow is he'. But at Cape Town, we find the diary's most comprehensive and varied single account. It is the story of the meeting with a Danish ship: first, the rumour of a ship, then the sailors looking out for it, then the flag and finally, the meeting with the Danes. It is a dream, Møller writes (Møller 1855b: 232).

After this, it is more intimate scenes that attract him, alongside portrayals of local sights and attractions. Almost spying, he points his telescope at touching outdoor family scenes that at first glimpse remind him of a Danish domestic idyll. He observes with experimental awareness so as to maintain his domestic feelings and not let himself be swallowed up by the emotional coldness of the foreign (Møller 1855b: 235). The portrayals almost seem to be written exercises to hold onto emotions he is otherwise afraid of losing.

Later, in Batavia, in the teeming and truly alien environment, the domestic no longer needs to be triggered from the outside. It becomes an inner yardstick for his experiences. The distance from Frederiksberg Garden to Vesterbro in Copenhagen becomes a comprehensible yardstick for him when conceiving foreign space (Møller 1855b: 247). The domestic loses its fascination close to, but pops up in Cape Town as a spontaneous national reunion with the flag and the whole caboodle. Later on, it turns into paparazzi experiments with his telescope and ends up as an internalized assessment scale.

That was the first aspect, the psychological one. At the same time, he moves in the other direction, towards an aesthetic self-awareness – how is he to represent the domestic place on such conditions? It starts discreetly. As he sails through Øresund between Denmark and Sweden, he contrasts the 'naked backbone' of Kullen, the promontory across in Sweden, with 'the smiling Danish coast' (Møller 1855b: 226) and by doing so has already outlined the contrast that is also going to characterize the poem to be written about one year later. The foreign as a negative contrast is a general prerequisite for experiencing the domestic as positive. It is not only a special structuring of the experience of Denmark from Indonesia. Møller also knows quite well that localities acquire identity via construction. In order to avoid offending the Norwegian pilot, he thus quickly invents a positive local description of the Norwegians (Møller 1855b: 231). When he sees a Danish ship in Cape Town, Denmark has quite simply become a 'dream' (Møller 1855b: 232). The vision he has built up at a distance controls the shaping of the local Danish landscape, not the landscape in itself.

At Cape Town, he becomes increasingly aware of these relations. He makes a little experiment. To really be able to see Table Mountain, one must not stand on deck when the ship approaches it. Hence, he remains in his cabin until it is really close. The actual experience then becomes a sudden almost epiphanic intensification of the expectation more than a concrete observation (Møller 1855b: 234). The real is a recreation of an expectation that is nourished at a distance. Now he is ready to write his poem about Denmark.

This psychological and aesthetic development Møller experiences on the deck of his ship, which is a place where everything changes places: the sailors fool each other, he turns his innards inside out when he is seasick, during gales trunks and equipment are tossed around. And even more radically: time ceases to exist and also the spatial function of the ship as a temporary home is turned upside-down: 'The seafarer is a snail in reverse; for the snail carries its house, but the house carries the sailor' (Møller 1855b: 226). In addition, one's 'own-being [becomes] as good as dissolved'. This Møller recognizes 'as in a mirror' when seeing someone else seasick, a strapping fellow who nevertheless is powerless, alive and yet dead and Møller himself even misunderstands the Danish language (Møller 1855b: 227). Everything is itself and something else at one and the same time.

That is also how he portrays the ideal Danish place: It is home, but only because it is seen from the outside and described via a reversed global mirror, as on board the unstable environment of the ship. The stability of the local is portrayed on the alienating and unstable conditions that characterize the foreign place. The great project of the nineteenth century is to use literary forms of presentation to remove the external instability from our field of vision, and on that basis conjure up the new meaning of the uniform national landscape as a common point of identification in a world that is breaking up. It still has a strong cultural impact today, even though globalization has removed its basis in reality, but not from the emerging national ideological revival of the twenty-first century.[4] We are not to throw these texts or their utopian project overboard. It has helped to shape us and our relation to globalization. But we are to read them with the instability as our point of departure, not the idealistic presentation of the place. This sceptical approach was difficult, although possible, back then. In the modern globalized meaning of place, it is the only possibility.

The landscape as a meeting place

Møller let the boy pick red berries in Dana's garden. If we sow a packet of radish seeds behind the house, he can also have red, Danish radishes. But unlike the berries, the radishes we buy and eat are often imported and cultivated far from the landscapes that surround us in our daily lives. Møller's 'crops in the field' are today first and foremost to feed animals with, not to make 'Danish bread'. Perhaps neither the seeds nor the boy's radishes come from what we would normally call a landscape. The seeds have passed through various laboratories, experimental fields and reports, marketing and consultant guidance sessions before they are sprinkled in the soil. And the radish soil is perhaps that of a greenhouse in an outsourced production unit and has itself also been fetched from elsewhere. So sources of energy from a third landscape must be used, to heat the greenhouse and transport the material and end-product around the world before we sow seeds and crunch radishes. We are not talking about luxury products such as medieval spices from the Orient or the explorers' chocolate from South America. This is everyday fare.

The Danish and any other national landscapes, then, are considerably larger than the local landscape we go around in or just visit occasionally. Not just because we get seeds and fruit from other places, but also because the local landscape that surrounds us is crucially affected by this extended landscape. Crops appear and disappear, as so do forms of behaviour in those who cultivate the soil, and those who eat the radishes, not to mention those who own the farms and its land. This does not take place on the basis of the possibilities offered by the historical local landscape in the 1,000-year-long alternation imagined by Ørsted, but on the basis of the global conditions of the extended local landscape.

The biggest change in the Danish landscape is that large parts of it do not lie in geographical Denmark. Some still lie in what is economic Denmark, though, since there is certainly Danish money in the greenhouses outside the country's borders where radishes are fetched from as well as in the transport sector that fetches them. Not to mention Danish-owned tourist resorts welcoming Danish tourists and other tourists whatever their origin looking for a subtropical sun and a sandy beach. But part of the extended landscape is not found in either geographical or economic Denmark – desert sand with oil, palms with bananas or vineyards with grapes. Today, we are connected to all of this via our daily imported foodstuffs, the great majority of which once used to come from the local landscape. No matter where the border of our landscape is located, it is globally conditioned right down to its concrete details. The Danish landscape is no exception, but just an example of a global reality.

When we are to decide which of the many landscape layers are the Danes' right place, it is not self-evident if we only follow Ørsted's rule of using our common sense and listen to the language spoken there. Is the landscape that cannot be used without all the foreign products and habits also a landscape for those who migrate from these distant places? That is the way of thinking that lies behind the attempts by the global tourism industry to give all local landscapes an international touch, so that people do not feel much too foreign when they pass by for the space of a week. Hotels are preferably to have the same global standard, and so have the busses transporting the tourists out into the nearby landscapes and to the airport. But what about the new Danes with other landscapes on a retina of many generations and in their narratives? Does the *Folk High School Song Book* provide refugees and migrants settling permanently in Denmark with anything? Not, at any rate, with the spontaneous common sense that Ørsted would most like; it requires another reservoir of supplementary experiences that they bring with them. It is a laborious learning process that does not end at the same place as for other Danes, even if it ends positively at all. And Denmark is not exceptional case.

If we, however, stick to the landscape of geographical Denmark, it is not all that easy to demarcate as in the songs. Leave the city behind and you're there, we used to sing. Yes, but only if the politically determined urban and rural zone has placed the border there, and changes haven't taken place since we last were there. The border is moving all the time, as well as the development of cities and their influence on the rest of the landscape. And at the same time, the landscape has acquired two separate functions that the ideal landscape without further ado united: production with field-rolling farmers, munching cows and crops in the field and the aesthetic entertainment landscape out of which we brewed a national identity in songs and images, or just relaxed in our leisure time between the working hours we spent in completely different localities. Today, however, the division is crystal clear: on the one side, a production landscape for forestry, agriculture and fishing, and on the other side, an entertainment landscape for jogging, sea views, family trips and holidays. The two functions on the basis of the same landscape are not in themselves an ideal harmony, rather tend to conflict with each other. It requires good will and good legislation to establish harmony. This nature is unable to manage itself, as Møller envisioned.

The situation also means that the two functions are not primarily demarcated in relation to each other but in relation to other social functions that each of them runs parallel with. Like all other production sites, the production landscape is determined by natural resources, legislation and economy. It contains a type of activity among all other kinds of activity in the globalized industrial Denmark. The entertainment landscape is also a kind of activity in the global tourism industry that produces experiences for indigenous Danes and foreign visitors alike. But from the point of view of the individual user, we mostly are dealing with the consumer's choice of entertainment on a par with cinemas, cafés and sports events, and with the landscape at the end of the charter corridor or the adventurous *tracking tour* in the Andes Mountains. On rainy days, we pick the cinema.

Each of the two types of exploitation of the landscape is thus also more structured by social time rhythms than by the nature's changing seasons and weather at the place in question. The entertainment landscape often has fixed opening hours for the public and generally speaking does not exist at night. It is shut, just like all other entertainment sites, unless special relations favour something else. Bird watching is open in the evening just as discos stay open longer on Saturdays. The production landscape works in shifts between worms at night and humans in the daytime, and the farmers, via cooperation, can gain organized working hours and holidays.

So the ideal landscape today has acquired two functions that are external to each other – production and entertainment. They are first and foremost social and cultural functions and are therefore more connected to other related social functions than to the course of nature. And these functions have been closely interwoven with modern global reality, cutting across city and country and across national borders. It is this dynamic meeting place that is our local place today, no matter where we live. It is a result of movements between the landscape itself and other places, and it is itself in constant motion.

How can we give it words and meaning so that we can connect with it on modern conditions? There is no point in feeling homesick about Dana's garden from the globalization presumably out there, as Møller in the Orient feels homesick for Denmark – for globalization is everywhere. J.M. Coetzee, in *White Writing* (1988), poses a related question:

> Africa is a land of rock and sun, not of soil and water ... The landscape remains alien, impenetrable, until a language is found in which to win it, speak it, represent it. ... Is there a language in which people of European identity ... can speak to Africa and to be spoken to by Africa? ... Many English–colonial doubts about identity are projected and blamed upon the English language itself, partly because, as a literary medium, English carries echoes of a very different natural world. (Coetzee 1988: 8)

The British in South Africa have a landscape that already has significance for the indigenous peoples, but now it has to contain their lives too, both parties alienated from each other but with a simultaneous local presence. Coetzee's problem corresponds to that of Honoré de Balzac, who wanted to find a form to present an emerging metropolis as a human life space. Balzac stood with a new city that was emerging on top of the one he knew with a long history. Localities which for centuries have carried key, identity-bestowing meanings, reflected in experiences, languages and images and expressed in poetry and narratives, are now transformed under global conditions, no matter whether this takes place at home as in Balzac's case, or outside as with Coetzee. Both use literature to help find new significances, giving the new experience of place an adequate form in the language we also use in our daily practice in these places.

Their answer is not a uniform global literature, for the localities represent different ways in which traditions are remoulded under global conditions. It is this upheaval literature is concerned with in presenting the meeting places, more than finding an alternative ideal place to replace the old one. Its various forms of presentation show new cultural needs of expression and challenge the forms of knowledge, ideas and presentations of reality we are familiar with. This experimentation will keep literature busy for quite some time yet.

Travelling on the spot

When we now move to the vast almost deserted areas of Australia, one of those who takes part in the experimentation is the British globetrotter Bruce Chatwin. In his distinctive travel book *The Songlines* (1987), he travels to Australia in order to find out what the Aboriginals feel about places.[5] He has heard that they are not restless modern nomads, even though they have been alienated on their own land, nor do they worship the clearly marked out ideal landscape. Nor is the difference between city and country of any significance to them. Bruce – the name of the main character in the book – has also found out that their relation to places unites movement and locality. At the same time, Bruce is curious to see how stories and songs not only describe stays and movements in the landscape but integrate them into each other. Words and rhythms are eyes to see with and feet to walk with. It is this connection that the title indicates. Songlines are both songs and actions, and both the routes and the places.

It is this connection he attempts to understand, mainly so as to gain some anchorage points in his own rootlessness – on the one side, a permanent travelling activity where he is just as tired of settling as of continuing, and on the other side, a curiosity for places with a local distinctive stamp beyond global homogenization as well as for all kinds of texts about places and their importance. He is a European individualist who is constantly expanding his own scope and his own experience, placing his personal imprints so to speak on as much of the globe as possible. Not in order to wreak havoc anywhere or to grab things, but in order to make the Earth his own experience. The planet is not just there, it is also mine.

Bruce's trip to Alice Springs at the very centre of the continent is the focal point of the action. Bruce meets the exiled Ukrainian Arkady. He works as a private consultant for a firm that is going to build a railway line through the area, and through some of the places that are sacred for the Aboriginals. They are either to be avoided, or negotiated settlements have to be reached. Arkady can manage that, but not the engineers doing the actual railway construction. So here, Bruce has come across precisely what he needs. With Arkady's help, he travels around, meets other exiled individualists, asks the Aboriginal leaders about their traditions and meets the Australians who as art dealers, social workers, teachers, shopkeepers or lawyers work with the Aboriginals. They live under wretched conditions, with shattered traditions and a severely tested self-awareness in small communities around Alice Springs. As knots in the thread of action, substories are wound around each of these life-stories.

This aspect of the book is a diluted version of the classic exploratory voyage of discovery, with the traditional description of strange places and people in stark contrast to the superior Europeans. Yet, the book is not a weak version of that endeavour, not because it is bad but because it is honest about Bruce's own status as a traveller. He is a stranger in this place, and he wants to examine local conditions from that position and to respect the independent identity of people. But there is not a new place or people to discover, not even a dangerous journey. Everything has taken place long since, and he cannot add one iota to what is known about the local conception and use of place and movement. Anthropologists and tellers of local history have presented everything that there is. He is not an anthropologist, only out to satisfy his own personal thirst for knowledge. He wants to know what the others know, but in his own way. It is an individual project he is involved in.

For that reason, he does not consider the local Aboriginals differently from the way he does the whites of mixed race he meets. As he himself, they are all anthropological cases on individual conditions at the intersection between a background story and loosened traditions in Australia, England, Ukraine or other places and, on the other hand, a present-day existence as an individualized mixture of the conditions of the past and present. Like us readers. What we are looking at is our own local world, just brought to a different place, both places existing on connected globalized conditions.

Bruce moves from one informant to the next so as to build up his knowledge of the meaning of the places and collect them into one meaning. The old voyages of discovery were also cognitive projects, sometime scientific projects into the unknown. But then the aim was to understand what was truly foreign, and the result was often that a new self-understanding occurred as a spin-off effect. That is how Møller's poem is constructed, and the way the enlightened Europeans of the Renaissance reacted to reports from the West Indies – Thevet, Léry, Las Casas, Montaigne, Swift and many others. They did not see foreign individuals but a flock of indistinguishable beings who, by being non-Europeans, were instances of cultural foreignness as such. But for Bruce, all of them are different under the same conditions, he himself included. No one is so different that it is inconvenient, but enough for it to be possible to gain new understanding of one's own individual global life.

So Bruce behaves like those he comes in contact with. He uses his previous personal history in spare parts to extract usable knowledge from the scattered information he gets about the Aboriginals' relation to place. He shifts from chapter to chapter in time and space when he meets something that makes him think of his family, his previous life in Senegal or his meetings in Switzerland with Konrad Lorenz, the expert on animal behaviour. We zoom around as if propelled by a remote control and find ourselves now in Africa, now talking to Lorenz in his Swiss office and now in other places from Bruce's globetrotting activities. The traditional thread running through a travel account is cut into pieces via his recollective leaps to other places. After all, he does not need to have total knowledge about the places, only enough to be able to form his own connection. Nor can he achieve it. Much knowledge he tries to get at in Australia is taboo and may not be passed on to him, and the storytellers have also become forgetful, just as part of the tradition which like elsewhere is now stiff with arthritis. The form of presentation with gaps and leaps grasps this situation. For this reason, his project can neither have the form of a traditional travel account nor be a scientific report.

But he does find out certain things. The use of songlines is, briefly told, that one carries out a sung repetition of a creation myth in the form of a journey. Original beings, shaped like animals or resembling humans, have roamed through the Australian continent and, through poem and song, have named and mapped the otherwise deserted and featureless land. Afterwards, they have become one with their land and have left behind their songs, maps and own bodies as plants and animals, places, mountains, river courses and all the other forms and elements of the landscape. In that way, they are inscribed in the so-called dreamtime of creation as an eternity into the landscape, and mankind is to keep it alive. Humans populate this earth and find their way by re-performing and repeating these songs and also using some dreamtime animals as their totems. 'If the songs are forgotten, the land itself will die' (Chatwin 2005: 52). The tradition must be constantly repeated and thereby renewed. That constitutes its eternity. Not a description, but a performance and execution of something that with body and song moves through the land time and time again. One cannot simply say: there is a songline. It is only there when shaped in the actual performance of the song.

Each human is connected from birth to an element in the landscape that goes back to the dreamtime, and therefore has special songs to look after and special repetitions to carry out which the tribe is responsible for him or her to be taught. Individual practice embedded in a collective logic. The strange thing now is that precisely the particular tone of the language of the song can be recognized as distinct from all the other many Aboriginal languages. No songlines are without an aesthetic awareness that carries them across language barriers. The individual songs can thus be added to each other and criss-cross an entire continent with a geographical mapping that one is literally able to use to find one's way. Goods and people have to be physically moved in that way for thousands of years, for example, the ceremonially important ochre. The songs replaced each other like batons in a relay. So no one song must be allowed to drop out. 'All our words for "country" … are the same as the words for "line" … – A man's verses were the title deeds to territory', Bruce is told (Chatwin 2005: 56, 57).

No one has a complete overview of the songlines as a whole, only those parts of the network into which one is woven oneself. So, one always has to sing for and with others in order to proceed. Hence, the songlines and *The Songlines* are dialogical. Bruce too has to piece his own understanding together from many sources without having access to all the information. Just as the Aboriginals individually have to put *their* songs together by practising them on the basis of what they have picked up, so he gets closer and closer to what these songlines are, and thus also becomes increasingly aware of the impassable distance he himself has to his own understanding of life. If he wants to enter into this practice of repetition, he must himself take part. He must personally run the risk the Aboriginals run of not being understood when the song is put into practice. Yet, the structure of that part of the country they are responsible for stands or falls according to their knowledge. Bruce must make up his own song to find a way. The result is the book we are holding in our hands.

Bruce's songlines

He is just about as much an outsider as the railways engineers are who, with Arkady's help, are to build a railway line. Bruce cannot make that kind of linear traffic artery through the landscape. It is completely without tradition and deprived of memory. He has to maintain the connection between word and action and between place and movement in his own concrete form of presentation. He cannot dance around in the landscape and imitate the locals. He has after all not received his name or his totem there. So he has to locate himself in the place as a foreigner and even so establish his own connection. For that reason, the book has to deal both with his attempt to find out about the songlines by travelling around and to produce, or rather *be* his own way through the world.

This means that the book has to have a dual structure. He braids together two layers – one is the narrative I have reproduced here, the other is the actual book as a concretely progressing course of events that is realized while we read it. His name is therefore also double. Bruce is the author on the front page, responsible for the actual book, and is also the main character in a novel-like travel account. The latter is in search of knowledge, and on that basis, the former performs his own songline with the book *The Songlines*, then meaning both 'the songlines' and 'my songlines'.

This interpretation is of course my reaction to the actual performance of the book that I establish in my reading of it. Bruce does not tell me directly, neither Bruce the author nor Bruce the protagonist. That would have been contrary to the very nature of the songlines. They are only contained in an actual aesthetic practice. And it is thus that they are to be repeated, dance upon dance, reading upon reading. The two layers of the book only come into position as Bruce gradually becomes aware that he is not to know what the locals do, but to carry it out himself in his own way, also without getting to the bottom of the Aboriginals' innermost taboo-laden knowledge.

In the first quarter of the book, approx. seventy pages, Bruce is the curious new arrival who goes round and asks those he is able to come into contact with. It resembles a slightly modified version of a questionnaire survey. He asks questions, gets answers and tries to conclude and ask further. There is something of a smart Alec about him, and he never really gets beyond a standard knowledge that he could have got simply by reading any introduction to Aboriginal culture. But it is nice to get it from the horse's mouth, even so. After this section, there are a couple of pages in italics where he tries to retell or make up himself a story about the creation process of the dreamtime, with the mythical kangaroo as the main character. After about a further seventy pages, we have arrived halfway through the book. Here he is out in the landscape himself and cannot find the way properly. So he tries to make use of his earlier experiences, not only what the others have told him about the local prior conditions and traditions. So he takes us along on an interpretative memory leap to Lorenz's study in Switzerland.

There now comes another solid slab of text, again approx. seventy pages, and once more in italics. It is a collection of Bruce's notes from a major project to write a book about places. There are extracts copies from all kinds of books, apt quotations about places and journeys from cultures all over the world, many from Europe, from ancient and more recent times, all of them fragments that have 'said something to him'. There are things about the origins of humanity, lack of freedom to travel, the urge to travel, nature, the thirst for knowledge, boundless identity, in short everything that is part of the basic material and practice of the songlines. These are his own scattered songline resources. It is these that are collected in the book when transformed into the story of his search, but they also become the actual book as a process of elucidation that we repeat as readers through materially marked different sections of the book.

The aesthetic awareness becomes ever clearer. We hear about the difficulty in buying his particular notebook in Paris, with the absolutely right sensual qualities that one can feel when holding it in one's hand, its form, smell, colour and material. The final seventy pages alternate between the continued travel account in Australia and inserted sections that directly reflect his dual project: to set out travelling and to repeat the process in the form of the book:

> Yet, I felt the Songlines were not necessarily an Australian phenomenon, but universal: That they were the means by which man marked out his territory, and so organised his social life. All other successive systems were variants – or perversions – of this original model. (Chatwin 2005: 280)

He is, therefore, also able to use his own prior experience along with the new experiences he makes. He stresses initially his European scepticism. The songlines correspond to his having to attempt to convince himself and others that 'a featureless stretch of gravel was the musical equivalent of Beethoven's Opus 111' (Chatwin 2005: 14). His own book can be interpreted as *his* song about *his* territory. It is not a piece of a continent he establishes and finds his way in. As a European traveller, he inhabits a cultural space with a flexible place-anchorage. The book becomes Bruce's songline that maps out the life-space of a modern, globalized European in a repetition of both the Aboriginals' songlines and his own tradition, so that we too can experience it. That it is *his* performance of the place for us is expressed in the final italicized section:

> And here I must take a leap into faith: into regions I would not expect anyone to follow.
>
> I have a vision of the Songlines stretching across the continents and ages; that wherever men have trodden they have left a trail of song (of which we may, now and then, catch an echo); and that these trails must reach back,

in time and space, to an isolated pocket in the African savannah, where the First Man, opening his mouth in defiance of the terrors that surrounded him, shouted the opening stanza of the World Song: 'I AM!' (Chatwin 2005: 280)

It is pure re-performed classical mythology transformed into personal identity through song. The point is that he does not try to put one over us. He does not imagine that we grasp the full content, but that we witness him performing it for us as a formation of identity. We are once more as in Chapter 3, with Blixen singing 'Here I am where I ought to be' or in the field of maize when she rhymes for her indigenous workers, and with Mahler at a performance of *The Song of the Earth*, which performs the eternity his composition enacts. After this, the book concludes with Arkady's wedding and a visit to three emaciated old people from a local tribe, on a mattress in the Australian desert, in the process of dying. They wave feebly. Death cannot be experienced, as Blixen also stated when leaving Africa in the ultimate loss in her life, but it too can be performed.

Participation

In Chapter 3, we left Joachim Heinrich Campe in the middle of roaring Paris, on the edge of the revolution, and Farah in Kenya in the middle of the living room with Blixen. The former stared with his entire body like one great eye at cosmopolitan Paris. Here, he was at the centre of the world. He did not have to do anything, just come with all his senses open, forget everything about who he was and where he came from, just be there. Anyone who took over his place would experience the same thing, without any particular effort: to enter as a provincial and emerge as a world citizen. It all takes place of its own accord, as long as one puts in an appearance.

The latter, Farah, is far from the centre and hears a strange story about a Jewish merchant from Venice somewhere far off in a distant time. Summoning all his supplementary experience of empathy, values, traditions and attitudes, he transforms the meeting with Blixen and her story to a meeting place with an echo of the two cultures that meet as well as the whole world they come with. The living room is changed into a global meeting place, and the two persons move on with the experience of it having taken place, not simply because they were there but because they themselves invested what they had inside them together with the unexpected and the unknown they encountered. Campe was a cosmopolitan, the two others were globalists.

Bruce knows that his final vision is his particular investment in the place where he finds himself, so that it can become a meeting place in the world. But qua content, it seems very similar to the account Campe gives of his experience in Paris. Alice Springs is not Paris, believe me. The difference is that Bruce transforms himself and the place by participating in the meetings between cultures that the place makes possible. He does not surrender anything without investing something, whereas Campe is simply at an exhibition. Bruce gets all his individual and collective memory sharpened and actualized by having to use it under other conditions than back home, while Campe forgets everything and dreams of becoming a new, universal human being.

Hence, Bruce's message is a different one from Campe's, whether we can follow his vision or not. Campe sees in his mind's eye certain particular big cities as cosmopolitan places. All of them provide a uniform experience of collecting together the worldwide trends within their borders. The rest is provincial, devoid of cosmopolitan tendencies. Only those who come to the right places are cosmopolitans. When Bruce shows that if even Alice Springs, on the edge of the desert, can be the framework of a global experience, then all places are potential global meeting places. Globalization is a real possibility right there where you find yourself. And that is even before mobile phones and the internet.

In addition, he says that the global meeting places are not uniform but precisely concrete and different. They are the result of the local preconditions, human and historical, but also of conditions on the far side of the city border and of people who are actually present. The Aboriginals are marginalized existences, poor and with a memory like a sieve about their history and with uncertain paths into white society after the colonial period. And the white people, too, fall between all the stools one can place out for them.

That, however, is what the local preconditions are, already characterized by the rift of earlier times between local conditions and influences from outside. It is the people who are there that make the globalized experience concrete, not necessarily in a positive way, but concrete all the same. You *are* not but *can be* global anywhere. New York is no more privileged a place by being global than Winesburg, Ohio. But New York is a privileged place by being one of the places that shape what being global is, also in Winesburg, Ohio. And therefore perhaps a more exciting place to be as a participant in global reality than Alice Springs. But not more global, only global in a special way. Literature does not have to deal with New York or Paris to be global.

In that way, places become fundamentally unstable. They have always been so, come to that. Empires have emerged and submerged in the course of history. But this has happened over so large a time span that they have exceeded the length of a human life. Those who have lived while the upheavals have been rapid and violent have experienced living in an abnormal and turbulent period and, under all circumstances, an unpleasant time. That was the case for Møller around 1820. Today, even radical changes take place to the appearance, functions and meanings of our places as a normal process within the space of one human life. This changes our perception of the relation between place and movement.

The Indian-American sociologist Arjun Appadurai suggests in *Modernity at Large* (1996) that we describe places as temporary hubs for flows at various levels and of various types. To describe them, he uses the old ending '-scape', as in 'landscape', 'cityscape', 'seascape' and 'playscape'. This applies not only to a physical place but constitutes a whole that is linked together in a particular domain by certain rules of the mutual connections and movements between the individual elements. A 'landscape' was defined in the Middle Ages on the basis of the law that held the land, people, buildings and activities of an area together, not on the basis of geography. The Dane Law was law as landscape in medieval England and landscape as law. Later, aesthetic laws also play a part, in the conception of the landscape, as in the cases of Møller or Campe. These places are held together by aesthetic principles for a holistic experience.

Appadurai outlines five such -scapes. They organize flows of particular things, so that they can form hubs around the Earth, places with soft and flexible boundaries. Where the strongest flows meet are the places that make a difference in globalization, such as New York, Shanghai or Rio de Janeiro. They contribute to changing the direction of the flows, and to the hubs being able to move geographically and culturally. Other places are affected by the same flows, but without being able to affect or move them in the same way.

It may sound a bit odd to combine flows and -scapes, a movement with a site, but the point is to find a new word for a new phenomenon. New types of place must not be mixed together with the place praised by Ørsted and Møller, but at the same time, the term must be such that we can connect a new kind of place, like financescape, with known meanings. So Appadurai chooses the ending -scape, which we already know, and connects it to new phenomena. The term 'landscape' (or landskip) for a particular slice of our surroundings as well as its aesthetic representation was also new in the fifteenth century when our view of the relation between nature and culture and man's role in connecting the two took a new turn, so the manoeuvre is not unknown when things change. Appadurai lists financescapes, ehtnoscapes, ideoscapes, technoscapes and mediascapes. They cover flows of money, demographic movements, ideological movements, technological dispersals and streams of information (Appadurai 1996: 33).

As mentioned, it is a sketch, and Appadurai, perhaps slightly naively, only mentions things that flow and that occasionally flow together and form temporary local fixed points. It always ends up sounding as if it all happens of its own accord. However, there has to be someone that causes it to happen where it actually happens. It is those people and places that are the focus of literature, not the flow in itself. It is by actively taking part in these flows, at an individual and collective level, that we can help change them, stop them or modify them, no matter whether we are borne along the flowing current or not. Everything can take place anywhere, but everything does not actually do so. Place-bound individuals are thus far from being a matter of indifference in globalization, and the traditions they carry with them likewise so. They are in the flows and essential to their intensity and directions. Only from this perspective can we understand flows as more than flows, as cultural transformations (cf. Urry 2000; Elliott and Urry 2011).

The French anthropologist Claude Lévi-Strauss has pondered on this fact. He has lived through the whole of the twentieth century as a personal and cultural experience, fortified by his work as an anthropologist. He has been a key researcher and cultural personality in France and the world, maintaining the tension between the local and the great outside world as a basic characteristic of human self-understanding, with consequences for ethics, politics, science and art.

He started his work in Brazil in the region where the Tupinambas once lived before they were exterminated. These were the people who the first discoverers described as cannibals, but, as we saw in Chapter 5, also as civilized people in their own way. Here, the Europeans saw their own cruelty during colonization reflected which represented a major challenge to their own self-understanding and action at home on the continent. After this, we became constantly split between our view of ourselves viewed through the lens of European values, and the view that was revealed on the basis of our negative actions, at home and abroad, fostered by the same values but ending up reversing them. There, then, young Claude turns up to do half a year's fieldwork in the 1930s. Waving his hand at Jean de Léry he knew he was entering the area where the Europeans' view of themselves had already been turned upside-down once before.

At the end of his memoir *Tristes Tropiques* (1955), he evaluates this experience of being inside and outside at one and the same time, of seeing himself with the eyes of others and his own eyes, and he considers this as being a fundamental way of understanding humanity. He too uses the idea of a flow as an image but in a more comprehensive sense than Appadurai:

> As he moves forward within his environment, Man takes with him all the positions that he has occupied in the past, and all those that he will occupy in the future. He is everywhere at the same time, a crowd which, in the act of moving forward, yet recapitulates at every instant every step it has ever taken in the past. For we live in several worlds, each more true than the one within it, and each false in relation to that within which it is itself enveloped. Some of these worlds may be apprehended in action, others exist because we have them in our thoughts: but the apparent contradictoriness of their co-existence is resolved by the fact that we are constrained to accord meaning to those worlds which are nearer to us, and to refuse it to those more distant. Truth lies rather in the progressive expansion of meaning. ... As an anthropologist I am no longer, therefore, the only person to suffer from a contradiction which is proper to humanity as a whole and bears within it the reason for its existence. Only when I isolate the two extremes does the contradiction still persist. ... Like the pebble which marks the surface of the wave with circles as it passes through, I too must first throw myself into the water if I am to plumb the depths. (Lévi-Strauss 1961: 395, 396)

Bruce Chatwin's *The Songlines* form such rings on the water while he is throwing himself out into them in order to link his own and the local world that surrounds him, without isolating them as extremes. Møller does so only indirectly while he trundles off on his ship, and everything is turned upside-down. But he does so. Literature is a form that presents the experience of living in several simultaneous worlds in motion and view things from a number of simultaneous points of view that go beyond our own framework. As such literature is a concrete model for global thinking, it gives our places meaning as changing meeting places which are more real and comprehensive than anonymized flows.

On the Move

Freeze!

Freeze! Freeze! the out-of-breath policeman shouts repeatedly when the criminal is about to be caught up with. That order also covers, generally speaking, the attitude of movement that has been familiar to us from thousands of years.[1] Unease about movement, especially movement away from home, is deeply anchored in our culture. In ancient times, that wisdom was transferred into sayings and other maxims: Cobbler, stick to your last! East, West, home's best. Those who were banished, were reduced to wandering unprotected and outlawed creatures on the restless highways, as happened to Oedipus as far back as ancient Greece after he had solved the riddle of the gods, been in bed with his mother and put out his own eyes. We feel for him and the likes of him in awe, fear and pity, but would not like to share their fate. The Flying Dutchman, Robin Hood and Romeo are other examples of people outlawed or banished but leaving more ambiguous impressions. It has never been possible to encapsulate just like that the old scepticism regarding those who went gallivanting about into one unambiguous meaning.

When we draw nearer to modern times, movement is on its way to accentuate its twilight-grey shades of meaning. The 'sentimental' European travellers of the eighteenth century in the manner of Laurence Stern's erratic travelogue or the adventurous travellers of the nineteenth century like Lord Byron combined an ambiguous attitude to both moving and staying. Not unlike Bruce Chatwin, many of them were fuelled by equal quantities of delight in and a dread of travelling transformed into sensitive and often impressionistic travel accounts carried by an unstoppable curiosity towards all things foreign and new, like modern technology.

However, from an age-old collective perspective, cultures are founded by those who travel. It can either be mythical heroes, who set out and founded new cities and societies, or gods who created the universe and all its kingdoms and lands, to which they subsequently offer their divine services. Some people can't quite manage to stop the movement, while the game is good, like nomads, gipsies, hunters and collectors. They were, and are, considered in myths, literature and broader cultural contexts to be people that were only tolerated among the home-grown, referred to special areas or thrown out into the nature that many felt they had hardly just left. Besides which, they really ought to settle down and get themselves a decent job. They do not define the cultural norms that have dominated the cultures of the world since the first peasants and urban societies.

From that point of view, travellers become heroes in one culture, but tyrants and terrorists in another – expulsions and exterminations are a constant undercurrent in the long history of movements: from the Israelites in Egypt and Babylon via the war expeditions of the Huns in Europe and the fate of indigenous peoples in the colonies up to the Palestinians on the West Bank and other global influxes of refugees. All cultures have collective movement narratives about their own foundation and the simultaneous destruction of others. The founding of a culture is such a dual movement, with the local narratives normally forgetting the destructive side they are responsible for. Other places than Scandinavia are sure to have other stories about the havoc wreaked by the Vikings across Europe than the glorious accounts the sagas wants to relate.

At the individual level, things look different. Movements are for selected exceptions, those who become heroes in our narratives, like Ulysses, the boy who set out in order to get to know fear, the journeying troubadours, Vikings, dark-skinned desert knights, explorers and many more besides. They exceed all the norms one can bring to mind that cement a society together. Despite this, they come home with riches or create pictures that can lift our self-awareness off the hinges. They are tempting and dangerous at one and the same time. We must admire them, as long as we don't imitate them. Yet, they supply an inexhaustible supply of material for stories that also contribute to the identity formation of the settlers.

The narrative is one form of presentation where the many ambiguities of movement acquire a meaning that can build a bridge between its ambiguous collective necessity and its equally unsettling individual exception. Another is the border-crossing movement happening on the spot. It too creates its heroes. This is sport where athletes attempts to go beyond the border of what is physically possible for the human body, or just the lazy everyday body of most of us, from the Olympics of Antiquity in honour of the gods, via tournaments in honour of the family up to modern sport or fitness training in honour of myself. Just as movement across geographical borders has become a possibility for everyone in their commuting everyday lives and charter travel leisure, sport has also become every person's business – in a youth and health obsessed culture even an obligation.

If one had said to people prior to the ending of the eighteenth century that they must make sure to exercise their bodies sufficiently, they would have stared at one in disbelief. How else could one work or even move around? The human body sets the standard for all movement, also when it placed itself on the back of a horse, in a carriage, in a sedan chair, on a ship – or later on a bicycle. It determined the tempo of work, transportation and communication. No one dreamt that things could be any different. Neither Aladdin's genie of the lamp nor Leonardo da Vinci's flying machines were of this world. Even with the introduction of writing, the use of paper, jungle drums and a few pigeons, it is still the movement of the human body that sets the general form for the speed. For that reason, the messenger has since ancient times had a central cultural function, with his messages and accounts, and even his own god, Hermes. Coming from outside, the messenger and postman stirred up movements within the protective walls of the town and camp. In stories and dramas, he creates decisive sudden movements in the action. He has long since been replaced by telephones and electronics, both in storytelling and everyday life. It was not unhazardous to be a messenger. He could be the first victim if the message was a bad one. Today, we turn off the mobile phone or unplug.

Knowledge, stories, gossip, commodities, money and news – everything moved via the body. It was the self-evident driving force for all mutual movements in communication, war, trade and love. It was the tacit standard for distance and movement in such measurements as inches, feet, handfuls and days of journey whether on foot, horse or in a carriage – if not derived from the human body at least from the body of other organisms, all of which are more meaningful than such abstract measurements as decilitres and kilometres an hour. Lastly, the body was the nucleus of the imagery one used for life from cradle to grave being a journey or a voyage, for cognition being a journey into the unknown, and for a mind drifting away, or when we hold our heads high, do not knuckle under, but put our backs into something. In short, the body was the medium that all movement and distance in space and time had as its starting point. The movement takes place in one direction at a time, for that is what the body is capable of, first away, then back home. The away movement is the dangerous one, the return home movement is the calming and generally speaking more positive one, for there movement stops, although a changed home may take us by surprise. So, the two movements can be considered independently of each other as two single, one-way movements, each with their separate meaning and cultural value.

This conception defined not only patterns of human movement but also antiquity's understanding of the organization of all of nature across cultural boundaries based on the essential placeness of all things, as defined in Aristotle's theory of nature. Moreover, it indicated how people could find their place in it. This is not all that simple, for people run counter to the common theory of nature. Things of every kind only exist in accordance with their nature when they are at rest in the place that is natural to them. But of all things, human beings are special creatures. They can move of their own accord to places where they do not belong, and even have a tendency to do so from sheer pleasure and their own will – into the domains of the gods or to foreign parts outside the jurisdiction of countries or gods. They simply cannot help themselves. And that is the worst of it all. In that way, they admittedly destabilize societies, but individually they also get onto the wrong paths. The classical tragedies and narratives deal with what happens because people cannot stay calm and stay put. And it is quite unequivocal: things go wrong for them, but not until after they have opened our eyes to sides of reality, we otherwise would not know anything about.

By the mid-nineteenth century, we are approaching different times from the old ones, although old meanings have not been lost. New meanings are under way, with modern technology such as trains, cars, planes, telegraphy, the telephone, electronic and digital media, and they shake the classical foundations of our understanding of movement. Jules Verne's novels from the end of the nineteenth century about circumnavigating the globe on land and under the sea, journeys to the moon and the centre of the Earth, deal with how movement is stretched out between body and technology. He gives meaning to movement in the transition between the monopoly of the body to define the meaning of movement and the new role of technology as the extension of the body. He did so before technology makes itself completely independent, detaching itself from the body as a troublesome deadweight for technology's possibilities for movement as we know it today (Giedion 2013).

The body is now no longer the foundation for our understanding of movement, and certainly not the only yardstick. It is just one medium among others. Sometimes, it is necessary for certain forms of motion; in other instances, it can be selected or deselected as we like. Even the movements that belong to the standard method for procreating children can be replaced by more complex and comprehensive movements between deep-freezing, test tubes and surrogate mothers. We are also familiar with this development at the more trivial everyday level: shall we walk or take the car to the cinema? Naturally, only after we have been on the internet, fetched the newspaper or phoned or texted to someone solely with the use of text-hooked movements of the thumb. One of the friends has seen the film in London, or just passed the cinema on his way home to see what films are on. It also depends on where the film is being shown. Perhaps we don't have to move somewhere else at all, but just buy a DVD for home use or access Netflix or some other streaming service.

On that basis, we consider each movement and each medium for movement as the subject of a choice between alternatives which leads to the same goal. In other words, measurement of movement becomes relative. This corresponds to what we all have already experienced at the train station. Our train is standing still, and the train next to it starts to move. For a moment, we are unsure if we are moving in one or the other direction, or if we are standing still. Our body and senses cannot determine it, but move in more than one direction at the same time. Every movement, in the same way, is an interaction between other movements, media and possibilities for movement.

In literature, that kind of movement acquires meaning via many interwoven narratives. In the traditional understanding, the body was the *entire* basis for the meaning movement acquired. The limbs and strength of the body are our innate possibility to move and expand our world. But in recent times, the body is only *part* of the basis for that meaning, and it is determined by the choice between alternative media for movement, not by the special capacity of the body.

The distance is still determined by the medium of movement that we choose, even though it no longer needs only be the body. For that reason, there are always several distances between the same places. To travel away and return home do not have to be equally long, for we can choose to walk to our destination and return home by car. Not to mention the distance to another continent. It is always too far away to walk or to swim to, and as a rule too far away to sail to; it is normally a suitable distance to fly to, and sometimes too great a distance to phone to because of the time difference, while it is never too far away to send an e-mail or a text message to. The abstract measurements such as metres or kilometres an hour can sometimes be a useful neutral common denominator to avoid this confusion when we talk about distance in terms of time and effort, so that for a moment, we can raise ourselves above the medium of movement whether it is the body or other media.

The cultural meanings of movement are still caught by a conflict between the classical scepticism regarding movement and more recent forms of movement in the globalized communication culture. That is why the national landscape and one's home plus the entire classical mode of thought has received new nourishment over the past two centuries, while at the same time, science moved in the opposite direction by being transformed into the technology that creates our new possibilities for movement beyond the local anchoring of the body. Many anti-globalization movements and political parties live off the tension that can only express itself as an unease that things are moving a bit too quickly, and in particular moving with them.

When the meaning of movement is to be renewed, the most important challenge is therefore to connect the ever-topical historical belief in the reality of stasis and the place with the new and as yet incalculable consequences of the patterns of movement in a globalized world between body, means of transportation and media. Today, it is not a question of only giving meaning to the new aspects of this movement, as the media gurus attempt to do when, with laser light in their eyes, they rave about all distances and places having been done away with, and that we can be everywhere at the same time. The two tendencies of meaning influence each other, and it is this mutual exchange to which literature attempts to give meaning – not to an isolated modern form of movement without reference to local life.

One-way movements and cross-movements

The clash between the traditional and modern conception of movement can be violent, as in the short tale by the Anglophone South African Nobel Prize-winner Nadine Gordimer's short story 'The Ultimate Safari' (1991). It is one of the many colonial stories of expulsion and suppression, but without facile moralizing and with larger perspectives. The former because we see the events through the eyes of an eleven-year-old girl, old enough to catch sight of the important details while fleeing with her family, but not old enough to understand what she sees. She has neither patterns of experience nor models of knowledge at her disposal. And the perspectives widen out, because there are several kinds of movement going on at the same time.

War is taking place around the girl's village in Mozambique, a result of the fluid war situation in many parts of the continent, usually on a more or less clearly outlined international backdrop. It takes the form of local tribal warfare in one place, governmental terror elsewhere, late colonial wars in a third place, and everywhere with a hazy division between bandits, rebels, mercenary troops, fortune hunters and shady governmental forces. Her mother and father have disappeared into the black hole of war, and she is now attempting to flee with what is left of her family, along with a couple of hundred other villagers. A local leader takes them on an exhausting and hazardous journey on foot in the dead of night. The family finally arrives at another village where people speak the same language as herself. They stay there as refugees.

The shortest route to temporary safety is through the large national park, Kruger Park, in the northeastern corner of South Africa. The girl has no idea whether she is inside or outside the park, and why this place is a specially demarcated area with a fence round it. But she notes with surprise that some people have that opinion. She simply passes through a familiar landscape with plants, rivers and animals like those around her own village. Dangerous, perhaps, but first and foremost is familiar, even in the nocturnal darkness of the flight: 'But it looked just like the bush we'd been walking through all day, ... I didn't know we were away' (Gordimer 1994: 145, 151). In the new village, she is surprised to find that they speak her language: 'That's why they allow us to stay on their land. Long ago, in the time of our fathers, there was no fence that kills you, there was no Kruger Park between them and us, we were the same people under our own king, right from our village we left to this place we've come to' (Gordimer 1994: 151).

But she knows that Kruger Park is something special in some way or other. The real dangers are not due to the animals, but to the fence, police, guards and laws that forbid them to pass through the area or find food for themselves there. From sheer fear of being caught, her group does not even have time to wait for her grandfather who is left behind sucked up by the dark and the high vegetation. The park has been made by white people, she understands, and she knows that men from her village 'used to leave home to work there in the places where white people come to stay and look at the animals' (Gordimer 1994: 145). There are many different movements going on here: work and flight determined by the Whites, the Whites on safari, and then a repeat of the way they used to cross the bush on foot back in the village. This life has now been lost, as the disappearance of her grandfather beyond their control demonstrates. He was more than a person. He was a physical guarantee of the connection to the village, their entire past and the possibility of returning to it.

The girl does not understand why things are like this, but she registers that Kruger Park does something or other to her and her people. It separates people with the same language, so that to be together requires them to travel great distances in the shadow of war. It makes her land the White Man's land and most of all it changes their role on their own land. Although 'our country is a country of people and not animals', they are obliged 'to move like animals among the animals' (Gordimer 1994: 145, 146). When they emerge from the far side of the park, they have become placeless, determined only by the movement they have taken out into the unknown: 'There is nothing. No home,' the grandmother says in the new village (Gordimer 1994: 153).

Here, they are exposed to a new experience, the one that gives rise to the grandmother's fatalistic remark. 'Some white people came to take photographs of our people living in the tent – they said they were making a film' (Gordimer 1994: 152). The refugees are now animals among the animals, elements in a wild landscape, and chance pieces in the political jigsaw puzzle of other humans and perhaps misery pornography in TV prime time. Well-meaning, indifferent or aesthetic – we do not know.

In their flight, the girl and her family have now become entangled in a number of other movements than their cumbersome tour on foot away from home. Through modern media, they move out into an even larger world they cannot even dream of in their wildest imagination, even though they know it exists. With the film, they will probably come to America and other places 'far from here', after the agents of this world and its media corps have returned to their many homes. In contrast, the news media crew belongs to a world where moving back and forth across the globe is commonplace with bodies, machines and media. We could easily hear over lunch in any Western eatery: 'Oh really?! Have you just been to South Africa – why haven't you said anything about it? We might have met there.' Here, the refugee camp is a meeting place between mutually exclusive patterns of movement, yet all determined by the same global conditions. The girls started out in a one-way street and ended up in a busy intersection without knowing where all the roads come from or lead to.

There is also a further level of movement. The girl cannot reach that kind of conclusion herself. Yet, her limited point of view calls on the reader's supplementary experience, so that we can add perspectives that reach into our context of reading. Gordimer helps us on our way. The narrative has a short motto from a British tourist ad: 'The African Adventure Lives On ... You can do it!/The ultimate safari or expedition/ With leaders who know Africa./ – TRAVEL ADVERTISEMENT, Observer, LONDON, 27/11/88)' (Gordimer 1994: 143). The advertisement is addressed to white tourists, but it turns the girl's safari experience upside-down with devastating irony. She is on her first, last and greatest safari, the ultimate one, while the tourist is offered the safari of a lifetime, a one-time experience one absolutely must not miss, but which nevertheless can be repeated year after year. Just like the film team's shootings and the short story, the advertisement also applies to us.

The tourist trip is not a movement that is first an outward one and then a return home. From the outset, it is a double movement, one in which the travelling tourist's body moves in one direction but only because information and images about Africa have already moved the opposite way to reach them via other media. The movement assumes the form of an exchange in which wild animals through the media and money are exchanged in view of their symbolic values: the Western dream of a slightly exotic life in brief luxury or mild primitiveness, with hot water and a view of elephants, retained in the digital photographs that are sent home by e-mail while *en route*. We travel out on photographs and return home with photographs. So, in fact, there are not two movements but one collected movement, a *cross-movement*. This logic also goes deeper. Jorge Semprún related in Chapter 4 that not until fifteen years after his physical return from Buchenwald was he capable of carrying out the double movement between away and home as one movement. This occurred when he was able to transfer the journey to another medium, to literature. Only with *The Long Voyage* did his separate physical movements become combined into one cohesive double movement in his life.

From the girl's point of view, there is only a physical movement in one direction, a *one-way movement* away from her home, with no possibility of returning, for there is 'nothing', her grandmother tells her. If she had been able to return home, it would have been an entirely new movement in the opposite direction. The girl has changed from stasis to a movement she cannot stop. She can only reside in the language she shares with people in the new village. From now on, her body is no longer the most important determination of her movements. For the white tourists or the film people, and for the readers, there is a multiple movement in several directions at the same time. The physical movement of the body and the movement via the media move in their separate directions, but they cannot be separated, nor from the planes that have brought the film teams and the white safari tourists out there and provided jobs for some members of the girl's family. Less visible, but just as real, international political movements with the streams of capital from the armaments and tourist industry as well as other industries trail through the landscape along different but intersected trajectories together with the war that has set the girl in motion in the other direction. The girl is merely a pawn, although she *is* an integral part of the entire pattern of movements.

This whole intersection of movements also transports knowledge, information, symbols, images, memories, prejudices and ideas around in global movements – of war, nature, philanthropy, ethnicity and morals without fixed abodes but yet strongly influenced by the great entanglement of cultures. Literature focuses on this complex situation to give the movement meaning today. To distinguish unequivocally for everyone between the journey out and the journey back is impossible. But one thing is certain: the fundamental structure of movement is not the series of separate one-way movements that can be strung together or lined up as parallel movements but intersected cross-movements.

The traditional meaning of movement, however, is connected to one-way movements. In this context, movement is often conceived as being 100 per cent determined by the will of the traveller or someone else and is considered to begin from scratch. We have found those responsible, and we have a complete understanding of the movement. In the folk tale, the young man sets out without any equipment except a little good luck and his common sense. The movement only starts when the body sets itself in motion, and the movement always has a well-defined starting point that we can track down without taking into account what happened before the take-off. The girl thinks this too, but the story shows that this is not the case. There are always many preceding movements, not only the war, that determine our movements here and now, even if we are not aware of it. We do not set out from one particular place and start out on something new, but always react to the outcome of several overlapping cross-movements. Preceding every one-way movement, there are a series of cross-movements that decide its nature, medium and direction.

In Gordimer's text, the two basic conceptions of movement clash, turning the African village into a meeting place for cultural differences of global scope, determined by the conflict the various cross-movements are part of. Those kinds of conflicts are perhaps the closest we get to the modern meaning of movement. The body is still part of the basis that shapes the meaning, simply because the medium of movement cannot always be chosen. Sometimes, it can only be the body. We therefore hear about the arduous trip from village to village and the death of the grandfather. But in other case, the body is a matter of indifference. We do not hear a word about how the film team arrived in Africa or returns home. And it does not matter either. As regards them, only the movement through the film they shoot is important. The team consists of professional film people at work, and they can simply be replaced by others. Their individual physical presence does not make any vital difference. It is that world the reader lives in. And it is that world the girl clashes with and that destroys her and her family, just as effectively as the war she is fleeing from.

Between past and present

This connection between body, movement and distance is the prerequisite for the short story, even though it is not treated directly as a theme. The Indian-American writer Amitav Ghosh's *In an Antique Land* (1992) is more radical. Does the presence of the body ever make any difference at all to the cross-movements into which people all over the globe are whirled? That is the unexpressed question that underlies the movements of the novel between the Middle Ages and the present, across continents from India and the Middle East across Africa to Europe and the United States, and between international big cities and local villages. The novel leaves the answer hanging in the air.

Ghosh's book is not difficult to read, only to categorize. There are historical details from past and present, there are autobiographical details about an Indian main character whose name in Arabic is Amitab, and who narrates everything and digs into early history, and there are glimpses from various wars from the crusades to the build-up to the war in Iraq of the 1990s. The book belongs to the mixed genre of fact and fiction that some people call faction, but it is probably best just to call it prose. It is one of the works that needs the reader's supplementary knowledge to become anchored in reality, and that contains many substories and characters, so that we cannot help but activate that extra knowledge. Painstakingly and precisely, Ghosh uses the characters to flesh out the cultural clashes that have created narratives, history and life stories and keep doing so.

First and foremost, Ghosh wants to give us ideas about the connection between movement and distance across time and geography. The framework is two time periods: the Middle East in the Middle Ages during the crusades and in 1980–1990. There are a couple more time pockets, but they are only additions to the two main periods. It is the narrator who controls the movements between the places and, in particular, the movement between past and present. He is a young Indian anthropologist who is studying in present-day Egypt while living in a couple of villages, the small Lataîfa and its slightly larger competitor Nashawy. But it is mostly certain documents he comes across, both in Egypt and in the United States, which fire his imagination. They contain a medieval story about certain ambulating Arab and Jewish merchants who travel between Egypt, India and Aden. The story partly occurs in the same places where Amitab is staying. And these overlaps, combined with the documents, make certain movements possible between past and present parallel to the spatial trajectories, allowing them to reflect their similarities and dissimilarities in each other, discretely but precisely. All these movements taken together determine the lives of the places and characters. It is the diversity and nature of these movements that structure a book which, at first glance, can be seen to be only loosely put together.

The two periods emerge through the many movements as comprehensive cultural meeting places. The stable medieval world of trading from the Middle East and further east, that is disturbed by the battles of the crusades, seems partially opposed to the modern world of global conflict which only now and then has room for peaceful movement and coexistence. The former is mainly an open international space for movements that can be established and re-established; the latter mainly a global battle zone the dissimilarities of which penetrate via rumours and the media right into the way in which individuals interact with each other in the small villages.

Amitab follows the story of the two merchants, the Moslem Khalaf ibn Ishaq and the Jew Abraham Ben Yiju, during the latter half of the twelfth century. The crusades are raging between Christians and Moslems, but their story has to do with friendship and commerce, journeys with the exchange of goods and letters and meetings with mutual acquaintances and families. They circulate along with other persons at intervals of several years between Aden, Mangalore on the west coast of India and Cairo, that is still called 'the mother of the world' (Ghosh 1992: 80). All these places make up one place, a meeting place because of the movements that hold it together – materially, culturally and personally:

They made it their business to keep themselves well informed: From season to season, they followed the fluctuations of the prices of iron, pepper and cardamom in the markets of Cairo. They were always quick to relay news to their friends, wherever they happened to be, and they are sure to have kept themselves well abreast of the happenings in Syria and Palestine. (Ghosh 1992: 16)

The basis for this part of the book is the two merchants' personal letters that Amitab has access to. Some of them come originally from the Jewish synagogue in Cairo, *geniza*, and others from the United States, yet others have emerged in the nineteenth century, and others again, while the desert battle was in full swing between Rommel and Montgomery in 1942. Ravaging crusades also swept past during the merchants' age, but still on the periphery of the flourishing and open civilization of knowledge, tolerance and trade that the letters bear witness to, even though there is also a slight suspicion of cheating in money matters under way. The path of the sources to the public is a similar story: the manuscripts were mainly found in Cairo, worked on by a German academic who, in the midst of the Nazi madness of the mid-twentieth century, was a connoisseur of Judaism and Islam and travelled in the area. The documents are historical sources, and the story of their being found and interpreted is based on hard evidence, and as such quite simple to grasp.

The modern story with Amitab as a participant deals both with his studies and results and with his personal contacts and friendships with the inhabitants of the two Egyptian villages. Here the world is different from the open medieval world of intercontinental commerce, small and self-sufficient, but yet hospitable towards the visiting, young and not particularly experienced Indian researcher, who is about twenty years old. He takes great trouble to learn the local Arabic dialect and, from back home, has gained a little insight into local habits and customs. The lack of knowledge and understanding is presented with humour when the individual characters get into a clinch with each other, but the sinister perspectives when the war between Iraq and Iran and the run-up to the Gulf War re-echo in the background.

We meet the bigoted insufficiency of their mutually deficient ideas of each other's cultures and their conflicts, without the tolerant accommodating attitude of the medieval universe. The ideas have always run ahead of the characters, who lose their open-minded potential in the shadows which the prejudices cast ahead of them. Mixed ideas about Egypt have already come to Amitab before he leaves India in the opposite direction. Ideas about him have arrived before he himself appears on the scene, and make unnecessary the reverse journey by the Egyptians. What would the point be of going there? The half-truths from rumours and the media that have already moved into their world are more than enough.

Amitab and the inhabitants meet against the background of these simple cross-movements that turn the small village into a meeting place between cultures in a global perspective. Their meeting is both slightly coincidental and has nothing to do with mutual cultural interest. Amitab's work on the manuscripts does not have anything directly to do with his stay in the village. He just lives there. And the villagers do not have any special wish to receive precisely an Indian. But now he is there, and so he activates all the meanings that have already moved between Egypt and India, and the locals do the same. The great distances and movements are translated into the small everyday movements and accentuations of the distance between the inhabitants and Amitab while he goes around and is slightly queer in an inoffensive way.

Through the balance between smile and uneasiness in the depiction of the dialogues between the individual characters and in their mutual lack of knowledge, the reader is drawn into the narrative. This balance spans the fumbling but conciliatory way the characters treat each other and their differences. They all try to make their chance simultaneous presence seem necessary by relating actively towards each other, but with a distinct echo of the non-conciliatory global conflicts in the build-up to the Iraq war in the early 1990s. It looks innocent, but, like many other direct and indirect experiences from a global world in motion, it is charged with wide-ranging implications.

The body on the sideline

In the village, they are convinced that when Amitab has learned about Islam, he will drop his Hinduism and 'God willing, he will soon be one of us' (Ghosh 1992: 45), find himself a wife and return home and tell his fellow countrymen to stop their barbaric customs of cremation and omitting to circumcise boys and girls: 'When you go back, you should tell them about our customs and how we deal with such matters' (Ghosh 1992: 169). This traditional, local clash of cultures comes to a head when they discuss if India or Egypt has the best weapons compared to the West. Now, there are global topics at stake, fed by the movements of information circulating in the mass media. Amitab has an argument with the Imam:

> 'We have them too!' I shouted back at him. 'In my country we have all those things too; we have guns and tanks and bombs. And they're better than anything you've got in Egypt – we're a long way ahead of you.'
>
> 'I tell you, he's lying', cried the Imam, his voice rising in fury. 'Our guns and bombs are much better than theirs. Ours are second only to the West's.'
> (Ghosh 1992: 236)

The wrangling continues for some time before they are separated. Amitab realizes that he and the Imam have made verbal mincemeat of each other due of a conflict that, superficially, has nothing to do with them. Both of them have lost, because they do not personally manage to decide the conditions for the movement between their two cultures, not even when they meet face to face, body to body. Instead, they actualize contrary cultural movements of global dimensions that spread out above their heads, as well as inside their heads and language. The place they are standing on becomes a meeting place for these conflicts, a global encounter, not a locality on its own cultural conditions. They just happen to be present together in the same place.

The characters are in constant motion between the two villages and, as far as Amitab is concerned, also between the villages and Cairo or Alexandria, so that he can take care of his medieval project. He also travels on to Europe and the United States with the same aim, and returns once more. At the same time, his paths are crossed by those of the medieval merchants when he settles for a while in Mangalore on the Indian west coast. Meanwhile, the conflicts of the Middle East make their impact on the village, sending some into the army and others as guest workers to Baghdad to earn money to keep the family fed back home. And not all of them come back. Isma'il returns with travel in his blood, and Nabeel stays over there without Amitab ever seeing him again, even though he promises to visit him in Baghdad. But the war between Iran and Iraq and the threatening conflicts afterwards help to prevent this.

All the physical movements of the characters back and forth are not, however, what most commands attention. They just take place, as for the film team in Gordimer's short story. The troublesome transportations of the medieval period are hardly mentioned and present-day flights and train journeys not at all. The body as a medium of movement is uninteresting in itself and completely determined by the more important cross-movements that are borne by the media and travelling rumours about each other's norms and habits. The only thing of interest is what happens there where the travellers make a stop, and where they behave as they do because they all are a part of these movements, whether they travel or are tied to their homes, as most of the villagers are. The body is only used to confirm the untranscendable distance in time and space and only used as an exception, a temporary surmounting of the distance in individual conversations between friends and intimates.

All movements in the Middle Ages and the present are primarily linked to mutual exchanges and communication at the places where the movement intersect and coalesce. The body here is only one medium for the exchanges among many other possible ones, and not a particularly obvious one. The basic structure of the cross-movements is exchanges, not the one-way movements that have the body as model. With or without a body, the cross-movements have communication as their basic form, and the distances manifest themselves first and foremost as communicative distance. It is not us who live in a communication society, but the communication society that lives in us by structuring our patterns of movement and the movement of the bodies in relation to each other.

The medieval scenes are based on the letters that govern the movement patterns of the merchants in the past and enable Amitab to understand them in the present. He himself must make do with trying to get on in inadequate Arabic. The movements in the village during the book are completely dependent on the media and technology which, arriving from outside, create movement and communication: a tractor, a TV, a water pump that supplies the water, electricity that links the village with the outside world, conscription to the army, and travelling stories. Most detailed is the endless series of questions and difficult answers that are exchanged between the villagers and Amitab, and that show their language deficiency and inability to convert the ideas circulating as limited knowledge and prejudices about each other into a basis for mutual understanding. This situation exposes a distance that is greater than bodily movements can overcome, even when they have moved in right close to each other.

When the body was the most important and only medium of movement, it constituted the actual possibility to move beyond the local boundaries with regard to geography, knowledge and experience. It marked the limit of the scope of movement and determined the positive or negative difference to the meaning produced by any movement. Its scope was gradually extended with newer technologies and media and as a kind prostates which reinforce the power of the body. This is what the village experiences with tractor, telephone and TV arriving during Amitab's stay. But technologies and media can also deprive the body of its privileged status as the fundamental medium of movement. For when other media than the body basically decide the framework for possible movements and a radius that the body cannot fulfil by itself, it ultimately becomes an impediment to movements otherwise determined by the body but now getting their meaning by being measured against new technologies and media.

With or without hair

That is also what happens in Lataîfa. The body is superfluous or slightly in the way, even when the characters are facing each other and actually talk about the body as an expression of distance and movement between the two cultures in India and Egypt. Here, it blocks the path to communicative movements by creating misunderstandings and increasing the distance. Amitab is an innocent youth. One day he sees a couple of ducks mating in Lataîfa and is well aware what they are up to, but is surprised that he can actually see in detail what is happening. And the 17-year-old Jabil gets, so to speak, under his skin (Ghosh 1992: 61–64). Sex, gender and the body are universal subjects, but also those which most clearly and spontaneously reveal cultural differences between views of the body: "'You were watching like it was a film, ya Amitab," [Jabil] said, laughing. "Haven't you seen ducks do that before?" "No," I said. His laughter was infectious …' (Ghosh 1992: 61).

When Jabil then starts interrogating Amitab about his knowledge of sex, he feels that Amitab is more ignorant than is acceptable. But it is first and foremost the Arabic word that Amitab does not know, something Jabil – who has never been outside the village – cannot grasp. "'You mean you've never heard of …?" It was the same word again' (Ghosh 1992: 61). – What Amitab eventually knows or does not know, he does not at any rate know the Arabic words for intimate physical details. Jabil now wants to know about circumcision in India:

> Of course you have circumcision where you come from, just like we do? … 'Some people do', I said …. In Arabic the word 'circumcise' derives from a root that means 'to purify': to say of someone that they are 'uncircumcised' is more or less to call them impure.
>
> 'Yes', I answered, 'yes, many people in my country are "impure"'. I had no alternative; I was trapped by language.
>
> 'But not you …' He could not bring himself to finish the sentence.
>
> 'Yes', I said. My face was hot with embarrassment and my throat had gone dry: 'Yes, me too.'
>
> He gasped and his incredulous eyes skimmed over the front of my trousers. (Ghosh 1992: 62)

A similar scene takes place immediately afterwards, now about how things are in Amitab's home country when it comes to shaving bodily hair in both visible and invisible places. And here also, to Jabil's amazement, they are not quick to resort to the razor.

It is not only because of the local petty-mindedness that things go wrong. Amitab himself is something of a cage bird without much life experience. He has only read about what things are like in Lataîfa and is unsure about how he is to behave. Is he to stand out, try to ingratiate himself or just refrain from getting involved? He is incapable of letting the situation create the contact. At the same time, the Arabic language ties him in knots. Jabil compares with a film when he interrogates Amitab about what he has seen with the ducks. It is words and media that create both contact and misunderstanding, not what they actually see and sense in each other and around them. Their presence together is entwined in communication structures, media and ideas that have already set themselves in motion across the continents. These structures define what is motion and distance, not the body.

That evening, Amitab has found the word for mating and can join in the conversation, but by then it is too late to explain that he was not as ignorant as

Jabil believed. Jabil tells the other boys how things are, and they are ready for a new round of stories:

> 'No', said Jabil, 'he's like a child, I told you. That's why he's always asking questions.' 'Shouldn't we tell him?' one of the boys said. 'How's he going to grow up if he doesn't beat the ten?' 'It's no use', said Jabir. 'He won't understand; he doesn't know a thing. Look, I'll show you.' (Ghosh 1992: 64)

Body and sex are shared human facts beyond language, but precisely because the cultural differences are very much to the fore in the various languages and ideas, the boys do not get down to this level. Instead of the boys, without too much difficulty, being able to see Amitab in the flesh and with or without hair, what happens is that words, prejudices and stories proliferate at every new turn of the conversation. On the surface, the communicative movements cross each other, but in reality, they mark a gradual widening of the distance the words try to bridge. And over and above the individual conversation on the spot there lies the idea of the body as a place for honour and shame that they all share and that prevents them from simply taking a look. That is why the word 'impure' is difficult for any of them to get past their lips.

On the other hand, there is the infectious laughter, the boys' eagerness to know and Amitab's desire to understand and his ability to smile and the others' eye for the laughable. He thinks that Jabil's disbelief is probably because he imagines the pubic hair sprouting out of the bottom of his trousers. Smiles and laughter create spontaneously and briefly a local pocket where the cross-movements meet and make contact, simply because the boys and Amitab are present together and actively try to reach each other. In the laughter, the large and small movements in words, media and ideas transform Lataîfa into a temporary meeting place between India and Egypt. Here, cultural norms, religion, technology and international conflicts and arms race meet. These continue when some of the young men of the village are sent off to war or out into the world as migrant workers. Before, the older boys actually did experience that they could create a brief solidarity between people of different identity with an echo in the great outside world, without removing the differences. Movement *is* possible.

However, Amitab's real project is neither the trade routes nor the correspondence of the great merchants or an anthropological field study.

Already at the beginning of the book, he points out that a slave is mentioned in the correspondence between the merchants, though just in passing. But he was there somewhere or other and moved around with his masters. It gradually transpires that the slave's name was certainly Bomma, a name with roots in the culture around Mangalore, where both the merchants and Amitab have lived for a period of time. Hence, Bomma and Amitab are fellow countrymen, and both of them are pawns in the large patterns of movement. Amitab is himself merely a young scholar and a somewhat naive young man who is constantly dependent on other people's knowledge and instructions in order to get around. The movements are controlled by the exchanges of words, things and knowledge he comes across when he turns up. In Mangalore and in the letters, the connection goes both ways at the same time between past and present, with Amitab and the slave as the connecting link. One notices his indirect interpretation of himself and his place in the story when he discovers the slave's name and domicile: 'It was thus that Bomma finally came of age and was ready at last to become a protagonist in his own story' (Ghosh 1992: 254).

Amitab's story also relates that the narratives of movement do not deal nowadays with the great heroes as in the classical narratives but with themselves as the small links in the chain which, with small jerks, actively participate wherever they are. Nabeel went off to Baghdad, just as Bomma and Amitab set sail out into the world. The main thing is not only the great synthetic moments when past and present, near and far meet and indicate that the cross-movements can be intensified into meeting places. It is the small movements of everyday life.

One of the last movements Amitab carries out is a telephone call from New York to his friend Nabeel from the village. Nabeel is now in Baghdad as a migrant worker. It is a conversation that peters out, gets lost in the sands. Disturbance on the line, a bad connection and difficulties for Nabeel to receive a call from the United States in Saddam Hussein's Iraq around 1990 get in the way. On those conditions, America is not particularly 'far away', but can move to Baghdad via the telephone with the same maybe harmful effect for Nabeel's physical life conditions as if a real-life American had stood there personally. Nabeel's employer grunts. Amitab promises to come and visit him personally, but he does not succeed. He only gets to the village. 'Nabeel had vanished into the anonymity of History' (Ghosh 1992:

353), just like the slave Bomma and maybe Amitab himself. Those are the last words of the book. There were no letters, conversations, exchanges with Nabeel as a participant.

Just before the book ends, we see the closest Amitab gets to an understanding of his own movements:

> My mind went back to that evening when I first met Nabeel and Isma'il; how Nabeel had said: 'It must make you think of all the people you left at home when you put that kettle on the stove with just enough water for yourself.' It was hard to think of Nabeel alone, in a city headed for destruction. (Ghosh 1992: 353)

The personal meetings and sensitivity of the everyday world also gathers together near and far, present and past on a smaller scale, but in the same way as the great meetings of cultures. This is what Amitab experiences with Nabeel and in the story of the slave and thereby of himself. The memory of the concrete meetings as movements filtered through different media at one and the same time live on in Amitab's way of moving and understanding the world, until it too will disappear at some point along with the others he has met in the course of his travels.

So, it is possible as a single individual on the edge of history to create the horizontal exchange between coexisting places across the globe and the vertical one between past and present. We carry the possibility to create global meeting places with us wherever we move. When Amitab is back in the village, he speaks with one of his old acquaintances, Shaikh Musa, about Nabeel and Jabil:

> 'Do you know why they left?' I asked. 'Was there any specific reason?'
> Shaikh Musa shrugged. 'Why does anyone leave?' he said. 'The opportunity comes, and it has to be taken.' (Ghosh 1992: 152)

The movement does not start and end at a distinct place, and the medium within which we realize the possibility for movement is not always the same. Such is life, local life too, even when there is no deep underlying philosophy. It is up to us to grab the opportunity if the closed environments open up for the movements in many media and directions that cross each other. For that reason, we will conclude in a different village than Lataîfa.

The back of beyond

In the depths of the Welsh countryside lies Black Hill, close to the village of Rhulen, in the back of beyond. The hill has given its name to Bruce Chatwin's debut novel *On the Black Hill* (1982). It takes place in the first eighty years of the twentieth century and takes place in that place only. If anything has ever been a native soil novel, a green, green-grass-of-home novel, an agrarian novel or regional literature, this is it. We do not move from the spot. And a tiny spot on the map it is. Far off, infinitely far off is the end of the neighbour's land.

We follow two twins, Lewis and Benjamin, who resemble each other like two clods of soil. They are like Siamese twins. If one of them is in pain, the other one feels is, no matter where he is. The place enters one's body and is stronger than distance and movement. They live on the farm where they were born, with the ironical name 'The Vision', with fittings and furnishings as in their parents' time. But one remembers and holds onto one's money. Without ever having seen an elephant, people have a rogue elephant's quality memory. When an affront has smouldered for a number of years and is ready to be repaid, it is as fresh as on the insult's first day.

Despite this, there is a draught from the outside world, with colonies, world wars and technological changes. Even the brothers finally go up in a plane and, utterly thrilled, see their farm from the air on their eightieth birthday on display from the slightly turbulent angle of eternity. Now they see things as if for the first time and from outside. This occurs when nephew Kevin gives them a ride. He has got a girl pregnant, tried smoking pot and mainly likes to hang out and not do any work. But the young couple gets the farm even so, and immediately sets about getting rid of all the junk from the turn of the century. Whether it is a vision or not remains unknown, but new times have come, and here the novel stops, while the last of the old people in the area disappear – and we do not know what these new times will bring.

The mother of the twins, Mary, has lived in India as a young woman and has a keen eye for the world with books, a piano, cultivated tastes and exciting recipes. Benjamin also becomes proficient in a kitchen. She has fallen for the taciturn Amos and has married below her class. The local lawyer never forgets this social mishap. And even Benjamin has for a while, away from Lewis and

'The Vision' done a stint in the army at the end of the First World War. But he never got any further than the nearest camp, was impossible to discipline from sheer introversion, was bullied and was a broken man after that. The world outside is behind an invisible wall impossible to climb.

The name of the farm, 'The Vision', comes from the former owners, the Bickerton family, who had earned money dealing with India and bought an estate with the farm belonging to it. Gradually, the members of the family got scattered across Europe and even further afield. But that does not affect the place. It could just as easily have been included in Ghosh's novel or Gordimer's short story. The people of Black Hill and Lataîfa would have understood each other and the girl's grandmother in Africa. The three texts deal with the same cracked local world, but from different angles.

The narrator here feels solidarity with people, with the same sparing use of hand-kneaded language as theirs, without picturesque descriptions and with an irony that more expresses a non-understanding scepticism towards the limited universe than a know-all arrogance. It is not a special world Chatwin is describing, just a world with individuals. The narrator in Ghosh, on the other hand, constantly has to adopt an attitude towards issues to do with strange Indian customs and somewhat reluctantly exposes how limited Lataîfa is, despite the people in the place he feels affectionate about. In Gordimer, the reader looks at the world at the same time with the wondering gaze of the girl and from the reality of films and tourist trips in which we live. But in Chatwin's book, the characters are just as impenetrable to each other and to us as the world outside is to Benjamin, Lewis, the Watkins family and the others. Reading the book calls for the inclusion of the reader's supplementary experience underneath the words and between the lines if we are to be able to understand the novel as a form of presentation of the movement between the place and the world outside and not primarily of the place and its characters.

We can do that in this short passage about the end of the Second World War. A German POW, Manfred, has arrived. He has settled in well, for all that about the war and the bombings of London and reflex-determined hatred of the Germans is unknown here. He is a stranger and is judged as one usually does such individuals – how well do they settle in? He is a farmer like the rest of them, so the distance from the world outside is not altered by a little bit of war or a German who, what's more, is really good with poultry.

So, on a lovely spring morning, the war came to an end, but a bold headline in the *Radnorshire Gazette* shows more local priorities:

51½ lb SALMON GRASSED
AT COLEMAN'S POOL
Brigadier tells of 3-hour
struggle with titanic fish. (Chatwin 1982: 188)

Also, Manfred couldn't care less about the fall of Germany, although he brightened up a few months later when seeing in the *News of the World* a photograph of the mushroom cloud over Nagasaki:

'Is good, *Ja?*'
    'No.' Benjamin shook his head, 'it's terrible.'
    '*Nein, nein!* Is good! Japan finish! War finish!'
    That night the twins shared the same nightmare: Their bed-curtain had caught fire, their hair was in flames, and their heads burnt down to sooty fragments. Manfred showed no signs of wanting to return home when the first contingents of prisoners were sent back. He spoke about settling down in the area, with a wife and a poultry farm. The twins encouraged him to stay. (Chatwin 1982: 89)

Like the rest of the novel, this passage must be read with two pairs of glasses. The narrator leaves things, on the whole, to us. Through one set of lenses, the world is as enclosed as an open-air museum, but at the same time with a will to survive that silently accepts the foreign in small doses and changes it. It is put into position in relation to the local norms and stays in the place assigned it.

Yet, the text can also be read as a warning that the outside world is going to swamp the local people and their lives, without their being able to do anything about it. Their adaptation is a pure farcical illusion with a frailty they haven't the faintest idea about, and it contains a hidden disdain for the world outside. The danger only announces itself in their subconscious dreams and a war on the margins of their world, not in the attitudes and actions of broad daylight. But it is there. Throughout the novel, we have to keep the two possibilities open and can never settle complacently in either of them. We move across the border between inner and outer in a permanent exchange, communication and negotiation – a movement that also defines this place, even though the inhabitants are left standing on the platform after the train of globalization has left. Chatwin writes about the same kind of places in the weightless *The Songlines* as in the mulch-heavy *On the Black Hill*, despite the fact that they occur in widely different locations and use different forms of presentation. The modern meaning of movement lives in this opposition, and as yet has hardly gone beyond these complementary points of view.

All three texts discussed in this chapter give meaning to movement in a literary form of presentation that builds on a double structure where bodily movements and movements via a multitude of other media determines each other under constantly changing conditions. The double structure is mainly administered by different textual levels of which the narrator's level, at times indirectly, gives the outer world a place in the local world. At the same time, the local world is opened for a move beyond the local place, threatening for some, irresistible for others; unrecognized by some, obvious for others, but a real choice for everyone. In other words, the form of presentation makes movement an inescapable choice, also for those who wouldn't dream of making that choice.

But to read the enclosed space from this double perspective means we have to force an entry into it, almost in the same hostile way as the outside world that the characters, like Gordimer's grandmother, seek to keep at arm's length. We do not display solidarity as readers. In Ghosh, we read from the perspective of the open world which he, via the hesitant Amitab, places outside the small villages and their partially non-understanding everyday participation in it. At one moment, we take the view of a sovereign narrator with active decisions and overview, at another anonymously that of the slave Bomma, Nabeel, Jabil and Amitab himself, or Gordimer's girl who also make choices. Actually, all of them choose but at times without any clear sense of choice or comprehensive understanding. But even so they choose to move and allow themselves to be moved in a world with its indistinct and borderless conditions and subsequently to disappear out into anonymity once more.

In Chatwin, however, we have to prise open the world and the characters who would prefer us not to meddle. This corresponds, as we saw in Chapter 3, to what Karen Blixen writes in her essay 'Blacks and Whites in Africa'. In Kenya the most meaningful meeting for me took place – here I came to meet the dark, indigenous people …. We had not sought each other out, I had not come to the country to study the Blacks, and they would have preferred me to have stayed away. But brought together by fate, we now came to belong together in our everyday lives. We were humans under shared fortunes – if the rain failed us Whites, it was also disastrous for the Blacks, if the water gave out on our safaris, all of us would thirst together. (Blixen 1985: 57)

This shared everyday life rests on different conditions for those involved in it, but everyone is linked to a movement across the distance between the local and that which lies on the far side of our various localities. Sometimes, it calls for an empathetic sense of solidarity to understand this togetherness, at other times a confronting counter-understanding. It is always a cross-movement in which various mediated movements are active, while at the same time, the movements change the distances over which we move. Such conditions are ours today, and they pin the responsibility on us too – for the meaning the movement is to assume, and for the consequences those meanings have anywhere we may happen to be while we tentatively move forward with new directions and contacts.

Perspectives: World Literature or Literature around the World?

Small town, global impact

Readers may have wondered why I have discussed the relation between literature and globalization with 'experience of globalization' as my key word and not simply use the heading 'world literature'.[1] I left this term in Chapter 1. It is now time to include it in a broader perspective. I will do so by time-travelling back to an important place, Weimar, in the nineteenth century, probably with my half-bruised body confined inside an uncomfortable and slow-moving horse-drawn coach, rehearsing my capacity to translate from and into German and hoping to meet the famous cosmopolitan Goethe, already part of European cultural memory before his death.

Without Johann Wolfgang von Goethe, Weimar would have been an unknown place, even a non-place, somewhere on the Eastern outskirts of Central Europe. With Goethe, Weimar became for more than a generation a cultural centre for both the German-speaking part of Europe and for Europe as a whole, also after he passed away in 1832. The city was the capital, *Hauptstadt*, of one the many small German principalities, Sachsen-Weimar. Actually, it was more *Haupt* than *Stadt*. The head was that of Goethe, reflecting most of the world on the inside, while the city in Goethe's lifetime harboured just 8,000 inhabitants.

But in face-to-face encounters and in his correspondence, Goethe gathered important thinkers, artists and diplomats from all over Europe across the national boundaries of his day. You did not wash your hands for a couple of days after having shaken hands with the famous man. He was a diplomat, a civil servant and a polyhistor in the cosmopolitan spirit of the eighteenth century and actively engaged in such modern sciences as geology and biology as well as in philosophy, arts and letters (Noyes 2006). But first and foremost, he was instrumental in the development of the conception of human life, which under the name of *Bildung* constituted the widespread and still active foundation of education and personal formation in general, particularly in Central and Northern Europe. Although he did not coin the term of 'world literature', he was instrumental in its later fame.

After Goethe's death, Weimar continued to be a symbol of German and European culture, for better or worse with a global impact. The city almost needed a 'time-out' after the Goethe's lifelong activity, and the broad cultural profile then narrowed down to the arts. European composers like Franz Liszt and Richard Wagner walked the streets and visited *salons* and concert halls. Then, shortly after 1900, Weimar became the home of an art and crafts school, exerting an influence on art, science and politics as profound as the outcome of Goethe's work. Known as the Bauhaus school, it became a driving force in twentieth-century architecture, urban planning, design and visual culture across the globe, its creations becoming icons of aesthetic modernity. This effect was obtained mainly because Bauhaus with innovative creativity combined the traditional craftsmanship with modern industrial production in design, materials and forms of production, also with wider social and political perspectives. The activities of Bauhaus had global consequences for our urban environment in streets, workplaces and homes. Modern design – and also what we in modern globalization call creative industries – would not have existed without Weimar and Bauhaus.

But Weimar's post-Goethe afterlife also had other consequences. One of the first constitutions on the European continent was born there in 1816 as a cautious beginning before democratic constitutions gained ground later in the century. In 1919, in the aftermath of the First World War, Germany tried to become truly democratic. This attempt was the Weimar Republic, which ended when Hitler and the Nazis gained power in 1933 and shortly after started another world war. Of course, the Nazi regime was well aware that Weimar both recalled former Germanic greatness and a more recent political breakdown, and they cultivated the positive symbolism of greatness with such a perverted zeal that it produced devastating negative effects in the material, political and moral European world, the global repercussions of which are still felt. As early as 1937, the concentration camp Buchenwald was built – almost in Goethe's back yard. Jorge Semprún's novels, *The Long Voyage* included, circle around this place, wondering how world culture precisely in this place could be transformed into world torture.

The former Eastern German communist regime also tried in 1968 to launch a new constitution in Weimar, with more allusions to the myth of Goethe than with real contributions from his work. Finally, in 1998 the Goethe archives, the old part of Weimar and the Bauhaus site were declared by UNESCO a part of the world's cultural heritage, while Weimar and its now 65,000 inhabitants became the European cultural capital of 1999. When a small city like Weimar is repeatedly able to be a kind of global centre under different historical conditions and with different implications, there is no place which cannot assume that role, too. The place in itself does not determine the range of its cultural perspective, only the quality of its visions.

World literature in a provincial town

Such visions Goethe developed through his primary activity, literature. It was the source of all his other activities. Towards the end of his life, he had a series of conversations with Johann Peter Eckermann, who collected even the smallest of the great man's words and published them after the latter's death as *Conversations with Goethe* [Gespräche mit Goethe] (1836). This account of their conversations offers an important insight into the making of the conception of human culture during the long period when Europe was gathering strength before leaping into modernization in the mid-nineteenth century, when industrialization, urbanization and the outline of modern democracies took shape and further developed into modern globalization.

However, for literature the most important idea Goethe gleaned from his eighteenth-century precursors Christoph Martin Wieland and August Ludwig von Schlözer was that there is a world literature.[2] Only some scattered remarks over a couple of pages, but they have had a lasting effect and been further elaborated by others in various directions and applied by Goethe in some of his essays and poetry. Today, the idea is important for how we try to come to grips with literature in the context of modern globalization. On 31 January

1827, Goethe tells Eckermann that he has just finished reading a Chinese novel and found it both understandable and profoundly interesting. It contains elements in the description of characters, in the relation to nature and to the cultural environment, which are in harmony with the way European literature describes similar phenomena. We do not know exactly which text he has in mind, but we know that he read various translations and re-elaborations of Oriental literature. It may be Peter Perring Thom's collection of texts *Chinese Courtship* (1824), or most likely Jean-Pierre Abel-Rémusat's translation from 1826 of the anonymous seventeenth-century novel *Yu Jiao Li* [The Two Cousins] (Purdy 2014).

Goethe concludes that if the Germans do not direct their attention towards the larger world, they will remain enclosed in 'a pedantic twilight' (Eckermann 1959: 175). Moreover, he states that 'National literature does not say very much any more. The age of world literature has arrived, and today all of us must help this age to come into existence' (Eckermann 1959: 174). But behind the programmatic words, Goethe still finds that the old Greeks set the standard. They possess a power of expression beyond any historical, linguistic, cultural and national limits and differences. What Goethe envisions, in line with the emerging universalism of the eighteenth century, is a number of works which belong to a literary domain of their own, situated above national boundaries and rooted in universal human values. Great literature gives the readers access to that domain, no matter where and when it is written or read.

The attempts to articulate a universally valid conception of the human being were an urgent issue on the cultural agenda in Goethe's lifetime after human rights had been put into writing, and after the French and the American revolutions had tried to realize them under violent and bloody circumstances: France in war with herself and the rest of Europe; America in war with England. Goethe was more preoccupied with the gradual realization of the universal potential of humanity in the individual human being rather than with revolutionary movements and national boundaries. The most basic universal human potential is the capacity of each individual to fully realize himself or herself – mostly himself – as an individual being in a gradual process fostered by the encounter with society and nature, also called *Bildung*. A widely accepted idea with a long afterlife was that the nation constituted a natural framework for the collective organization of this process. Our national language, which we acquire naturally, as it were, enables each individual to realize his or her full potential in relation to others and in relation to the ideal human freedom. That is why *Bildung* was gradually adopted as the guiding principle for the national education systems that were established all over Europe from the early nineteenth century onwards, in northern Europe in particular. For the same reason, national literature played a decisive role, and national literary history emerged as a coherent representation of how each nation evolves through its connection with the universal ideals of mankind. This connection is realized when the particular national language is moulded in the universal forms of literature.

Literature is regarded as universal because of its acclaimed capacity to express what is common to all humans across individual differences and cultural and national boundaries. Hence, a world literature is possible, a literature which in the particular national languages articulates universally valid human conditions and which, therefore, is accessible to all people independent of linguistic differences, translations and other forms of cultural communication. Together with national literary history, a general and comparative study of literature emerged, the aim of which was to study the connections between the national literatures and to reveal the shared universal features in all literatures as well as to develop a conceptual framework for that study. This reduplication of a national study of literature with a general and comparative study of literature reiterates itself in some of the other new domains of cultural studies which were born at the same time opening comparative perspectives: linguistics, anthropology, biology and others.

Goethe's statement on world literature occurs against the backdrop of these ideas. He is clearly more interested in the relation between the individual and the globally manifested possibilities for human development and for new forms of cultural evolution than in the national aspects. In his conversations with Eckermann, he remarks that the high quality of the Chinese novel he has just read derives from the fact that it resembles his own idyllic narrative in verse *Hermann und Dorothea* (1797). However, Goethe is more than just narcissistic. What he indirectly shows is that there is always a local and personal starting point which we use as a necessary supplementary experience when we reach out to understand a global context we cannot experience directly by ourselves. Goethe tries himself to write poetry in Oriental style, firstly in the collection *West-östlicher Diwan* (1819, enlarged 1827), 'diwan' meaning in Persian a collection of poetry. In the title, he mentions his own homeground first, *West*, but this is not meant to be a projection of himself, rather a challenge to himself. Every local culture, with its own language, is a valid point of departure for a global perspective. That is the function of the 'West' in the title and the book. Any locality can be challenged productively from the outside, irrespective of size and location. No population, be it German or not, in any location can legitimize an attempt to hide in 'a pedantic twilight.' This is the critical essence of Goethe's self-reflection.

Local literature as the prism of world literature

This is the point where Georg Brandes interacts with Goethe when he further develops the idea of world literature in the short article 'World Literature' [Verdenslitteratur] (1899), written by invitation to a German celebration of Goethe's 150-year anniversary (Larsen 2011b). Goethe walks on a tightrope between a classical universalism and a modern global perspective, looking to both sides. In the universal perspective, it is either the human being who addresses the ideal or divine dimension of life or, alternatively, God or nature that speaks to us through poetry. Brandes does not take this stance. Although humans can share with each other common issues and concerns in literatures from many cultures, the heart of the matter is that the actual multitude of their differences and varieties counts more and is dependent on broader and transnational historical processes in culture and society. This is the modern global perspective.

For a start, Brandes reminds us of the progress of science as a global intellectual process and of the travelogues from scientific expeditions during the nineteenth century. He adds that transport, communication, the modern press and also translations accelerate the global process, and he could also have listed the newly established international time zones, the telegraph lines and the world's fairs. There is no universal idealism at work here, but concrete globalized cultural contacts and interactions.

Therefore, he moves his focus away from the universal content of world literature above national literatures which Goethe had placed centre stage. A literature which is written to be immediately understandable everywhere may for that very reason 'lose in vigour' (Brandes 2013: 27), simply because it is not rooted anywhere. And if something is written in order to be marketed as world literature, it is therefore highly probable that it will be completely irrelevant. It is more likely that world literature primarily has to be seen as a local literature, which just happens to be written in a language which, for the time being, and more or less accidentally, enjoys a global extension. Smaller languages may therefore hide literature known only to a few, but with the potential for a qualitative world literature impact. The point Brandes wants to bring home is that a world literary perspective is enacted inside and not beyond national and local literatures:

> The world literature of the future will become all the more captivating the more the mark of the national appears in it and the more heterogeneous it becomes, as long as it retains a universally human aspect as art and science. That which is written directly for the world will hardly do as a work of art. (Brandes 2013: 28)

World literature is not a certain group of texts, but rather a dimension of literature that is brought out by the way we read it in relation to different and concrete contexts beyond the local framework, along with other texts and cultural phenomena and therefore, as Brandes points out, in a context of heterogeneity. When literature is approached in this way, it becomes a cognitive model for global thinking and opens windows, doors and barriers for the wind that blows from the greater world into the specific locality of everyone. This is a view practised within the world literature paradigm in literary studies today when it comes to the relation between literature and globalization. This book may be called an example of this practice, with the important twist that literature, its own forms and historical vicissitudes are not, as in most world literature studies, at the centre; the core is the challenge that our experience of globalization poses to literary works and literary studies.

Literature around the world

Brandes also touches on another important point: the worldwide dissemination of literature and knowledge. As already stated, he mentions the importance of transport, communication and the modern press. Today, we could expand his list: the import and export of educational systems, electronic media, exchange of students, backpackers, media conglomerates and other elements of modern communicative globalization. When Brandes still emphasizes the primary importance of the local anchoring, his general claim for world literature is double and can be formulated in the following way: first, local anchoring is a necessary but not a sufficient condition for literature to be world literature, and second, its widespread circulation through the channels available in any given age is only a sufficient, but not a necessary condition for the status of texts as world literature.

In his first major work, the first volume of his *Main Currents in Nineteenth-Century Literature* [Hovedstrømninger i det nittende Aarhundredes Litteratur] (1872), he uses the metaphor of a telescope to express his view:

> The comparative view possesses the double advantage of bringing what is foreign so near to us that we can assimilate it, and of removing what is familiar until we are enabled to see it in its true perspective. We neither see what is too near the eye nor what is too far away from it. The scientific view of literature provides us with a telescope of which the one end magnifies and the other diminishes; it must be so focussed as to remedy the illusions of unassisted eyesight. The different nations have hitherto stood so remote from each other, as far as literature is concerned, that they have only to a very limited extent been able to benefit by each other's productions. (Brandes 1906: 9)

Most important here is the clear acknowledgement of the fact that the tension between the local and the global aspects is articulated by the textual structure itself and thus a topic for various interpretive theories and methodologies centred on the texts, though requiring complementary approaches. No monopolizing theory will suffice to answer the challenge of the double view, least of all to legitimize the establishment of an almost transcendental canon. That is why this book has focused on readings focusing on border-crossings of various types and suggested the term 'form of presentation' to embrace the textual dynamics of this cross-over.

Furthermore, this perspective assumes that there are texts out there with a modest circulation which have the potential to be world literature, only waiting to be known outside their local confinement determined by language, culture and media. Hence, I have mixed 'known' with 'lesser known' writers by insisting that the reading of all of them makes them equally important examples of world literature, that is, literature that gives form to an experience of globalization as a local-global relationship, provides it with an individual appeal, opens a historical dimension beyond modern globalization, and displays an astute aesthetic self-awareness that intensifies the reading as a concrete interaction here and now.

Some texts will make it outside the local enclosure, others not; some will make it with a huge delay – like Aboriginal dreamtime narratives made known through the global success of Aboriginal painting and Bruce Chatwin's *The Songlines*; others will gain ground with a smaller delay – like Imre Kertész's *Fateless* that jumped from anonymity in 1975 to world fame via the Nobel Prize in 2002. Although translated, some are still waiting, like Ludvig Holberg's *Erasmus Montanus*. In all three cases, the tension between the local perspective and the global conditions is an integral part of the text, although the road to their dissemination often seems accidental. Such texts may require new reading strategies and theoretical approaches to acquire a larger reading audience and thus spur a general reorientation of existing literary traditions. This happens when new genres occur, like witness literature, literatures of migration or hyper fiction, or when special focus points like memory, translation, body, place and movement attract scholarly attention.

A final perspective

The global dissemination follows at least four roads, each of which is manifested in the texts themselves in various ways, and which encourages new ways of future readings manifested as rewritings, interpretations, adaptations or translations and other types of integrations in cultures at work. Some of the roads are being taken by literary studies, others are still without dense traffic, but together they structure a map for the future:

Comparativity

The European tradition of comparative literature has fostered the modern studies of world literature studies as well as other variants of literary studies that engage in a critical discussion of the cultural aspects of globalization. However, comparative literature was born together with the ideas of the virtually autonomous national literatures, each with their own primary literary history, supported by only secondary side-glances at influences from abroad and vice-versa. The two keywords for this endeavour are, first, the idea of influence, cast in more or less strict, causal terms echoing models of knowledge launched by the emerging hard sciences, and, second, the idea of the primacy of national literatures. The European understanding of national literatures and their histories dominated the discipline, but, in spite of its name, it did not suggest a differentiated notion of comparison. The discipline subscribed to the ideas of nation defined by sovereign territory and national language, and the idea of history as linear progression towards the present nation. First, national literatures were established, and then comparative literature could work as a go-between.

Just a brief look at a world map shows that numerous literatures will never enter a comparative literature built on this shaky foundation. Large parts of the oral tradition, many genres from around the world, other conceptions of what constitutes literature as well as literatures which are not contained in cultures based on the ideal national model, all of this will be excluded together with multilingual cultures, colonial and postcolonial domains, literature not written in anything like national languages like Pidgin, Creol, Faroese, Sami and the about 1,500 languages of Africa and similar compounds of languages in other continents.

A modern comparative study will have to take another point of departure. First of all, it will have to adopt a broader notion of comparison, which I would call comparativity (Larsen 2015a), with an open eye for points of comparison across cultures that go beyond, but do not exclude proto-causal influences. Literature is interconnected in networks of parallels and similarities of many kinds and on many levels, and therefore readings that focus on more differentiated relations between texts are closer to the multiple realities of relations between cultural sites and periods. In this way, they contribute to a new sense of cultural interconnection between the cultures of the globe beyond the primarily dichotomic take on classical comparisons between individual national literatures.

Second, a relevant study of comparative literature today will abandon the narrow European definition of a nation as its ideal model of an independent literary community. It will work with looser geographical demarcation lines changing with the comparative project at hand and respecting the many different ways communities are defined and have been defined across the world and generated literary creativity. The reality of the European nation state is of course not revoked, but the true life of literature has always unfolded across such dividing lines. This perspective has guided the choice of texts and the focus of the analyses in this book (cf. Walkowitz 2006; Gelder 2010).

Translation

In most cases, translation is seen as a decontextualized technical procedure, which, often in vain, transfers a text from one language to another by diminishing its potential or even distorting it. In view of the fact the most languages and cultures are deeply dependent on and shaped by translation processes in various media, this view is obsolete and out of touch with the reality of texts and cultures. As shown in Chapter 6, translation is a productive cultural intervention propelled by the mutual challenge of two or more languages and media, which contributes to the reconfiguration of all the involved languages. In the texts themselves, translation is traced as the meeting of two or more cultures, and hybrid or broken languages are increasingly becoming an important feature in many texts. Being a cultural practice and not an exercise of technical skills, translation in its many media-specific forms also makes visible the boundaries of languages and cultures. This development reflects how the text articulates the globalized dimension of local cultures, both the translocal potential of all cultural products and their resistance to a decontextualized globalized circulation (Apter 2013; Walkowitz 2015).

Broken language is of course a feature known from earlier texts, particularly in prose and comedy. A blend of sociolects and dialects is used to pinpoint characters as foreigners and mostly as ridiculous. The interpretive framework behind this use of linguistic contrasts is the classical tripartion of styles into high, low and medium style, each of which corresponding to a cultural value system. An early example is Honoré de Balzac's reoccurring

Baron de Nucingen, who speaks Balzac's homemade construction of a hybrid French-German lingo. More recent texts go a step further than a simple mixing of styles. Here, the broken language is a sign of an individual or local refraction of a global migrant reality, for example Henry Roth's *Call It Sleep* (1934), Derek Walcott's *Omeros* (1990), Aleksandar Hemon's *Nowhere Man* (2002), Jonathan Safran Foer's *Extremely Loud & Incredibly Close* (2005), Jonas Hassen Khemiri's *Montecore* (2006), Xiaolu Guo's *Chinese-English Dictionary for Lovers* (2007), Dinaw Mengestu's *How To Read The Air* (2010), Chimamanda Adichie's *Americanah* (2013) and many more.

Anonymous mediation

The effect of literature is often embedded in everyday language and images, used and understood by people who never have actually read, borrowed or bought the literature in question. Such occurrences are due to a complex and accidental proliferation of meaning that cannot be explained with reference to the reading of specific texts by elite readers and the use of specific channels of communication and dissemination by particular select publishers. Quotations from Homer or the Bible, images of national landscapes, fictional characters like Gulliver or stereotypical actions like having a fight with windmills are used and understood by people who may not know at all the origins of what they say or imagine. Tracing the origin will, however, not give us a clue to understanding the process by which the actual use takes place (Hopper 2007; Hoskins 2009; Larsen 2015b).

Such more or less random cultural traces may originate in the school curriculum, in popular songs or in journalists or politicians who are also not aware of their sources. Once written, literature belongs to its language, a translated language included, and some of its phrases continue to work in that language beyond the intentions or knowledge of the author, publisher, critic and any other user. Through translation and intercultural communication, such linguistic effects may be transported to other cultures in unpredictable ways. The same goes for films: the visual languages of a film and other media inspire those who shape our visual surroundings in the urban layout, posters, fashion and so on, a visual impact which is also part of the lives of people who never enter a cinema.

The process also expands to the supermarkets. When we look at the shelves in a supermarket, we can easily find foodstuffs with a Max Havelaar label. This name was first used in this context by a Dutch NGO organization that wanted to brand coffee produced in ways which are economically and ecologically beneficial to the local producers. Later, it spread to a more general fair trade labelling. Although the origin is the protagonist of Multatuli's controversial colonial novel *Max Havelaar* (1860), a man who stood up against Dutch colonial rule in Java, the way the label and the brand have become globally successful has nothing to do with any knowledge of the novel, but everything to do with the media-communicated interests in conscientious consumerism as an ideology with practical consequences. Literature is integrated in what Siegfried Giedion in relation to the history of technology calls 'anonymous history' (Giedion 2013).

That the mediation of experiences of globalization is essential has been evident throughout the book, and also that it transcends film and TV adaptions to which many of works analysed here have been submitted. Literature has reached a global dissemination almost in spite of is internal structures and meaning and entirely conditioned by the media landscape through which it has travelled the world. In many literary texts, the randomness of this accidental attribution of place and meaning to literature is transformed in the texts into the general, almost fuzzy logic of the interaction of characters, of time and place, and of the open-ended plot structure of many contemporary novels (Larsen 2011c). This partly anonymous process is difficult to study and explain in detail, but it is a fundamental factor in the global dissemination of literature. Chapter 5 on memory dealt with this problem in particular, but the anonymity disguised as everydayness of the global experience is an undercurrent in most of the chapters and is studied in the growing area of digital humanities (Schreibman et al. 2015).

Existential reconfigurations

Many literary works that try to come to grips with the cultural complexity of globalization tend to turn the characters and their voices into suppressed local peoples or anonymized products of hidden globalized power structures. But also texts that do not thematize the settings and direct mental or cultural consequences of the overall processes of globalization are reflections of globalization. Instead, they dig deep into the basic existential components of human life that are being reconfigured by the larger processes, and thus push any direct references to global realities to the margins of the texts: the memory that gives cohesion across time, translation that bridges between cultures, the body as the centre of experience, the place as the site of experience and the movements as the possibility of changing the horizon of experience. Such texts deal first and foremost with the effects on the way individual experience of globalization is shaped, although shaped differently in different locations across the globe. Literature has always played around with this dimension of human life, and literature has a potential to also do so when the dynamic centre of gravity of all of them is the crossing of borders between the local and the global (O'Brien and Szeman 2001, Damrosch 2008).

At least two emerging interdisciplinary fields involving literary studies are important here; one has to do with the evolving studies of affect, passion and emotions as both existential and cultural parameters being reshaped in a globalized culture (Sætre et al. 2014), and the other is the rapidly increased interest in the post-human taking issue with not only pervasive technologies but the basic ontological question of what it means to be human today (Thomsen 2013).

On all four roads into the future of literary studies, the circulation process indicates the sufficient condition for the global dissemination of certain works of literature, sufficient in the sense that it is a real and powerful process. Yet, it is not necessary in the sense that this process is not clearly rooted in the textual structures. For readers of literature as world literature, the task is to establish theories, methods and reading practices that allow us precisely to see the reflections of such real processes in the texts and not discard them as irrelevant to their literariness. From this perspective, world literature does not mean literature around the world, but confronts us with a fascinating challenge to our approach to literature, its conditions of existence and its use in the world of modern globalization. Literature is like the duck-billed platypus, it cuts across all borders, belongs nowhere and everywhere and concerns us wherever we live.

Appendix: The Story of the Duck-Billed Platypus

Why the platypus is special! Traditional Aboriginal people from all parts of Australia regarded the platypus as very special. It was taboo, and therefore not hunted for food as most of the animals were. This Dreamtime legend explains why. It comes from the folklore of the Wiradjuri people, who lived in traditional times in the area known as Central New South Wales.

Very early in the dreamtime, the ancestor spirits were deciding on totems, and the animals, the water creatures and the birds were all vying for what they thought was the top position.

The birds had decided to invite the platypus. 'She belongs among us', they said. 'She lays eggs, and she has a bill like a duck.' 'Oh no, I am glad to be invited to your meeting, but I am not really a bird. But I'll think about it', she said as she scampered back to her waterside hole.

Soon after this, all the animals held their own meeting. 'I think', the kangaroo said, 'we should invite the platypus to join our group. She is different from us in some ways, but she runs on land and is covered in fur as we are.' Platypus was surprised and happy to be receiving so much attention, but told them as she told the birds, that she had to think before she could make a decision.

It was not long before a big fish called a meeting for all the water creatures. So they too invited platypus to their meeting. 'She has webbed feet and can swim remarkably well'. The platypus was most surprised to find another group at her door. Platypus replied: 'I will give you my answer next week.'

So next day, she went to discuss this strange situation with her friend, the spiny echidna. The echidna thought carefully, and then advised platypus not to join any of the groups. They talked awhile, and the platypus could think of no better answer. So the platypus sent separate messages to the birds, the animals and the water creatures. She invited each group to a place near her home, and insisted that they all must come together in friendship.

When platypus emerged from her hole, a hush fell over the whole crowd. 'You are all my friends. I understand the birds because you have to keep your eggs warm as I do. I understand the water creatures because like me you dive to the depths and explore the underwater world as I do. And I feel akin to the animals who run on the land and grow fur like I do. But I am grateful that Byamee, the father-of-all has seen fit to make me a little bit like each one of you. So it is my hope that each time you see a member of my family, you will be reminded of Byamee in sky world, the father-of-all, who made each one of us.'

At this time, the Aboriginal people could each interchange bodies with their particular totem animal. They heard what the platypus said. They heeded her message, and agreed that she was unique and should be regarded as very special. The story was told to each generation, and the Aboriginal people of all areas, century after century, have continued to respect the platypus.

In traditional times, whenever people saw a platypus scurrying around the creekbank or swimming in the river, they regarded it as an omen of good luck. Perhaps that is why most of us feel a special thrill when we see one nowadays.

From a mural in Sydney Aquarium, Australia

Notes

Introduction

1   On epistemology and the platypus, see Eco (2000/1997).

Chapter 1

1   On Shakespeare's obscenities, see Kiernan (2006).
2   Most of the recent works on literature in a global perspective, important as they are, focus exclusively on the contemporary scene, for example, Ramazani (2009), Jay (2010), Ascari (2009), Leonard (2013).
3   Rewriting is an example of this practice, for example, Parker and Mathews (2011) and McConnell and Hall (2016), both on later, particularly contemporary literary rewritings of mainly European classics in a global perspective; in a longer historical perspective also known in, for example, the rewritings of the Phaedra- or Oedipus-stories throughout European cultural history.
4   I will discuss world literature in my conclusion. Those who cannot wait can take a look at the two handbooks from Routledge: *The Routledge Companion to World Literature* (D'haen et al. 2012), *World Literature. A Reader* (D'haen et al. 2013) and the historical overview (D'haen 2011).

Chapter 2

1   General literature on globalization, mainly in a predominantly economic and political perspective, is abundant. Although my topic is not globalization as such, the comprehensive anthology Lechner and Boli (2004) has been useful together with more recent and also broadly scoped references like Scholte (2005), Baylis and Smith (2013) and Eriksen (2014), partly overlapping with studies on 'transnationalism', used as a term from early twentieth century (Vertovec 2009, for a contemporary, and Howard 2011 and 2012, for a historical perspective).

As will be clear in Chapter 3, most important for this book have been the works by Ulrich Beck (2000, 2006, 2007, 2009 and Beck and Bonß 2001) and his contribution to Beck, Giddens and Lash (1994: 1–55). More relevant in a literary studies perspective are references with a special focus on culture like Featherstone (1990), Tomlinson (1999), Mudimbe-Boyi (2002), Saussy (2006) and Hopper (2007), and works on particular globalized cultural topics with direct literary repercussions, which will be dealt with in later chapters: topics of a relative recent date like cosmopolitanism (Chapter 3), cognitive uncertainty (Chapter 4), cultural memory (Chapter 5) and translation (Chapter 6), and more classical topics like body in a new perspective (Chapter 7), place (Chapter 8) and mobility (Chapter 9). The reader *Literature and Globalization* (Connell and Marsh 2011) is useful, but, as is often the case in this field, it is mostly preoccupied with theoretical scaffolding while actual textual engagements that do not only illustrate, but modify and challenge the theoretical positions are in short supply. The present book is a modest attempt to remedy this situation.

2   The school closed in June 2010, www.cde.ca.gov/re/sd/details.asp?cds=386847 83830163&Public=Y (accessed 29 December 2016); yet the alumni association continues to exist, http://www.classmates.com/places/school/Newcomer-High -School/17937651 (accessed 29 December 2016). Young immigrants are now spread in the San Francisco area. In 1995 the Newcomers High School in Long Island, New York, took inspiration from San Francisco and is still in full swing, http://insideschools.org/component/schools/school/1265 (accessed 29 December 2016). The opening and closing of special schools or classes for migrant children mirror the ambiguous approach to the reception and integration of migrants in the everyday life of globalized societies, not least in recent years, where an intensified migration has triggered xenophobic feelings around the globe.

3   Beyond the function as a rhetorical device the importance of metaphors for human cognition is dealt with by, for example, Holland and Quinn (1987), Lakoff (1988), Fauconnier (1997), Larsen (1997), and for scientific thinking by, for example, Peirce on abduction (Peirce 1998), Schön on generative metaphor (Schön 1993), Leatherdale on analogy with a historical perspective (Leatherdale 1974).

4   On the global outreach of fake news, see for example http://fakenewswatch .com (accessed 29 December 2016). On fake news as a money machine, see for example *Financial Times*, 16 December 2016, https://www.ft.com /content/333fe6bc-c1ea-11e6-81c2-f57d90f6741a (accessed 29 Dec 2016). On the US presidential election, see for example *Washington Post*, 9 December 2016, https://www.washingtonpost.com/business/economy/

russian-propaganda-effort-helped-spread-fake-news-during-election-experts
-say/2016/11/24/793903b6-8a40-4ca9-b712-716af66098fe_story.html?utm
_term=.a261457230a5 (accessed 29 December 2016); the FBI report of 29
December 2016, see www.us-cert.gov/sites/default/files/publications/JAR_16
-20296A_GRIZZLY%20STEPPE-2016-1229.pdf (accessed 31 December 2016);
or, beyond the United States, see for example *The Guardian*, 2 December 2016,
https://www.theguardian.com/media/2016/dec/02/fake-news-facebook-us
-election-around-the-world (accessed 29 December 2016). On potentially
fatal effects, see, for example, *CNN*, 26 December 2016: In response to the
fake news about a nuclear threat, the Pakistani prime minister tweeted that he
was prepared to respond proportionally, http://edition.cnn.com/2016/12/26/
middleeast/israel-pakistan-fake-news-nuclear (accessed 29 December 2016).
I hope all these websites are reliable!

Chapter 3

1   Other important works on cosmopolitanism are Appiah 2009, in a contemporary
    perspective, and Schiller and Irving 2015 with both a historical and a
    contemporary outlook.
2   Quotations without pagination in the following part of the text are from pp.
    139–140.
3   Beck updated his analysis in *World at Risk* (2009) with a stronger emphasis on
    environmental issues. For a critical introduction to Beck, see Mythen (2004).
4   Quotations without pagination in the following part of the text are from p. 3.
5   There is a rich literature on the earthquake, for example, in English Kendrick
    (1956), Svensen (2006: 34–54) and Larsen (2006), in German Löffler (1999), and
    in French Poirrier (2005).
6   Quotations without pagination in the following part of the text are from p. 150.

Chapter 4

1   Together with Holberg's utopian novel *Nicolai Klimii iter subterraneum* (1741),
    his book on world history *Synopsis historiae universalis* (1733) saw a particularly
    broad European dissemination before 1800 in Latin and in many translations,
    also posthumously, English included. Before 1800 *Erasmus Montanus* was

published twice in Dutch, twice in Swedish and three times in German; English translations in 1884, 1916 and 1990; Danish-Brazilian film production *The Earth Is Flat* (1977), http://www.imdb.com/title/tt0132255 (accessed 4 January 2017).

2   Given the transnational nature of collective trauma and the global media awareness of war atrocities, trauma and literature form an essential topic in contemporary literary studies. The field was opened by Felman and Laub (1992), continued in, for example, Rogers et al. (1999), Ibsch (2000), Whitehead (2004), Richardson (2016) and, since 2010, in the *Journal of Literature and Trauma Studies*.

3   Quotations and references without pagination in the following part of the text are from pp. 18–25. This scene is also the centrepiece in the TV-movie *Le Grand Voyage* (1969), see Hoffmann (2005). On Semprún, see Razinsky (2016).

4   *Le mort qu'il faut* has not been translated into English.

5   The Hwang Woo-Suk case in 2006, http://www.nature.com/news/specials /hwang/index.html (accessed 4 January 2017) and revisited in 2014, http://www .nature.com/news/cloning-comeback-1.14504 (accessed 4 January 2017).

6   See also a psychological and ethical analysis in Bok (1989) and an epistemological and ethical analysis in Nietzsche (1973).

7   An insightful discussion of knowledge, experience and uncertainty in view of globalization can be found in Beck and Bonß (2001: 96–121) in the contributions by Sabine Weishaupt, Mathias Heymann and Ulrich Wengenroth.

Chapter 5

1   Classic memory scholars like Friederich Nietzsche, Henri Bergson, Sigmund Freud and Maurice Halbwachs shaped modern memory studies by insisting (1) on memory as an act in the present of remembrance, not primarily a storehouse of the past; (2) on memory as a dialectics between memory and forgetting, not an autonomous process of pure recall; and (3) on memory as a dialogical process, not a matter only of individual consciousness. Since then, recent developments in memory studies of importance for this book also open the field to issues of globalization, transnationalism and migration on the shared fundamental condition that place-bound memories are being contested and have to be reconstructed to be instrumental for identity formation, a condition that applies to dwellers and movers alike who coexist in the same place. See works like Levy and Sznaider (2002, 2010), Agnew (2005), Erll and Rigney (2009), Rothberg

(2009), Gutman et al. (2010), Philips and Reyes (2011), Larsen (2011a), Cesari and Rigney (2014). Among the numerous anthologies, see Olick et al. (2011) (texts) and Erll and Nünning (2008) (interdisciplinary articles).

2   On *ars memoria*, see Blum (1969), Yates (1974), Eco (1988), Berns (1993), Carruthers (1994).

3   On Yahoo!, see https://en.wikipedia.org/wiki/Yahoo! (accessed 29 December 2016).

4   Full English title from 1568: *The new found vvorlde, or Antarctike wherin is contained wo[n]derful and strange things, as well of humaine creatures, as beastes, fishes, foules and serpents, trées, plants, mines of golde and siluer: garnished with many learned aucthorities, trauailed and written in the French tong, by that excellent learned man, master Andrevve Theuet. And now newly translated into Englishe, wherein is reformed the errours of the auncient cosmographers.* On Thevet, see Lestringant (1994a); on cannibals, see Lestringant (1994b).

5   The full English title from 1555 is close to Boemus' own: *The Fardle of Facions conteining the aunciente maners, customes and lawes, of the peoples enhabiting the two partes of the earth, called Affricke and Asie.* The 1610 title clearly points to the compilatory nature of the volume and the translator's own additions: *The manners, lauues and customes of all nations collected out of the best vvriters by Ioannes Boemus …; with many other things of the same argument, gathered out of the historie of Nicholas Damascen; the like also out of the history of America, or Brasill, written by Iohn Lerius; the faith, religion and manners of the Aethiopians, and the deploration of the people of Lappia, compiled by Damianus a Goes; with a short discourse of the Aethiopians, taken out of Ioseph Scaliger his seuenth booke de emendatione temporum; written in Latin, and now newly translated into English, by Ed. Aston.*

6   Excerpts from Léry were added to Boemus (1610).

7   Quotations without pagination in the following part of the text are from pp. 11–18. On Swift, cannibals and genocide, see Rawson (2001).

Chapter 6

1   See http://www.hutong-school.com/defense-chinglish; http://www.fluentu.com /chinese/blog/2013/01/16/chinglish-signs (both accessed 5 January 2017).

2   Translation studies have developed as a burgeoning research field, transcending practical linguistic skills and the ancillary position of a translation vis-à-vis a superior origin. The increased emphasis on cultural contexts and intermedia relations has a direct importance for literary studies in general and for literary

studies in a globalized perspective in particular. To mention but a few works of special importance for this book: (1) anthologies and handbooks by Lefevere 1992 (on translation throughout cultural history), Malmkjaer and Windle 2011 (historical, contemporary and interdisciplinary perspectives), Venuti 2012 (on twentieth-century theory); (2) publications that develop the field as an interconnectedness of languages, media and cultures (Lefevere 1990; Bassnett and Lefevere 1995, 1999; Cronin 2003; Bermann and Wood 2005; Apter 2006, 2013; Bellos 2011; Bassnett 2014; Walkowitz 2015; Larsen 2016a).

3 Accessed 5 January 2017.

4 Mahler, see Adorno (1992), Hefling (2000), Solvik (2005), and the website for *The Song of the Earth*, http://www.mahlerarchives.net/Archive%20documents /DLvDE/DLvDE.htm, containing both Bethge's text and the translations he relied on (accessed 5 January 2017). Mahler's text is quoted from the CD booklet included in Mahler (1998) while English translations are made for this chapter by John Irons.

5 On Chinese translations in a mainly linguistic perspective, see Balcom (2006), in relation to poetry, see the editors' two introductions in Barnstone and Ping (2005), in a broader linguistic and cultural perspective, see Luo and He (2009).

6 On big and small travels, see Leed (1991), Adams (1983), Wallace (1993), König (1996), Solnit (2006), in Europe originating in the Aristotelian peripatetic school of the Athenian Lyceum, but continued in the contemplative walks in the medieval cloisters.

Chapter 7

1 On the history of the body, see Mauss 1980 (first nation people), Corbin et al. 2005 (Europe), Corbin et al. 2011 (Europe), Feher 1989 (global).

2 This perspective has been developed particularly by phenomenology in the footsteps of the German *Gestaltheorie* of the 1920s and 1930s, and with Maurice Merleau-Ponty as the most influential figure, see Schütz (1955), Larsen and Johansen (2002: 165–172), Mearleu-Ponty (2013), Larsen (2017b).

3 On honour and shame in a contemporary and historical perspective, see Peristiany (1965), Gilmore (1987), Fisher (1992), Cairns (1993), Miller (1993, 2006), Nussbaum (2004).

4 See Morris (1991), Peters (1996), Benthien (2002), Chamayou (2008).

5 On *habeas corpus*, see http://legal-dictionary.thefreedictionary.com /habeas+corpus (accessed 5 January 2017).

Chapter 8

1   Place is a topic in cultural studies and memory studies emphasizing stable
    localities and their changes as well as in migration studies highlighting, in contrast,
    the ephemeral nature of place. Just to mention a few works that articulate this
    constitutive ambiguity: Casey (2009), Tomlinson (1999), Urry (2000), Aydemir and
    Rotas (2008). In the field of eco-criticism, place also occupies a prominent position,
    for example, Larsen (2007), Heise (2008). The notion of 'meeting place', introduced
    in Chapter 3 and used throughout this book, is inspired by the 'contact zones'
    proposed in Pratt 1992 (who adapted the term from linguistics) and it bridges
    between the stable and the ephemeral aspect of place.
2   English anthologies of Danish literature are Jansen and Mitchell (1971) and
    Bredsdorff and Mai (2010).
3   All Danish texts in this chapter are translated by John Irons.
4   There are numerous historical and critical analyses of nationalism, nations and
    nation states. On the relation to globalization, see Beck (2000, 2006).
5   On Chatwin's book, see Texier-Vandamme (2003); on Aboriginal songlines and
    dreamtime, see Munn (1973), Sutton (1998), Bradley (2010), Mudrooroo (1991)
    (a novel) and the website, http://aboriginalart.com.au/culture/dreamtime3.html
    (accessed 5 January 2017).

Chapter 9

1   Displacements with major cultural implications have often been labelled exile,
    diaspora or migration with the latter term being used more frequently today
    (Appadurai 1996; Cohen 1997; Agnew 2005; Knott and McLoughlin 2010;
    Elliot and Urry 2011). However, its emphasis on the general hybridity and
    nomadic nature of global identities often discards the parallel and equally strong
    development of localism, nationalism and regionalism. In literary studies the
    term 'migrant literature', referring to the hybrid origin of the writer, should be
    replaced, as suggested in Walkowitz (2006), by the more precise term 'literature
    of migration'. This term embraces the experience of mobility of both dwellers,
    whose life today is influenced by the mobility of others, and movers, depending
    on their own mobility, intensified by the coexistence of dwellers and movers in
    the same social and cultural space. Today, this situation has a strong influence on
    creative writing and other art forms.

Perspectives

1 With different backgrounds in Europe, the United States and Asia, the world
literature paradigm has developed over the last twenty years as a global
enterprise embracing research and education as well as broader outreach
on different levels. This endeavour has in many ways redefined comparative
literature today following in the footsteps of the early individual researchers
who kept the vision of world literature from the early nineteenth century alive
(G. Brandes, E. Auerbach, F. Strich, A. Guérard, R. Etiemble and others) (see
also note 2). The world literature paradigm branches out in different directions:
(1) *The theoretical, analytical and historical level*: Schöning (2000), O'Brien
and Szeman (2001), Damrosch (2003, 2008), Prendergast (2004), Pradeau and
Samoyault (2005), Thomsen (2008), Veit (2008), Beecroft (2015), Ette (2016a,
2016b). (2) *National level:* a world literature perspective on national literatures,
for example' Buell and Dimock (2007) (The United States), Dixon and Rooney
(2013) (Australia), Beebee (2014) (Germany), Mufti (2016) (India), Ringgaard
and Thomsen (2017), Larsen (2013) (Denmark) and also Lionnet and Shih
(2005) (global). (3) *Poetics:* Miner 1989 (transcontinental and historical),
Ramazani (2009) (mainly Anglophone and contemporary). (4) *Publishing and
dissemination:* Casanova (2004), Sapiro (2009). The anthology *The Longman
Anthology of World Literature* in 6 vols. (2004 and later) is a milestone in this
development. The French attempt to formulate a 'littérature-monde' takes place
in a postcolonial framework in relation to *la francophonie* (Le Bris et al. 2007).
In 2016 *Journal of World Literature* was launched in an attempt to unite the
different research interests across the globe.

2 See Pizer (2006), David (2012).

Bibliography

Included are works quoted or discussed, not works just listed. If there are two dates, the first refers to the edition used, the second to the year of first publication. Titles of individual authors are listed in the order of editions used.

Achebe, C. (1965), 'English and the African Writer', in *Transition* 18: 27–30.

Ackerley, C. and L. Clipper (1984), *A Companion to Under the Volcano*, Vancouver: University of British Columbia Press.

Adams, P. G. (1983), *Travel Literature and the Evolution of the Novel*, Lexington: University of Kentucky Press.

Adorno, T. W. (1992/1960), *Mahler*, Chicago: University of Chicago Press.

Agnew, V., ed. (2005), *Diaspora, Memory, and Identity*, Toronto: University of Toronto Press.

Appadurai, A. (1996), *Modernity at Large*, Minneapolis: University of Minnesota Press.

Appiah, K. A. (2006), *Cosmopolitanism. Ethics in a World of Strangers*, London: Penguin.

Apter, E. (2006), *The Translation Zone. A New Comparative Literature*, Princeton: Princeton University Press.

Apter, E. (2013), *Against World Literature. On the Politics of Untranslatability*, London: Verso.

Arendt, H. (1957), 'Karl Jaspers: Citizen of the World', in P. A. Schilpp, ed., *The Philosophy of Karl Jaspers*, 539–555, La Salle: Open Court Publ.

Aristoteles (1941/c. 350 BCE), *The Basic Works of Aristotle*, R. McKeon, ed., New York: Random House.

Ascari, M. (2009), *Literature of the Global Age*, Jefferson: McFarland.

Augustine of Hippo (2005a/c. 400 CE), *On Lying*, http://www.ccel.org/ccel/schaff /npnf103.v.v.html (accessed 4 January 2017).

Augustine of Hippo (2005b/c. 400 CE), *Against Lying*, http://www.ccel.org/ccel /schaff/npnf103.v.vi.html (accessed 4 January 2017).

Aydemir, M. and A. Rotas, ed. (2008), *Migratory Settings*, Leiden: Brill.

Balcom, J. (2006), 'Translating Modern Chinese Literature', in S. Bassnett and P. Bush, eds., *The Translator as Writer*, 119–134, London: Continuum.

Barnstone, T. and C. Ping, eds. (2005), *The Anchor Book of Chinese Poetry. From Ancient to Contemporary*, New York: Anchor Books.

Bassnett, S. (2014), *Translation*, London: Routledge.

Bassnett, S. and A. Lefevere, eds. (1995), *Translation, History and Culture*, London: Cassell.

Bassnett, S. and A. Lefevere, eds. (1999), *Constructing Cultures. Essays on Literary Translation*, Bristol: Multilingual Matters.

Baylis, J. and S. Smith, eds. (2013), *The Globalization of World Politics. An Introduction to International Relations*, Oxford: Oxford University Press.

Beck, U. (2000/1997), *What Is Globalization?*, London: Polity Press.

Beck, U. (2006/2004), *Cosmopolitan Vision*, London: Polity Press.

Beck, U. (2007/1986), *Risk Society. Towards a New Modernity*, London: Sage.

Beck, U. (2009/2007), *World at Risk*, London: Polity Press.

Beck, U., A. Giddens and S. Lash (1994), *Reflexive Modernization*, Stanford: Stanford University Press.

Beck, U. and W. Bonß, eds. (2001), *Die Modernisierung der Moderne*, Frankfurt a. M.: Suhrkamp.

Beebee, T. O., ed. (2014), *German Literature as World Literature*, London: Bloomsbury.

Beecroft, A. (2015), *An Ecology of World Literature. From Antiquity to the Present Day*, London: Verso.

Bell-Villada, G. H. (1996), *Art for Art's Sake and Literary Life*, Lincoln: University of Nebraska Press.

Bellos, D. (2011), *Is That a Fish in Your Ear. Translation and the Meaning of Everything*, London: Penguin.

Benthien, C. (2002/1999), *Skin. On the Cultural Border between Self and the World*, New York: Columbia Press.

Bermann, S. and M. Wood, eds. (2005), *Nation, Language and the Ethics of Translation*. Princeton: Princeton University Press.

Berns, J. J. (1993), 'Umrüstung der Mnemotechnik im Kontext von Reformation und Gutenbergs Erfindung', in J. J. Berns and W. Neuber, eds., *Ars Memorativa. Zur kulturgeschichtlichen Gedächtniskunst 1400–1750*, 35–72, Tübingen: Niemeyer.

Bethge, H. (2001/1907), *Die chinesische Flöte*, Kelkheim: yinyang Media Verlag.

Blixen K. (1979), 'Daguerreotypes', in *Daguerreotypes and Other Essays*, 16–63, Chicago: University of Chicago Press.

Blixen, K. (1985/1939), 'Sorte og Hvide i Afrika', in *Samlede Essays*, 56–80, Copenhagen: Gyldendal.

Blixen, K. (2013/1937), *Out of Africa*, Bowdon: Stellar Books.

Bloom, H. (2000), *How to Read and Why?*, London: Fourth Estate.

Blum, H. (1969), *Die antike Mnemotechnik*, Hildesheim: Olms.

Boemus, I. (1555/1520), *The Fardle of Facions*, https://ebooks.adelaide.edu.au/h /hakluyt/voyages/boemus (accessed 5 January 2017).

Boemus, I. (1610/1520), *The Manners, Laws and Customs of All Nations*, http://
    quod.lib.umich.edu/cgi/t/text/text-idx?c=eebo;idno=A16282.0001.001 (accessed
    5 January 2017).

Bohr, N. (1961), *Atomic Physics and Human Knowledge*, New York: Dover.

Bok, S. (1989), *Lying. Moral Choice in Public and Private Life*, New York: Vintage.

Bradley, J. and Yanyuwa Families (2010), *Singing Saltwater Country: Journey to the
    Songlines of Carpentaria*, London: Allen and Unwin.

Brandes, G. (1906/1872), *Main Currents in Nineteenth-Century Literature 1. The
    Emigrant Literature*. London: Heinemann.

Brandes, G. (2013/1899), 'World Literature', in T. D'haen, C. Dominguez and
    M. R. Thomsen, eds., *World Literature. A Reader*, 23–27, London: Routledge.

Bredsdorff, T. and A.-M. Mai, eds. (2010), *100 Danish Poems. From the Medieval
    Period to the Present Day*, Seattle: University of Washington Press.

Buell, L. and W. C. Dimock, eds. (2007), *Shades of the Planet. American Literature as
    World Literature*, Princeton: Princeton University Press.

Cairns, D. L. (1993), *Aidōs. The Psychology and Ethics of Honour and Shame in
    Ancient Greek Literature*, Oxford: Clarendon.

Campe, J. H. (1790), *Briefe aus Paris zur Zeit der Revolution*, Braunschweig:
    Schulbuchhandlung.

Carruthers, M. (1994), *The Book of Memory. A Study of Memory in Medieval Culture*,
    Cambridge: Cambridge University Press.

Casanova, P. (2004/1999), *The World Republic of Letters*, Cambridge: Harvard
    University Press.

Casey, E. S. (1997), *The Fate of Place*, Berkeley: University of California Press.

Casey, E. S. (2009), *Getting Back Into Place*, 2nd ed., Bloomington: Indiana University
    Press.

Cesari, C. De and A. Rigney, eds. (2014), *Transnational Memory*, Berlin: de Gruyter.

Chai, L. (1990), *Aestheticism. The Religion of Art in Post-Romantic Literature*, New York:
    Columbia University Press.

Chamayou, G. (2008), *Les corps vils. Expérimenter sur les êtres humains aux XVIIIe et
    XIXe siècles*, Paris: La Découverte.

Chatwin, B. (1982), *On the Black Hill*, London: Picador.

Chatwin, B. (2005/1987), *The Songlines*, London: Vintage.

Chew, T.-L. (2004), 'The Identity of the Original Poem Mahler adapted for *Von
    der Jugend*', in *Naturlaut* 3/2. 15–17, www.mahlerarchives.net/archives.html >
    Archives > Mahler's Works > Das Lied von der Erde (accessed 5 January 2017).

Chew, T.-L. (s.a.1), 'Tracking the Literary Metamorphosis in *Das Lied von der Erde*',
    www.mahlerarchives.net/archives.html > Archives > Mahler's Works > Das Lied
    von der Erde (accessed 5 January 2017).

Chew, T.-L. (s.a.2), '*Das Lied von der Erde:* The Literary Changes', www
.mahlerarchives.net/archives.html > Archives > Mahler's Works > Das Lied von
der Erde (accessed 5 January 2017).

Coetzee, J. M. (1988), *White Writing*, New Haven: Yale University Press.

Cohen, R. (1997), *Global Diasporas*, Seattle: University of Washington Press.

Cohen, S. (1996), *Aristotle on Nature and Incomplete Substance*, Cambridge:
Cambridge University Press.

Conrad, J. (1950/1897), 'Preface', in *The Nigger of the 'Narcissus'*, vii–xii, London: J. M.
Dent and Sons.

Connell, L. and N. Marsh, eds. (2011), *Literature and Globalization. A Reader*,
London: Routledge.

Corbin, A. et al., eds. (2005), *Histoire du corps*, 1–3, Paris: Le Seuil.

Corbin, A. et al., eds. (2011), *Histoire de la virilité*, 1–3, Paris: Le Seuil.

Cronin, M. (2003), *Translation and Globalization*, London: Routledge.

Damrosch, D. (2003), *What Is World Literature?*, Princeton: Princeton University Press.

Damrosch, D. (2008), *How to Read World Literature*, Hoboken: Wiley-Blackwell.

David, J. (2012), *Spectres de Goethe. Les métamorphose de la "littérature mondiale"*,
Paris: Les Belles Lettres.

D'haen, T. (2011), *The Routledge Concise History of World Literature*, London:
Routledge.

D'haen, T., D. Damrosch and D. Kadir, eds. (2012), *The Routledge Companion to
World Literature*, London: Routledge.

D'haen, T., C. Dominguez and M. R. Thomsen, eds. (2013), *World Literature. A
Reader*, London: Routledge.

Dixon, R. and B. Rooney, eds. (2013), *Scenes of Reading. Is Australian Literature a
World Literature?*, Melbourne: Australian Scholarly Publishing.

Eaton, R. (2002), *Ideal Cities. Utopianism and the (Un)built Environment*, London:
Hudson.

Eckermann, J. P. (1959/1836), *Gespräche mit Goethe in den letzten Jahren seines
Lebens*, Wiesbaden: Brockhaus.

Eco, U. (1988), 'An *ars oblivionis*? Forget It', in *Publications of the Modern Language
Association of America* 103: 254–261.

Eco, U. (2000/1997), *Kant and the Platypus. Essays on Language and Cognition*, New
York: Hartcourt Brace.

Elliott, A. and J. Urry (2011), *Mobile Lives*, London: Routledge.

Engdahl, H., ed. (2002), *Witness Literature*, Singapore: World Scientific Publishing.

Eriksen, T. H. (2014), *Globalization (Key Concepts)*, London: Bloomsbury.

Erll, A. and A. Nünning, eds. (2008), *Cultural Memory Studies. An International and
Interdisciplinary Handbook*, Berlin: de Gruyter.

Erll, A. and A. Rigney, eds. (2009), *Mediation, Remediation, and the Dynamics of Cultural Memory*, Berlin: de Gruyter.

Ette, O. (2016a/2001), *Transarea. A History of Globalization*, New York: de Gruyter.

Ette, O. (2016b/2005), *Writing-Between-Words*, New York: de Gruyter.

Fairchild, H. N. (1961/1927), *The Noble Savage*, New York: Russell and Russell.

Fauconnier, G. (1997), *Mappings in Thought and Language*, Cambridge: Cambridge University Press.

Featherstone, M., ed. (1990), *Global Culture. Nationalism, Globalization and Modernity*, London: Sage.

Feher, M., ed. (1989), *Fragments for a History of the Human Body 1–3*, New York: Zone Books.

Felman, S. and D. Laub (1992), *Testimony. Crises of Witnessing in Literature, Psychoanalysis, and History*, London: Routledge.

Fisher, N. R. E. (1992), *Hybris. A Study of Values of Honour and Shame in Ancient Greece*, Warminster: Aris & Philips.

Frankfurt, H. G. (2005), *On Bullshit*, Princeton: Princeton University Press.

Fugard, A. (1989/1980), *Tsotsi*, Johannesburg: Donker.

Gelder, K. (2010), 'Proximate Reading: Australian Literature in Transnational Reading Frameworks', in *Journal of the Association for the Study of Australian Literature: Common Readers and Cultural Critics* (special issue): 1–12, http://openjournals.library.usyd.edu.au/index.php/JASAL/article/view/9615 (accessed 5 January 2017).

Ghosh, A. (1992), *In an Antique Land*, New Delhi: Ravi Dayal.

Ghosh, A. (2000), *The Glass Palace*, New York: HarperCollins.

Giedion, S. (2013/1948), *Mechanization Takes Command. A Contribution to Anonymous History*, Minneapolis: University of Minnesota Press.

Gilmore, D. D. (1987), *Honor and Shame and the Unity of the Mediterranean*, Washington: American Anthropological Association.

Glissant, E. (1996/1981), *Caribbean Discourse*, Charlottesville: University of Virginia Press.

Goldsmith, O. (1992/1763), 'On National Prejudices', in J. Gross, ed., *The Oxford Book of Essays*, 94–97, Oxford: Oxford University Press.

Gordimer, N. (1994/1991), 'The Ultimate Safari', in R. Malan, ed., *Being Here. Modern Short Stories from Southern Africa*, 143–153, Cape Town: David Philip.

Gratz, W., ed. (1990), *A Literary Companion to Science*, New York: Norton.

Guo, X. (2007), *A Concise Chinese-English Dictionary for Lovers*, London: Chatto and Windus.

Gutman, Y., A. G. Brown and A. Sodaro, eds. (2010), *Memory and the Future. Transnational Politics, Ethics and Society*, London: Palgrave Macmillan.

Halliday, F. E. (1964), *A Shakespeare Companion*, London: Duckworth.

Hassig, D. (1995), *Medieval Bestiaries: Text, Images, Ideology*, Cambridge: Cambridge University Press.

Hefling, S. E. (2000), *Mahler: Das Lied von der Erde*, Cambridge: Cambridge University Press.

Heise, U. (2008), *Sense of Place and Sense of Planet*, Oxford: Oxford University Press.

Herrmann, E., C. Smith-Prei and S. Taberner, eds. (2015), *Transnationalism in Contemporary German-Language Literature*, New York: Camden House.

Hoffmann, A., ed. (2005), Coffret pédagogique sur „Le grand voyage" de Jorge Semprún (novel, film, interviews, history and other materials). Luxembourg: Centre de Technologie de l'Education.

Holberg, L. (1990/1723), 'Erasmus Montanus', in *Jeppe of the Hill and Other Comedies*, 145–192, Carbondale: Southern Illinois University Press.

Holland, D. and N. Quinn, eds. (1987), *Cultural Models in Language and Thought*, Cambridge: Cambridge University Press.

Hopkins, G. M. (1877), 'Pied Beauty', http://www.poetryfoundation.org/poem/173664 (accessed 5 January 2017).

Hopper, P. (2007), *Understanding Cultural Globalization*, London: Polity Press.

Hoskins, A. (2009), 'Digital Network Memory', in A. Erll and A. Rigney, eds., *Mediation, Remediation, and the Dynamics of Cultural Memory*, 91–106, Berlin: de Gruyter.

Howard, M. C. (2011), *Transnationalism and Society*, Jefferson: McFarland.

Howard, M. C. (2012), *Transnationalism and Medieval Societies*, Jefferson: McFarland.

Højskolesangbogen (2006/1894), 18th ed., Odense: Andelsbogtrykkeriet.

Ibsch, E., ed. (2000), *The Conscience of Humankind. Literature and Traumatic Experiences*, Amsterdam: Rodopi.

Jansen, F. J. B. and P. M. Mitchell, eds. (1971), *Anthology of Danish Literature 1–2*, Carbondale: Southern Illinois University Press.

Jay, P. (2010), *Global Matters: The Transnational Turn in Literary Studies*, Ithaca: Cornell University Press.

Kant, I. (1994/1756), 'Von den Ursachen der Erderchütterungen', 'Geschichte und Naturbeschreibung der merkwürdigen Vorfälle des Erdbebens, welches an dem Ende des 1755sten Jahres einen grossen Teil der Erde erschüttert hat', and 'Fortgesetzte Betrachtung', in W. Breidert, ed., *Die Erschütterung der vollkommenen Welt*, 100–146, Darmstadt: Wissenschaftliche Buchgesellschaft.

Kant, I. (2006). *'Toward Perpetual' Peace and Other Writings in Politics, Peace, and History*, New Haven: Yale University Press.

Keats, J. (1973/1816), 'On First Looking into Chapman's Homer', in *The Complete Poems*, 72, London: Penguin.

Kendrick, T. D. (1956), *The Lisbon Earthquake*, London: Methuen.

Kern, S. (2003), *The Culture of Time and Space, 1880–1918*. Cambridge: Harvard University Press.

Kertész, I. (1992/1975), *Fateless*, Evanston: Northwestern University Press.

Kertész, I. (2002), 'heureka! Nobel Lecture', www.nobelprize.org/nobel_prizes /literature/laureates/2002/kertesz-lecture.html (accessed 29 December 2016).

Kertész, I. (2005/2001), 'Who Owns Auschwitz?', in *The Yale Journal of Criticism* 14 (1): 267–272.

Ketham, J. de (1493), *Fasciculo de medicina*, Venice, https://ceb.nlm.nih.gov/proj/ttp /flash/ketham/ketham.html (accessed 9 January 2017).

Kiddel, M. and S. Rowe-Leete (1989), 'Mapping the Body', in M. Feher, ed., *Fragments for a History of the Human Body*, 3, 448–469, New York: Zone Books.

Kierkegaard, S. (1992/1843), *Either-Or*, London: Penguin.

Kiernan, P. (2006), *Filthy Shakespeare. Shakespeare's Most Outrageous Sexual Puns*, London: Quercus.

Klibansky, R., E. Panofsky and F. Saxl (1964), *Saturn and Melancholy*, London: Thomas Nelson and Sons.

Knott, K. and S. McLoughlin, eds. (2010), *Diasporas. Concepts, Intersections, Identities*, London: Zed Books.

Koselleck, R., ed. (1984), 'Organ', *Geschichtliche Grundbegriffe*, 4, 519–622, Stuttgart: Klett-Cotta.

König, G. (1996), *Eine Kulturgeschichte des Spazierganges*, Wien: Böhlau.

Kundziałek, M. (1971), 'Der Mensch als Abbild des Kosmos', in A. Zimmermann, ed., *Der Begriff der Repraesentatio im Mittelalter: Stellvertretung, Symbol, Zeichen, Bild*, 35–75, Berlin: de Gruyter.

Lakoff, G. (1988), *Women, Fire and Dangerous Things*, Chicago: University of Chicago Press.

Larsen, S. E., ed. (1990), *Ahelluva Country. American Studies as a Cross-Cultural Experience*, Odense: Southern Danish University Press.

Larsen, S. E. (1997), 'Metaphor – A Semiotic Perspective', in *Danish Yearbook of Philosophy* 31: 137–156.

Larsen, S. E. (2005), 'Self-Reference: Theory and Didactics between Language and Literature', in *The Journal of Aesthetic Education* 39 (1): 13–30.

Larsen, S. E. (2006), 'The Lisbon Earthquake and the Scientific Turn in Kant's Philosophy', in *European Review* 14 (3): 359–367.

Larsen, S. E. (2007), '"To See Things for the First Time". Before and After Ecocriticism', in *Journal of Literary Studies/Tydskrif vir Literatuurwetenskap* 23 (4): 341–373.

Larsen, S. E. (2011a), 'Memory Constructions and Their Limits', in *Orbis Litterarum* 66 (6): 448–467.

Larsen, S. E. (2011b), 'Georg Brandes: The Telescope of Comparative Literature', in T. D'haen, D. Damrosch and D. Kadir, eds., *The Routledge Companion to World Literature*, 21–31, London: Routledge.

Larsen, S. E. (2011c), 'How to Narrate the Other', in S. Y. Sencindiver, M. Beville and M. Lauritzen, eds. *Otherness*, 201–219, Frankfurt a.M.: Peter Lang.

Larsen, S. E. (2013), 'From the National to a Transnational Paradigm. Writing Literary Histories Today', in *European Review* 21 (2): 241–251.

Larsen, S. E. (2015a), 'From Comparatism to Comparativity. Comparative Reasoning Reconsidered', in *Interfaces. A Journal of Medieval European Literatures* 1 (1): 318–347, http://riviste.unimi.it/interfaces/index (accessed 5 January 2017).

Larsen, S. E. (2015b), 'Beyond the Global Village', in *The Journal of English Language & Literature* 61 (3): 383–398.

Larsen, S. E. (2016a), 'Translating Languages I Don't Know', in I. Z. Dinković and J. M. Djigunović, eds., *English Studies from Archives to Prospects Volume 2 – Linguistics and Applied Linguistics*, 149–164, Cambridge: Cambridge Scholars Publishing.

Larsen, S. E. (2016b), 'The Good Life Lost and Found: East, West, Home's Best', in J. Vassbinder and B. Gulyás, eds., *East-West. Cultural Patterns and Neurocognitive Circuits*, 141–168, Singapore: World Scientific Publishing.

Larsen, S. E. (2017a), 'Ludvig Holberg. A Man of Transition in the Eighteenth Century', in D. Ringgaard and M. R. Thomsen, eds., *Danish Literature as World Literature*, 53–90, London: Bloomsbury.

Larsen, S. E. (2017b), 'Body and Narrative. Mediated Memory', in L. Sætre, P. Lombardo and S. Tanderup, eds., *Exploring Text, Media and Memory*, Aarhus: Aarhus University Press (in print).

Larsen, S. E. and J. D. Johansen (2002), *Signs in Use*, London: Routledge.

Las Casas, B. (1992/1552), *The Devastation of the Indies. A Brief Account*, Baltimore: Johns Hopkins University Press.

Le Bris, M., J. Rouaud and E. Almassy, eds. (2007), *Pour une littérature-monde*, Paris: Gallimard.

Leadbeater, C. and J. Wilsdon (2007), *The Atlas of Ideas: How Asian Innovation Can Benefit Us All*, London: Demos, www.demos.co.uk/files/Overview_Final1.pdf (accessed 29 December 2016).

Leatherdale, W. H. (1974), *The Role of Analogy, Model and Metaphor in Science*, Amsterdam: North-Holland.

Lechner, F. and J. Boli, eds. (2004), *The Globalization Reader*, 2nd ed., London: Routledge.

Leed, E. J. (1991), *The Mind of the Traveler. From Gilgamesh to Global Tourism*, New York: Basic Books.

Lefevere, A. (1990), 'Translation: Its Genealogy in the West', in S. Bassnett and A. Lefevere, eds., *Translation, History and Culture*, 14–28, London: Pinter.

Lefevere, A., eds. (1992), *Translation/History/Culture*, London: Routledge.

Leonard, P. (2013), *Literature after Globalization*, London: Bloomsbury.

Léry, J. de (1990/1578), *Story of a Journey to the Land of Brazil Otherwise Called America*, Berkeley: University of California Press.

Lestringant, F. (1994a/1991), *Mapping the Renaissance World*, London: Polity Press.

Lestringant, F. (1994b), *Le cannibal. Grandeur et décadence*, Paris: Perrin.

Lévi-Strauss, C. (1961/1955), *Tristes tropiques*, New York: Criterion Books.

Levy, D. and N. Sznaider (2002), 'Memory Unbound. The Holocaust and the Formation of Cosmopolitan Memory', in *European Journal of Social Theory* 5 (1): 87–106.

Levy, D. and N. Sznaider (2010), *Human Rights and Memory*, University Park: Pennsylvania State University Press.

Lindqvist, S. (2007), *Terra nullius. A Journey Through No One's Land*, New York: The New Press.

Lionnet, F. and S.-M. Shih, eds. (2005), *Minor Transnationalism*, Durham: Duke University Press.

Löffler, U. (1999), *Lissabons Fall – Europas Schrecken*, Berlin: Walter de Gruyter.

Lowry, M. (1971/1947), *Under the Volcano*, New York: Signet.

Luo, X. and Y. He, eds. (2009), *Translating China*. Bristol: Multilingual Matters.

Mahler, G. (1998/1967/1908), *Das Lied von der Erde*. CD: C. Ludwig (contraalto), F. Wunderlich (tenor), Philharmonia Orchestra and New Philharmonia Orchestra, O. Klemperer (cond.) (Mahler's text is reproduced in the booklet), CDM 5 66892 2/ EMI Records.

Malmkjaer K. and K. Windle, eds. (2011), *The Oxford Handbook of Translation Studies*, Oxford: Oxford University Press.

Malouf, D. (1990), *The Great World*, London: Vintage.

Mauss, M. (1980/1934), 'Les techniques du corps', in *Sociologie et Anthropologie*, 365–386, Paris: Presses Universitaires de France.

McConnell, J. and E. Hall, eds. (2016), *Ancient Greek Myth in World Fiction since 1989*, London: Bloomsbury.

Mehlsen, C. and F. Lau (2007), *Globalisterne. De gør din verden mindre*, Copenhagen: Gyldendal.

Merleau-Ponty, M. (2013/1945), *Phenomenology of Perception*, London: Routledge.

Miller, W. I. (1993), *Humiliation and Other Essays on Honor, Social Discomfort, and Violence*, Ithaca: Cornell University Press.

Miller, W. I. (2006), *An Eye for an Eye*, Cambridge: Cambridge University Press.

Miner, E. (1989), *Comparative Poetics. An Intercultural Essay on Theories of Literature*, Princeton: Princeton University Press.

Montaigne, M. de (1580), *Essays of Montaigne*, https://ebooks.adelaide.edu.au/m/montaigne/michel/essays/index.html (accessed 5 January 2017).

Morris, D. (1991), *The Culture of Pain*, Berkeley: University of California Press.

Mudimbe-Boyi, E., ed. (2002), *Beyond Dichotomies. Histories, Identities, Cultures, and the Challenge of Globalization*, New York: State University of New York Press.

Mudrooroo (1991), *Master of the Ghost Dreaming*, London: Angus and Robertson.

Mufti, A. (2016), *Forget English! Orientalism and World Literature*, Cambridge: Harvard University Press.

Munn, N. (1973), 'The Spatial Representation of Cosmic Order in Walbiri Iconography', in A. Forge, ed., *Primitive Art and Society*, 193–220, Oxford: Oxford University Press.

Multatuli (1987/1860), *Max Havelaar: Or the Coffee Auctions of a Dutch Trading Company*, 2nd ed., London: Penguin.

Münster, S. (1544), *Cosmographia*, http://daten.digitale-sammlungen.de/~db/0007/bsb00074924/images/index.html?id=00074924&groesser=&fip=193.174.98.30&no=&seite=1 (accessed 5 January 2017).

Mythen, G. (2004), *Ulrich Beck. A Critical Introduction to the Risk Society*, London: Pluto Press.

Møller, P. M. (1855a/1820), 'Glæde over Danmark', in *Efterladte Skrifter* 1, 63–65, Copenhagen: C.A. Reitzel.

Møller, P. M. (1855b/1821), 'Optegnelser fra Reisen til China', in *Efterladte Skrifter* 2, 225–258, Copenhagen: C.A. Reitzel.

Nabokov, V. (1973), *Strong Opinions*, New York: McGraw Hill.

Nerrière, J.-P. (2005), *Parlez Globish! Don't Speak English*, Paris: Eyrolles.

Nietzsche, F. (1973/1873), 'Über Wahrheit und Lüge im aussermoralischen Sinne', in *Nietzsche Werke* 3 (2): 367–384, Berlin: Walter de Gruyter.

Novalis (1960), *Schriften*, 1, Stuttgart: Kohlhammer.

Novalis (1975), *Schriften*, 4, Stuttgart: Kohlhammer.

Noyes, J. K. (2006), 'Goethe on Cosmopolitanism and Colonialism: *Bildung* and the Dialectic of Critical Mobility', in *Eighteenth-Century Studies* 39 (4): 443–462.

Nussbaum, M. (2004), *Hiding from Humanity. Disgust, Shame, and the Law*, Princeton: Princeton University Press.

O'Brien, S. and I. Szeman (2001), 'The Globalization of Fiction/The Fiction of Globalization', in *South Atlantic Quarterly* 100 (3): 603–623.

Olick, J., V. Vinitzky-Seroussi and D. Levy, eds. (2011), *The Collective Memory Reader*, Oxford: Oxford University Press.

Osterhammel, J. and N. P. Petersson (2009), *Globalization. A Short History*, Princeton: Princeton University Press.

Ørsted, H. C. (1852/1836), 'Danskhed', in *Samlede og efterladte Skrifter* 7, 39–58, Copenhagen: A.F. Høst.

Parker, J. and T. Mathews, ed. (2011), *Tradition, Translation, Trauma: The Classic and the Modern*, Oxford: Oxford University Press.

Peirce, C. S. (1998/1903), 'Pragmatism as the Logic of Abduction', in *The Essential Peirce* 2, 226–241, Bloomington: Indiana University Press.

Peristiany, J. G. (1965), *Honour and Shame. The Values of Mediterranean Society*, London: Weidenfeld and Nicolson.

Peters, E. (1996), *Torture*, Philadelphia: University of Pennsylvania Press.

Philips, K. R. and G. Mitchell Reyes, eds. (2011), *Global Memoryscapes. Contesting Remembrance in a Transnational Age*, Tuscaloosa: University of Alabama Press.

Pizer, J. (2006), *The Idea of World Literature*, Baton Rouge: University of Louisiana Press.

Pliny the E. (1961), *Naturalis historia*, London: Heinemann.

Poirrier, J.-P. (2005), *Le tremblement de terre de Lisbonne*, Paris: Odile Jacob.

Pradeau, C. and T. Samouyault, eds. (2005), *Où est la littérature mondiale?*, Paris: Presses Universitaires de Vincennes.

Pratt, M. L. (1992), *Imperial Eyes. Travel Writing and Transculturation*, London: Routledge.

Prendergast, C. (ed.) (2004), *Debating World Literature*, London: Verso.

Purdy, D. (2014), 'Goethe, Rémusat, and the Chinese Novel: Translation and the Circulation of World Literature', in T. O. Beebee, ed., *German Literature as World Literature*, 43–60, London: Bloomsbury.

Rahimi, A. (2002/1999), *Earth and Ashes*, London: Vintage.

Ramazani, J. (2009), *A Transnational Poetics*, Chicago: University of Chicago Press.

Rawson, C. (2001), *God, Gulliver and Genocide*, Oxford: Oxford University Press.

Razinsky, L. (2016), *Writing and Life, Literature and History: On Jorge Semprún*, New Haven: Yale University Press.

Richardson, M. (2016), *Gestures of Testimony. Torture, Trauma and Affect in Literature*, London: Bloomsbury.

Ringgaard, D. and M. R. Thomsen, eds. (2017), *Danish Literature as World Literature*, London: Bloomsbury.

Rio Convention (1992), *Convention on Biological Diversity*, United Nations, http://www.biodiv.be/convention/cbd-text/preambule (accessed 4 January 2017).

Rogers, K. L., S. Leydesdorff and G. Dawson, eds. (1999), *Trauma and Life Stories. International Perspectives*, London: Routledge.

Rose, M. (1993), *Authors and Owners. The Invention of Copyright*, Cambridge: Harvard University Press.

Rothberg, M. (2009), *Multidirectional Memory: Remembering the Holocaust in the Age of Decolonization*, Stanford: Stanford University Press.

Sanders, M. (2007), *Ambiguities of Witnessing: Law and Literature in the Time of a Truth Commission*, Stanford: Stanford University Press.

Sapiro, G. (2009), *Translatio. Le marché de la traduction en France à l'heure de la mondialisation*, Paris: CNRS.

Saussy, H., ed. (2006), *Comparative Literature in an Age of Globalization*, Baltimore: Johns Hopkins University Press.

Schiller, N. G. and A. Irving, eds. (2015), *Whose Cosmopolitanism? Critical Perspectives, Relationalities and Discontents*, New York: Berghahn.

Scholte, J. A. (2005), *Globalization. A Critical Introduction*, London: Palgrave MacMillan.

Schreibman, S., R. Siemens and J. Unworth (2015), *A New Companion to Digital Humanities*, Oxford: Blackwell.

Schön, D. (1993), 'Generative Metaphor', in A. Ortony, ed., *Metaphor and Thought*, 137–163, Cambridge: Cambridge University Press.

Schöning, U., ed. (2000), *Internationalität nationaler Literaturen*, Göttingen: Wallstein.

Schütz, A. (1955), 'Symbol, Reality, and Society', in L. Bryson et al., eds., *Symbol and Reality*, 135–203, New York: Praeger.

Semprún, J. (1998/1994), *Literature or Life*, London: Penguin.

Semprún, J. (2001), *Le mort qu'il faut*, Paris: Gallimard.

Semprún, J. (2005/1963), *The Long Voyage*, New York: Overlook Press.

Shakespeare, W. (1983/1595), *Romeo and Juliet*, London: Routledge.

Shakespeare, W. (1989/1592), *King Henry IV*, 1–2, London: Routledge.

Shakespeare, W. (2005/1611), *The Tempest*, London: Thomson Learning.

Shakespeare, W. (2010/1598), *The Merchant of Venice*, London: Bloomsbury.

Sinnett, F. (1966/1856), *The Fiction Fields of Australia*, Queensland: University of Queensland Press.

Solnit, R. (2006), *Wanderlust. A History of Walking*, London: Verso.

Solvik, M. (2005), 'Mahler's Untimely Modernism', in J. Barham, ed., *Perspectives on Gustav Mahler*, 153–171, Aldershot: Ashgate.

Staden, H. (2008/1557), *Hans Staden's True History. An Account of Cannibal Captivity in Brazil*, Durham: Duke University Press.

Sutton, P. (1998), 'Icons of Country: Topographic Representations in Classical Aboriginal Traditions', in D. Woodward & G. M. Lewis, eds., *The History of Cartography* 2 (3), 351–386, Chicago: University of Chicago Press.

Svensen, H. (2006), *The End Is Nigh. A History of Natural Disasters*, London: Reaktion Books.

Swift, J. (1969/1729), 'A Modest Proposal', in C. Beaumont ed., *A Modest Proposal*, 11–18, Columbus: Charles E. Merrill.

Swift, J. (1975/1726), *Gulliver's Travels*, London: Everyman's Library.

Sætre, L., P. Lombardo and J. Zanetta, eds. (2014), *Exploring Texts and Emotions*, Aarhus: Aarhus University Press.

Tang X. (2002/1598), *The Peony Pavilion*, Bloomington: Indiana University Press.

Texier-Vandamme, C. (2003), '*The Songlines*. Blurring Edges of Traditional Genres in Search of a New Monadic Aesthetics', in *Commonwealth Essays and Studies* 26 (1): 75–82.

Thevet, A. (1568/1557), *The New Found Worlde, or Antarctike*, http://quod.lib.umich .edu/cgi/t/text/text-idx?c=eebo;idno=A13665.0001.001 (accessed 5 January 2017).

Thomsen, M. R. (2008), *Mapping World Literature*, London: Bloomsbury.

Thomsen, M. R. (2013), *The New Human in Literature: Posthuman Visions of Changes in Body, Mind and Society after 1900*, London: Bloomsbury.

Todorov, T. (1982), *La conquête de l'Amérique: la question de l'autre*, Paris: Le Seuil.

Tomlinson, J. (1999), *Globalization and Culture*, London: Polity Press.

Urry, J. (2000), *Sociology Beyond Societies. Mobilities for the Twenty-First Century*, London: Routledge.

Valéry, P. (1957/1943), 'Réflexions simples sur le corps', in *Œuvres* 1, 923–931, Paris: Gallimard.

Venuti, L., ed. (2012), *The Translation Studies Reader*, London: Routledge.

Veit, W. F. (2008), 'Globalization and Literary History, or Rethinking Comparative Literary History – Globally', in *New Literary History* 39: 415–435.

Vertovec, S. (2009), *Transnationalism*, London: Routledge.

Vinci, L. da (1998), *The Notebooks of Leonardo da Vinci*, Oxford: Oxford University Press.

Vitruvius (2002/c. 40 BCE), *On Architecture* 1–10, Cambridge: Harvard University Press.

Voltaire, F. (1912/1755), 'Poem on the Lisbon Diaster', in *Tolerance and Other Essays*, 255–263, London: Putnam's Sons.

Walcott, D. (1996/1974), 'The Muse of History', in A. Donnell and L. Welsh, eds., *The Routledge Reader in Caribbean Literature*, 354–358, London: Routledge.

Walkowitz, R. (2006), 'The Location of Literature: The Transnational Book and the Migrant Writer', in *Contemporary Literature* 47 (6): 527–545.

Walkowitz, R. (2015), *Born Translated. The Contemporary Novel in the Age of World Literature*, New York: Columbia University Press.

Wallace, A. (1993), *Walking, Literature, and English Culture*, Oxford: Clarendon.

Walther, L., ed. (1999), *Melancholie*, Leipzig: Reclam.

White, P. (1989/1958), 'The Prodigal Son', in C. Flynn and P. Brennan, eds., *Patrick White Speaks*, 13–17, Sydney: Primavera Press.

Whitehead, A. (2004), *Trauma Fiction*, Edinburgh: Edinburgh University Press.

Yahoo! (2016), https://en.wikipedia.org/wiki/Yahoo! (accessed 29 December 2016).

Yates, F. (1974), *The Art of Memory*, Chicago: University of Chicago Press.

Žižek, S. (2007), 'Mozart as a Critic of Postmodern Ideology', in *JEP. European Journal of Psychoanalysis* 24: s.p., www.psychomedia.it/jep/number24/zizek.htm (accessed 29 December 2016).

Index

CPSIA information can be obtained
at www.ICGtesting.com
Printed in the USA
LVHW080839160721
692666LV00002BA/129

9 781350 007567